Strategy SHELVED

Strategy SHELVED

THE COLLAPSE OF COLD WAR NAVAL STRATEGIC PLANNING

Steven T. Wills

Naval Institute Press
Annapolis, Maryland

Naval Institute Press
291 Wood Road
Annapolis, MD 21402

Library of Congress Cataloging-in-Publication Data

Names: Wills, Steven T., author.

Title: Strategy shelved : the collapse of Cold War naval strategic planning / Steven T. Wills.

Other titles: Collapse of Cold War naval strategic planning

Description: Annapolis, Maryland : Naval Institute Press, [2021] | Includes bibliographical references and index.

Identifiers: LCCN 2021005467 (print) | LCCN 2021005468 (ebook) | ISBN 9781682476338 (hardback) | ISBN 9781682476741 (ebook)

Subjects: LCSH: Sea-power—United States—History—20th century. | United States. Navy—Planning. | United States. Navy—History—20th century. | Naval strategy.

Classification: LCC VA50 .W55 2021 (print) | LCC VA50 (ebook) | DDC 359/.03097309045—dc23

LC record available at https://lccn.loc.gov/2021005467

LC ebook record available at https://lccn.loc.gov/2021005468

♾ Print editions meet the requirements of ANSI/NISO z39.48-1992 (Permanence of Paper).
Printed in the United States of America.

29 28 27 26 25 24 23 22 21 9 8 7 6 5 4 3 2 1
First printing

This work is dedicated to my wife, Alice, my son, John, and my daughter, Emily, who endured many evening hours, weekends, and several vacations without me so that it could be completed. My wife's encouragement sustained this effort, and I could not have accomplished it without her loving support.

CONTENTS

ACKNOWLEDGMENTS

The contributions of numerous active and retired officers, civilian officials, and academics were essential to the completion of *Strategy Shelved: The Collapse of Cold War Naval Strategic Planning*. The author is grateful to the following persons for their comments, support, and general assistance: Capt. Arthur "Trip" Barber, USN (Ret.), Capt. Roger Barnett, USN (Ret.), Irv Blickstein, John Brobst, Cdr. Mitch Brown, USN (Ret.), former deputy under secretary of the Navy Seth Cropsey, Capt. Richard Diamond, USN (Ret.), Capt. Thomas Fedyszyn, USN (Ret.), Cdr. Paul Giarra, USN (Ret.), John Hanley, Capt. R. Robinson "Robby" Harris, USN (Ret.), Prof. John Hattendorf, Capt. Wayne Hughes, USN (Ret.), Capt. William Spencer Johnson, USN (Ret.), Cdr. John Kuehn, USN (Ret.), former Secretary of the Navy John Lehman, Capt. Brad Martin, USN (Ret.), Rear Adm. Michael McDevitt, USN (Ret.), Cdr. Bryan McGrath, USN (Ret.), Greg Melcher, Vice Adm. Henry C. "Hank" Mustin, USN (Ret.), Charles Nemfakos, James O'Brasky, Adm. William Owens, USN (Ret.), Randy Papadopoulous, Bruce Powers, David Alan Rosenberg, Captain Robert (Barney) Rubel, USN (Ret.), Rear Adm. Joseph Sestak, USN (Ret.), Rear Adm. James Stark, USN (Ret.), Ingo Trauschweizer, Cdr. Stanley Weeks, USN (Ret.), Cdr. Steve Woodall, USN (Ret.), and Cdr. Harlan Ullman, USN (Ret).

The author especially owes a debt of gratitude to Capt. Peter Swartz, USN (Ret.), who graciously provided access to his archives, Rolodex, and insights on nearly four decades of naval strategy and policy. This work would not have reached its level of detail in the absence of Captain Swartz's contributions, for which the author will always be grateful.

INTRODUCTION

The significant implications of the dissolution of the Warsaw Pact for the U.S. military had become readily apparent by the middle of 1989. This was especially true for the U.S. Navy, whose Maritime Strategy—its operating doctrine since 1982—along with an attendant six-hundred-ship force structure revolved around countering Soviet threats worldwide. The naval analyst Ronald O'Rourke described the coming post–Cold War period as the Navy's "most significant crossroads in four decades." It produced a shift that "called into question many of the basic assumptions that [had] guided U.S. Defense Planning for naval and other military forces since the 1950s."[1]

Historical assessments of periods of fundamental strategic shifts are vital not only for understanding those particular moments, but those that preceded them as well. They can also serve to predict and understand future trajectories. *Strategy Shelved: The Collapse of Cold War Naval Strategic Planning* explains the fundamental alterations in strategic thinking, organization, and execution of global U.S. naval operations during the relatively short period between 1989 and 1994. While the transition from the Maritime Strategy to "... From the Sea" (1994), the first post–Cold War and post–Gulf War naval policy, was essentially successful, the U.S. Navy failed to sufficiently grasp and retain those Cold War–era elements of strategic organization that had proved effective at generating the strategy and operational analysis of the previous two decades. One can see in retrospect that this failure left the Navy ill-prepared to conduct the strategic assessment necessary to identify a new era of strategic competition in which both rising and revanchist near-peer competitors as well as non-state actors would threaten U.S. naval superiority in a growing number of geographic locations.

Periods of great change demand considered responses. While immediate strategic conditions may change and demand new solutions, it does not mean that the system of producing strategic thinking has to be altered. The U.S. Navy's system of producing strategic documents had successfully functioned since 1970, yet from 1989 to 1994 Navy leaders cast it aside. *Strategy Shelved* serves to warn decision makers of the perils of careless or needless change without adequate assessment of a proven successful system of strategy generation.

The U.S. Navy had spent the two decades before the 1990s reconstituting its Vietnam-era fleet. Beginning in the late 1970s, it began carefully crafting and refining what would become the Maritime Strategy and then updated the established doctrine several times before 1989. With 588 ships in the fleet in 1988, the six-hundred-ship building program was approaching fruition, albeit at the cost of significant deficit spending.[2] Staff in the Office of the Chief of Naval Operations (OPNAV) had largely been responsible for the creation of both the strategy and the planned six-hundred-ship force structure. The OPNAV staff was in effect a competitive marketplace of ideas, where strategy and analysis elements vied to develop products that would sway the Navy service chief to their desired outcomes. Three Chiefs of Naval Operations in particular—the admirals Elmo Zumwalt (1970–74), James Holloway III (1974–78), and Thomas Hayward (1978–82)—effectively balanced these groups and in doing so laid the building blocks for the Maritime Strategy and its associated six-hundred-ship navy. Many of the officers from the strategy and analysis cohorts would go on to more senior positions of greater influence, suggesting that the personnel involved in the project were just as much a successful "product" of this process as the strategy documents they created.

By the beginning of 1989, the product of the great effort to confront a global Soviet threat was declining in relevance. The Soviets had begun withdrawing from Afghanistan in May 1988 and would finish the operation by February

1989.[3] The revolutions that ultimately brought about the fall of communist governments in Eastern Europe and the fall of the Berlin Wall on 9 November 1989 signified the final days of the Cold War.[4] It was with some irony that the unofficial end of the Cold War occurred in a distinctly naval environment. In December 1989 at the Malta summit between U.S. president George H. W. Bush and Soviet premier Mikhail Gorbachev, warships anchored in the Grand Harbour represented their two countries. Bush stayed aboard the 6th Fleet flagship, the USS *Belknap*, for the duration of the summit. As a storm lashed at the *Belknap* throughout the president's stay, three strategic storms were gathering to engulf the U.S. Navy: the disappearance of the Soviet threat and the end of the Cold War, on which naval strategic planning had been based for more than four decades; organizational changes wrought by passage of the Goldwater-Nichols Act of 1986, and limited naval involvement in the 1990–91 Gulf War. These three events would play noteworthy roles in the Navy and Marine Corps devising proposed strategies and force structures for the 1990s and subsequent decades and in the resulting strategy and attendant force structure for the emerging post–Cold War era.

The Maritime Strategy had been designed around combating and defeating the Soviet navy on a global scale and in providing naval support in Europe against a hypothetical Soviet invasion across Central Europe. In the European contest, the Navy would attack the Soviet Union and its nuclear ballistic missile submarines operating in home waters and land Marines in Norway, the Balkans, and in the Soviet Pacific to divert Soviet resources and attention from Central Europe. This strategy came under the Navy's scrutiny in the late 1980s as the Warsaw Pact alliance began to fail and in light of the rising cost of the naval component of President Ronald Reagan's military buildup. By late 1989 Navy strategists believed a new plan was in order and set up a series of official and ad hoc, unofficial groups that from 1990 to late 1992 examined possible successor strategies. Many of the same individuals responsible for the creation of the Maritime Strategy participated in these discussions. "... From the Sea" had coalesced around a new area and principle of naval warfare—littoral operations, that is, operations in coastal areas and within range of sea-based air and missile weapons. This new focus of naval warfare represented a sharp turn away from the high seas, blue water combat anticipated against the Soviet navy in the 1980s. Naval forces would maneuver from sea to land, and in some cases the land forces and their actions would be more important than operations at sea. The Navy was still expected to maintain sea control in forward areas when required, but its focus would now be on supporting air-ground expeditionary operations along the greater Eurasian littoral.

While ". . . From the Sea" had been developed by the same staff organizations and in some cases many of the same people who had had a hand in drafting the Maritime Strategy, this new product proved to be much less effective over time than its predecessor due to the reorganization of the naval staff that came with the Cold War's end, Goldwater-Nichols provisions, and the Gulf War's negative effects on naval morale. The change in how naval strategy was produced and to the particular cohort of men and women engaged in that work also made the creation of subsequent strategic documents problematic at best, because the competitive environment of the 1970s and 1980s was in effect replaced by top-down consensus thinking for the sake of time, budgets, and convenience. Rear Adm. Bill Pendley, a former Pacific Command J5, director for Strategy, Plans, and Policy, has called the 1990s, "A lost decade in strategic affairs, planning for threats that were not there while ignoring the emerging threats of the New Era."[5]

The shift to a more joint form of strategic planning was perhaps inevitable, as the Goldwater-Nichols Act stemmed in part from the perception of inherent flaws in the collaborative and competitive process of negotiations within the Joint Chiefs of Staff geared toward achieving consensus. Some faulted the system as producing watered-down, consensus decisions and documents. A top-down, directive system was, therefore, considered to be a more effective approach in terms of budgetary efficiency over time. In effect, Goldwater-Nichols represented a victory for the acolytes of Robert S. McNamara, who as secretary of defense during the Kennedy and Johnson administrations stripped, to the extent possible, the individual military services of their budgetary and force creation powers in favor of a centralized, analysis-driven process directed by senior Department of Defense civilian personnel. The Goldwater-Nichols Act concentrated much of this authority within the office of the chairman of the Joint Chiefs of Staff rather than senior defense civilian leaders, but the outcome still cast aside the competitive process of the past decades.

The pre-1986 strategy, budgetary, and force planning system, however cumbersome, produced what is widely acknowledged as the finest strategic and operational U.S. military thinking since World War II. From this competitive, decentralized environment driven by the uniformed military leadership emerged the Army's AirLand Battle doctrine (1981), the Air Force's Basic Aerospace Doctrine (1984), the Navy's Maritime Strategy (1982), and the Marine Corps' Maneuver Warfare doctrine (1989). The list of similar products from the 1990s to the present does not include such illustrious entries. While Goldwater-Nichols was billed as a preventative measure against future, fruitless conflicts like the Vietnam War, the wars fought in Afghanistan and Iraq since 2001 and 2003, respectively, have not displayed much in the way of improved strategic thinking. U.S. forces achieved quick, operational victories only to become mired in counterinsurgency operations as challenging as those in Vietnam. The vaunted Iraqi "surge" of 2007 was a product of retired officers and think tank members rather than the chairman of the Joint Chiefs and the Joint Staff.

The Navy's shift in strategy from one based on threats, geography, and military capability in favor of one in which budgetary concerns represented a primary component mirrors that of the U.S. defense establishment in general in the 1990s. U.S. long-term strategic military planning lapsed during the 1990s, due to the absence of an applicable strategic vision following the collapse of the Soviet Union, the top-down, non-competitive decision-making environment as a result of Goldwater-Nichols, and perhaps the impression of an "easy" post–Cold War security environment based on the outcome of the Gulf War. Although long-term strategic planning reemerged to a degree after the 11 September 2001 al-Qaida attacks, it remained constrained by budgets and systemic organization. While some attempts at reforms have been made, there has been no movement to fundamentally alter the concepts and systems for running the business of national security that have been in place since the McNamara era, more than a half century ago. McNamara's systems analysis approach to defense planning migrated to the service staffs after his departure from the Pentagon and were largely reaffirmed by Goldwater-Nichols. The Navy's experience with this process was a negative one, as the service lost control over its force structure design, many of its operational concepts, and ultimately of the trained officers responsible for their creation.

The abrupt end of the forty-plus-year Cold War caught naval strategists unawares and plunged the U.S. Navy and the rest of the defense establishment into the most significant period of strategic change since the end of World War II and passage of the National Security Act of 1947, which laid the foundations for the current joint force. At that time, the Army and the Air Force had operational-level strategies that could be adapted to multiple situations and geographic environments, but the Navy had fully invested in a strategy that based force structure, deployment, and its principal basis for existence on a peer opponent. There was, of course, an immediate understanding that the world had changed with the dissolution of the Soviet Union and that the blue water Maritime Strategy was no longer applicable to the evolving situation. Deprived of a Soviet naval threat, the Navy and Marine Corps would spend 1989 to 1994 developing a new naval strategy and attendant force structure to replace the Maritime Strategy and the six-hundred-ship concept of the early 1980s.

Unlike in the late 1970s, when initial planning for what became the Maritime Strategy was conducted at the highest levels of naval leadership, post–Cold War strategic research began at the level of Navy captains, Marine Corps colonels, and junior flag officers. The Marines played an unprecedented role in the process, and a focus on support for operations ashore quickly emerged. Remarkably, however, despite advocating for major strategic changes, this same group of strategy planners did not recommend significant alterations to the Navy's force structure. Old warships no longer supported by generous Cold War budgets were retired, but the basic fleet of aircraft carriers, surface warships, and nuclear submarines remained intact.

As Chief of Naval Operations, Adm. Frank B. Kelso (1990–94) took the opportunity offered by the end of the Cold War to fundamentally reorganize OPNAV along lines more favorable to the maintenance of the remaining fleet strength than a continued focus on strategy. Although the Navy would have "... From the Sea" in place by late 1994, the same fleet built around the remarkably different Maritime Strategy to oppose the Soviet Union supported it. Presented as a white paper rather than a strategy, the new concept of "... From the Sea" was based on "shaping the future in ways favorable to U.S. interest," focused on "joint and combined operations" with the Marine Corps, and proposed that the Navy provide a host of non-warfighting capabilities, among them force presence, crisis response, and the ability to project power from the sea.[6] With "... From the Sea," the Navy's ultimate goal had been a replacement for the Maritime Strategy of the 1980s, but it is debatable whether the concept truly formed the basis of a new kind of post–Cold War force or merely made the best use of the existing, recently built force structure. *Strategy Shelved* leans toward the second supposition.

The advent of greater defense centralization and primacy of joint planning rather than single- or dual-service planning, a result of Goldwater-Nichols, also complicated Navy efforts at devising a new strategy. Goldwater-Nichols stripped away the few remaining controls the Chief of Naval Operations and the commandant of the Marine Corps possessed over operational forces. Other requirements of the law, especially the need for more joint rather than service-specific staff officer billets, shifted the services' personnel priorities away from those billets traditionally responsible for service-based strategic planning. Talented officers previously in service-planning positions naturally became attracted to operational joint positions to enhance their career prospects. While this effect was not immediate in the late 1980s, it would become more pronounced as "... From the Sea" evolved.

Goldwater-Nichols' elevation of the chairman of the Joint Chiefs of Staff to the position of principal military adviser to the president allowed that officer to exercise significant influence over purely naval-related strategies and force structures. Gen. Colin Powell, who served as chairman from October 1989 to September 1993, exercised the full range of powers provided by the legislation. He developed the Base Force according to his strategic vision of the United States retaining superpower status rather than threat-based scenarios in which U.S. forces might become involved in the post–Cold War world.[7] The chairman's assumption of traditional service force planning was part of the centralization that complicated the Navy's efforts to craft a post–Cold War strategy and an attendant force structure.

Most of the Navy's leadership had vigorously opposed the Goldwater-Nichols legislation. Much of joint doctrine emphasized "operational art," a term the Navy had long eschewed as not applicable to blue water naval combat. Army War College professor Antulio Echevarria suggested that some of the reluctance stemmed from the Navy's belief that it was able to "exert direct strategic influence" in the course of its campaigns.[8] After Congress approved Goldwater-Nichols almost unanimously, however, the maritime service felt it had to drop its objections to joint operations. While all the services sought to enact the mandate for joint operations that Congress had set out through the legislation, the Navy started from a position of relative disadvantage compared to the Army and the Air Force due to its long-standing opposition to joint concepts. Members of Congress and the George H. W. Bush administration tended to view the Navy as backward thinking in light of its resistance. This negative view of the Navy would also complicate the business of creating a new strategy.

The Persian Gulf War cast a long shadow over the post–Cold War U.S. military force. The Army and the Air Force ended the conflict secure in the knowledge that the outcome had validated their Cold War operational and tactical concepts. The Navy did not enjoy the same outlook. Iraq did not have a significant navy and mounted little opposition to U.S. Navy operations during the war beyond mine-laying operations in the Persian Gulf that damaged two U.S. warships. The Navy's inability to validate its principal Cold War strategy and operational doctrine cast a cloud of uncertainty over its efforts to develop a replacement for the Maritime Strategy. Congress and the press interpreted this uncertainty as the Navy being too "parochial" and unable to adjust to the changing times. The 1991 Tailhook scandal, exposing alleged sexual and other improper misconduct by aviation officers, further unnerved the naval leadership and put greater pressure on them to develop a new strategy eschewing the immediate past.

Despite these obstacles, the Navy produced a strategic concept for the post–Cold War world that largely met internal and external measures of success. The progression from blue water warfare against the Soviets to a transoceanic successor in support of operations ashore proved a logical development. Many of the same offices who produced and refined the 1980s Maritime Strategy developed and advanced the new strategy. The Navy preserved nearly all of its modern fleet units despite the numerical and budgetary limitations imposed by the requirements of the Base Force. As with the conclusion of past eras of conflict, some significant ship, aircraft, and submarine programs were canceled, and Cold War disciplines like antisubmarine warfare atrophied in the absence of a peer competitor.

The combination of the Cold War's end, Goldwater-Nichols, and operations during the Gulf War served to substantially alter the political-military climate in which the Navy had to create a new strategy. The Navy, deprived of its principal opponent, struggled to determine which capabilities to retain in the post–Cold War environment. Goldwater-Nichols provisions forced it to collaborate on an unprecedented level with the other services in determining its own strategic vision. As noted, the Gulf War failed to validate the Navy's Maritime Strategy of the 1980s and introduced further uncertainty into the process of creating a successor. Ironically, unlike during previous significant shifts in U.S. naval strategy, fleet force structure did not applicably change. Efforts by senior officers to protect the existing force structure as an offset against the return of an aggressive Russian fleet further complicated the process of strategic change. The shift from the Maritime Strategy to the concepts embodied in " . . . From the Sea" and "Forward . . . from the Sea" (1994) constituted the most significant change to U.S. naval strategy and operations since the end of World War II.

As the United States returns to an era of Great Power competition and thus the need to create a strategy to meet the challenges of a rising China and a revanchist Russia, it is useful to consider how the U.S. Navy deconstructed its Maritime Strategy. The examination of the end of the Maritime Strategy in *Strategy Shelved* can benefit current and future efforts at producing a triservice—Navy, Marine Corps, and Coast Guard—maritime strategy, transforming the Marines into a more "maritime"-focused service, and retooling the Department of Defense's focus on a global strategy in high-end warfare.

CHAPTER 1

NAVAL STRATEGY, 1945–1980

The Post–World War II Transoceanic Strategy

To appreciate the scope and magnitude of the change in how naval strategy was created and implemented between 1989 and 1994, it is necessary to take note of the development of national and naval strategy from the end of World War II through the late 1970s and reorganizations within the Department of Defense. The U.S. Cold War policy of containment is best described by the historian John Lewis Gaddis, who called it a "series of attempts to deal with the series of consequences that resulted from the Faustian bargain" of the U.S. alliance with the Soviet Union in World War II.[1] The actions of the Soviet Union from the end of the war through the Berlin Blockade of 1948–49 eventually compelled the United States to join with other nations in unified opposition to the Soviet Union, but the military strategy and attendant defense organization that emerged at the end of the 1940s to support containment were also shaped by competition among the U.S. military services for increasingly scarce resources, their differing historical concepts of unification and grand strategy, and arguments about which of them would employ atomic weapons and in what capacity. These issues, rather than any actions by a communist country, defined how the Department of Defense and its component military services structured their Cold War strategies and force structures to support containment. The U.S. Navy grappled with all three issues over the course of the 1960s and 1970s in trying to develop a naval strategy that preserved its force structure and independent fleet action, supported hypothetical strategic and actual ground operations in Vietnam (and before that in Korea), and confronted a global Soviet naval presence. These conditions would also affect post–Cold War strategy development, with the Navy once again facing concerns about force structure, independence of the fleet in the joint era, and how best to support operations ashore.

THE UNIFICATION STRUGGLE

The fight for funding in the immediate aftermath of World War II and initial Navy attempts to build a postwar naval strategy coincided with intense service disputes over the unification of the armed forces that resulted in 1947 in the creation of the National Military Establishment, which in 1949 became the Department of Defense.[2] The apparent failure of the Army and Navy to anticipate and prevent the Japanese attack on Pearl Harbor on 7 December 1941, the advent of atomic weapons, and a general sense that the United States' newfound global responsibilities as of 1945 drove both Congress and President Harry Truman to demand a defense reorganization, including some measure of unification among the armed forces. A series of congressional and military boards took up the issue of unification in the late 1940s, and their efforts caused division among the services on which course of action would best provide "national security"—a term coined by Secretary of the Navy James Forrestal at a 1945 Senate hearing—as well as meet service needs and requirements.[3]

The Army's experience with intra-service unification in the early 1900s, its theory of command and control, and its persistent lack of funding over the years appear to have significantly influenced its military and civilian leaders to propose a unification plan after World War II. The earlier internal unification process, conducted under Secretary of War Elihu P. Root, stamped out rivalries among the cavalry, infantry, and artillery branches by creating a chief of staff position senior to the branch chiefs.[4] After World War II, Army leaders advocated such an arrangement and the same general operational procedures for all the armed services to eliminate similar inter-service arguments.

The Army had pushed these concepts in inter-service planning discussions prior to the U.S. entry into World War II. For Army secretary Henry Stimson and Chief of Staff Gen. George C. Marshall the Root reforms were the "model to which they instinctively turned when they sought a structure to encompass both the Army and the Navy."[5] The Army put forward its concept for a unified military in a July 1941 paper on a proposed structure for the Joint Chiefs of Staff (JCS), which would be established the following February. Written by the War Plans director, Brig. Gen. Dwight Eisenhower, it stated, "The principles of strategy and employment of military forces are the same for all of the services."[6] General Marshall's attitude toward unification had hardened over the course of World War II in light of a number of conflicts with the Navy, especially ones involving the services' competing wartime budgets. At one point, Marshall wrote to the Army quartermaster general regarding the Navy's better budget situation, stating, "I know that they have more money because they are more popular with Congress and I believe they are less rigidly held to account for the details of their expenditures."[7]

The Army's concept for defense unification under a single chief of staff was known as the Collins Plan, named for its nominal author, Lt. Gen. Joseph Lawton Collins, although General Marshall had previously promoted many of its elements. Collins had commanded troops in both the Pacific under Gen. Douglas MacArthur and in Europe under General Eisenhower. The Collins Plan called for a secretary of the armed forces to replace all the cabinet-level service secretaries. In addition, a singular armed forces chief of staff, responsible to the president, would "direct the military activities of four operating commands: the Army, Navy, Air Forces, and a Common Supply and Hospitalization Service patterned after Army Service Forces. Overseas theater commanders would report directly to the Chief of Staff."[8] The World War II–era JCS would remain intact but have no control over operating forces. It would serve only as an advisory group to the president and the armed forces secretary.[9]

President Truman had served in the Army in World War I and was generally predisposed to that branch's viewpoints on unification. He also strongly favored a system with a single, supreme commander of the nation's armed forces to replace the wartime corporate JCS. Truman blamed the Pearl Harbor fiasco on there being separate command structures for the Army and Navy in Hawaii, felt that separate military departments contributed to duplication and waste, and believed that separate services bred "elitism and military cliques."[10]

High-profile infighting and accusations marred early attempts at compromise between the services. Advocates of separating the Air Force from the Army to create another independent service, among them Lt. Gen. James Doolittle and Gen. Carl Spaatz, had provoked the ire of the Navy by also calling "for the separation of naval aviation from the Navy and its incorporation into the new service."[11] There had been initial support from some senior naval leaders, including Adm. Chester Nimitz and Adm. William Halsey for a unified defense establishment, but that faded over concern that the Army (and later the Air Force) preferred unification to "deprive the Navy of its air arm or of a fully trained and equipped Marine Corps."[12] While Nimitz and Halsey liked the idea of a supreme commander at the operational level, they became opponents of the concept when confronted with harsh Army rhetoric about who had won the Pacific War. During a dinner in Norfolk, Virginia, to promote service harmony, Army Air Force Brig. Gen. Frank Armstrong claimed that Air Force B-29s had won the war against Japan and called the Marine Corps "a small, bitched up army talking Navy lingo" that needed to be put back into the Army, where the Marines could become "real soldiers."[13] Hyperbole aside, some senior naval aviators, including Adm. Forrest Sherman and Adm. Arthur Radford, were concerned about the welfare of naval aviation.

In 1945 the Marine commandant, Gen. Alexander Vandegrift, sent a circular to his generals in which he asserted that the "Marine Corps was in a fight for its life," and specifically addressing Gen. Howland Smith, remarked that "unification is more like a street brawl than a knightly joust."[14] In practical terms, the naval service was accustomed to determining its own strategy and its own acquisition and operations budgets without the interference of the other services or civilians, except for the president. As the military analyst Carl Builder, who has examined military traditions as a source of strategic thinking wrote, "The concept of independent command at sea is to be sought and honored by every true naval officer."[15] The Army's proposed unification plan violated this principle of naval independence.

Although unification of some kind seemed inevitable, Secretary of the Navy Forrestal was determined to preserve naval independence within a unified armed services organization. A Wall Street investment banker and former naval aviator, Forrestal had been appointed by his close friend President

Franklin Roosevelt in April 1944, after the death of his predecessor, Frank Knox.[16] Forrestal urged Navy admirals to "end their luxury of separation from national affairs and to take a more active and vocal role as advocates of their service."[17] Forrestal recruited Ferdinand Eberstadt, a friend and partner in business and government, to draft an alternative to the Army's Collins Plan. Eberstadt, who delivered his recommendations in 1945 believed that the Army's unification efforts "had deep political-economic and organizational implications that overshadowed the simple combination of the Army and the Navy into a single department" and that "unification was a complicated subject where opinions seem to be more plentiful than knowledge."[18] With a background in industry and finance, Eberstadt proposed retaining a corporate model of military leadership, considering it the best course of action to ensure military readiness "within the framework of our democratic system of government."[19] He also called for "separate departments that provide a greater representation of specialized knowledge," arguing that "they provide a varying aggregation of experienced judgement and [ensure] representation of varying viewpoints."[20] A single armed forces secretary, Eberstadt warned, "might become a puppet of the military establishment" and raised the possibility that the "civilian and military chiefs might be tempted to exercise prerogatives reserved by the Constitution to the President."[21]

The Eberstadt Report recommended the creation of coordinating bodies—i.e., the National Security Council and the National Security Resources Board—to promote corporate cooperation between the Army and the Navy. It also advocated that the Air Force be made a separate service. The report received praise within the Navy as well as from the broader defense community. Truman's first executive secretary of the National Security Council, Rear Adm. Sidney Souers, said that Eberstadt's work "provided a definite plan for unification instead of a merger," as proposed by the Army.[22]

Congress began examining both plans at the end of 1945 but could not agree on one or the other. An exasperated Truman finally suggested that Secretary of the Army Robert Patterson and Secretary of the Navy Forrestal settle the unification dispute in lieu of attempts to mandate what form unification should take. The service secretaries and the prospective Air Force secretary, W. Stuart Symington, worked out the services' biggest differences. The Navy received significant concessions from the Army in that the Marine Corps and naval aviation remained largely unaltered and under naval control. The service departments, including a newly independent Air Force, were organized along the corporate lines suggested by Eberstadt. These agreements enabled passage of the National Security Act in July 1947.[23] Patterson had been Truman's first choice for the new position of secretary of defense, but Patterson wanted to return to private life. Truman then turned to Forrestal, who accepted and was sworn in on 17 September 1947.[24]

Thus, the concept of force unification ultimately merged the service secretaries and their respective departments into a single department, the National Military Establishment, led by a cabinet-level civilian secretary of defense and responsible for military, naval, and aviation affairs; the service secretaries still reported to the president. The corporate board–like structure and collaborative decision-making policies of the wartime JCS were replaced by a single armed forces chief of staff, with deputies for ground, air, and naval warfare. Forrestal and Eberstadt had preserved many of the Navy's freedoms, but challenges to the creation and implementation of a postwar naval strategy loomed on the immediate horizon with the emerging Cold War. A contest over service-preferred platforms to deliver atomic weapons would threaten the Navy's credibility with lawmakers, the press, and the public, while an unexpected conflict in the Far East provided the naval service a boost in its campaign to obtain adequate funding for a global naval force.

PRESERVING A CARRIER-BASED FORCE

The compromise that produced defense unification gave birth to a crisis of roles and missions among the services. In the late 1940s, the Navy's strategy had coalesced around aircraft carrier–based aviation, antisubmarine forces, and amphibious ships capable of ferrying Marines or Army troops to distant combat locations. The Navy came into direct conflict with the Air Force, however, over the capability to use strategic nuclear weapons. This in turn affected the other services and called into question the Navy's planned strategy and attendant force structure.

The Navy's chief strategist was Admiral Sherman, who had spent much of World War II working for the Pacific Fleet commander, Admiral Nimitz, as his chief planner.[25] Serving as the deputy chief of Naval Operations for Operations, Sherman had developed the naval component of the first postwar joint plan to confront the Soviet Union, Operation Pincher, adopted in March 1946. Pincher provided the basic outline for a war against the Soviet Union in which the United States' nuclear weapons would be the key equalizer against large Soviet ground formations, which the United States and its allies could not match in quantity.[26] The Navy's role in Pincher would be to destroy the Soviet navy and merchant marine and blockade the Soviet coastline.[27]

In early 1947, Sherman unveiled to President Truman and members of the House and Senate Armed Services Committees the first, full Navy strategy for a global war against the Soviet Union.[28] Sherman's strategy generally followed what he had articulated in Pincher but put greater emphasis on the U.S. presence in the Mediterranean. The British Royal Navy, which from the 1870s until the end of World War II had patrolled the Mediterranean as if it were a local lake, was now in the throes of even greater postwar cutbacks than the U.S. military. In 1946 Sherman and other senior U.S. naval commanders had met with Admiral Lord Cunningham, the Royal Navy's First Sea Lord and chief of the naval staff. Cunningham bluntly informed his guests that Britain was "unable to support their whole Mediterranean forces anymore" and that "Britain would need help from the United States in Europe."[29] Given this situation, Sherman's strategy assumed a more robust U.S. presence in the Mediterranean than envisioned in Pincher. His presentation was generally well received, and although Sherman departed Washington in early 1948 to command the Sixth Fleet in the Mediterranean, Adm. Arthur W. Radford, vice chief of Naval Operations, continued to advocate and advance his global naval strategy. Sherman's efforts formed the basis of U.S. Cold War naval strategy and force deployment for the next forty years. Thus U.S. Navy units routinely set out from ports in the continental United States to forward deployed stations in the Pacific and Europe in case of conflict with the Soviet Union.

Sherman and Radford believed that the limited number of available atomic weapons demanded the presence of aircraft carriers for strikes against the Soviet homeland. It was this assumption that brought the Navy into direct conflict with the Air Force over atomic weapon delivery rights and forced the services into a round of roles and missions fights that appeared (erroneously) to have been settled by the National Security Act of 1947. Air Force leadership was convinced that the only effective means of deterring the Soviet Union from a ground attack in Western Europe was a "powerful strategic air offensive, which would lay waste to urban/industrial targets in the USSR that were vital to the Soviet war making capacity."[30] Such an offensive required a new, more powerful bomber that could carry both conventional and nuclear payloads. This concept became a key element in a series of joint war plans developed with the United Kingdom from 1947 to 1949.[31] The Navy viewed this approach as being at variance with U.S. national security interests because it abandoned large parts of Western Europe, the Mediterranean Sea, and the oil fields of the Middle East to the Soviets almost at the outset of war. Such abandonment, it was argued, could "seriously jeopardize the possibilities for ultimate victory."[32]

The Navy also disagreed with the Air Force's preference for massed strikes, rather than precision strikes, even in atomic warfare, perhaps as a result of the services' very different experiences in World War II, during which the Navy never conducted strategic bombing against cities. A 1948 draft Navy briefing stated, "National air power must consist of a land-based air force and a sea air force (carrier task forces), each developing the weapons and tactics for the precision, instead of mass, destruction essential to the successful prosecution of atomic warfare."[33] From early 1948 through 1950, these differing views on the prosecution of atomic warfare along with service roles and missions in general, a change in defense leadership, and the unexpected conflict in Korea initially threatened and then affirmed the Navy's Cold War strategic concepts.

Departing Chief of Naval Operations (CNO) Admiral Nimitz may have innocently launched this second round of conflict over roles and missions in his farewell "valedictory" speech in 1947, when he stated, "It is improbable that bomber fleets will be capable, for several years to come, of making two-way trips between continents with heavy loads of bombs. In the event of war within this period, if we are to project our power against vital areas of an enemy across the ocean before beachheads on enemy territory are captured, it must be by air-sea power."[34] Indeed, the Air Force chief of staff, General Spaatz, believed at the time that not only had Nimitz's statement "start[ed] off the fight again" over roles and missions,[35] but also that it violated Truman administration Executive Order 9877, Functions of the Armed Forces, which charged the Air Force with organizing, training, and equipping air forces.[36]

Forrestal, in his capacity as secretary of defense, tried to mediate the disputes through negotiation. To that end, the March 1948 Key West Conference and subsequent Newport Conference in August that same year produced some agreement between the Navy and the Air Force over the question of strategic air operations, naval air capabilities, and the employment of nuclear weapons. The Key West Agreement gave the Navy primary interest in combat operations at sea and the right to "conduct air operations as necessary for the accomplishment of objectives in a naval campaign," thus preserving the concept of carrier aviation.[37] The Air Force's primary interest was in all air operations, except those elements given to the other services, and it was given specific control of "strategic air warfare."[38] The Newport Agreement allowed the Navy to pursue atomic weapon capabilities, and the Navy agreed that the Air Force should assume responsibility for the nation's nascent atomic weapons program until further study on atomic energy organization could be completed.[39] Thus, the two conferences resolved some of the outstanding strategic issues between the Air Force and the Navy, but the truce remained uneasy. The historian Jeffrey Barlow quotes Capt. Fitzhugh Lee, an aide to Secretary of the Navy John Sullivan, telling his boss after the Key West event, "Strategic bombing means many things to many people. The basic issue as to whether or not carriers can be utilized for atomic bombing on selected targets remains unresolved."[40]

Interservice tensions had resurfaced with the greater centralization in the National Military Establishment, reductions in the defense budget, and the resignation of Secretary Forrestal in March 1949, due to ill health, and his replacement by the Air Force partisan Louis Johnson. The 1948 Hoover Commission, created to review federal government organization, had examined the fledgling, reorganized defense establishment, with Forrestal's confidant Eberstadt serving as primary investigator. Eberstadt recommended further centralization and strengthening of the defense secretary's position to avoid service disputes like those involving unification and roles and missions. Truman embraced the commission's recommendations, as did Congress in passing amendments to the National Security Act in 1949. The National

Military Establishment was duly renamed the Department of Defense in 1949, and service secretaries were placed directly under the defense secretary and relieved of direct reporting responsibility to the president.[41]

The 1949 legislation represented a measured approach. Concerns that the JCS and the new permanent position for the chairman resembled the German General Staff from World War II had led Congress to also limit their power and influence. The legislative amendments made the secretary of defense the principal assistant to the president on all Department of Defense issues, rejecting calls by Truman to make the JCS chairman the president's "principal military advisor." It also doubled the size of the Joint Staff supporting the JCS, from 100 to 210.[42] These actions did not, however, reduce service infighting over military strategy or conventional and nuclear weapons programs. Indeed, the reductions in the 1950 defense budget increased service competition for scarce resources. Truman had requested $14.2 billion, a significant increase from the $11.9 billion proposed for 1949, but included only half of what would be required to adequately fund the emerging containment force structure.[43]

Forrestal's replacement by Johnson, who had had financially backed Truman in the 1948 presidential election, further complicated the situation.[44] Johnson had been an executive at the Convair Aviation Company, producer of the Air Force's B-36 bomber, which in the competition for decreased defense resources would become the principal rival of the Navy's emerging supercarrier design.[45] Johnson, who took charge of defense on 28 March 1949, told Adm. Louis Denfeld, Nimitz's replacement as CNO, that he "would not allow anything to happen to the Navy," but while secretary he relayed to administration officials his view of the "whole damn Navy" as a "terrible outfit," their transgression being "anti-unification."[46] Johnson quickly made it clear that he was no friend of the supercarrier. Just eighteen days into his term of office, he requested the services' input on whether the supercarrier program should continue.[47] The chiefs of staff of the Army and the Air Force, Gen. Omar Bradley and Gen. Hoyt Vandenberg, respectively, issued negative appraisals of the Navy program. Johnson agreed and decided to cancel it. The CNO received notification just three hours before Johnson was to tell the press.[48] Secretary of the Navy Sullivan and his deputy, W. John Kenney, both resigned in protest. Sullivan's replacement, Francis Matthews, was not well regarded by his uniformed colleagues, who disparagingly referred to him as "Rowboat" Matthews, for his lack of naval knowledge and apparent unwillingness to educate himself about naval capabilities.[49] Navy leaders at all levels viewed the cancellation of the supercarrier as the White House and Department of Defense's tacit rejection of the naval strategic principal of precision airstrikes against specific military and industrial targets and acceptance of the Air Force's strategy of atomic attacks on cities.

Air Force leaks on the capabilities of the B-36 force to conduct atomic attacks were countered by the release of an anonymous, negative report on acquisition and testing procedures. The report had in fact been written by Cedric Worth, the civilian special assistant to the under secretary of the Navy, and his military subordinate, Cdr. Thomas Davies. These shenanigans led the House Armed Services Committee chairman, Carl Vinson (D-Ga.), to open an investigation into the allegations of problems in the B-36 program.[50] The August 1949 hearings and the related controversy over the Navy's attempts at damage control and efforts to preserve carrier aviation became known as the Revolt of the Admirals, due to the large number of senior naval officials who testified or submitted statements in support of naval aviation and its central role in naval strategy. The group included former CNOs—Nimitz and Ernie King—and Pacific Fleet admirals—William Halsey, Raymond Spruance, and Thomas Kinkaid. CNO Denfeld created his own research office, designated OP-23 by its director, Capt. Arleigh Burke, to support the Navy's role in Vinson's hearings. Burke, a respected surface officer, had been the primary author of a significant contribution to postwar naval strategy presented in the "National Security and Navy Contributions Thereto for the Next Ten Years," produced by the General Board of the Navy in 1948. Burke's assessment recognized the need for the Navy to be able to strike the Soviet Union through naval air attack, but also that such a capability "may well be beyond the capacity of the United States Navy."[51]

The House hearings became a de facto referendum on carrier aviation as a component of the military. In addition to retired officers, senior active duty officers such as the vice chief of Naval Operations, Adm. Arthur Radford, and Burke spoke of the effectiveness of naval aviation as a component of national power and of the potential shortcomings of the B-36 in its role as an atomic weapons delivery vehicle. Radford, in particular, questioned the use of atomic weapons against cities, the primary mission of the B-36. He suggested that it would result in a "pyrrhic victory" and was also "morally indefensible."[52] While senior naval leaders worked to defend the case for naval aviation, other naval officers pursued their own public efforts against the B-36. Rear Adm. Dan Gallery wrote "Don't let them Scuttle the Navy," an article critical of Navy opponents, and the aviator Capt. John Crommlein staged his own ad hoc, unauthorized press conference to highlight the plight of naval aviation. These actions, although widely supported from within the naval officer ranks, generally undermined the reasoned efforts of senior officers to persuade a generally sympathetic Vinson of the Navy's need for carrier-based aviation. Denfeld, despite instructions from Secretaries Johnson and Matthews to the contrary, gave dramatic testimony to Vinson's committee in favor of naval aviation. The Soviet Union had meanwhile exploded an atomic bomb in September 1949, further complicating the discussion on how the U.S. military would employ its atomic weapons.

The Navy appeared to have suffered a significant defeat by the time Vinson's hearings ended in October 1949. Vinson concluded that "not one scintilla of evidence" offered during the hearings suggested the presence of corruption or undue influence in the B-36 acquisition program.[53] The Navy Secretariat had been somewhat discredited by its inability to exercise control over its uniformed officers. Secretary Matthews fired CNO Denfeld for refusing to support the civilian chain of command by following the orders of Johnson and Matthews not to testify. Rear Admiral Gallery and Captain Crommlein were denied future active duty advancement. Vice Adm. William Blandy and Vice Adm. Gerald F. Bogan, who testified against Matthews for his lack of support for naval aviation, were given rear admiral assignments as "punishment" for their actions.[54] Captain Burke nearly met a similar fate when Matthews tried to block his elevation to rear admiral, but Truman in an out-of-character decision overruled him.[55]

The Revolt of the Admirals appeared on the surface to be a significant defeat for both the emerging naval strategy of strike warfare from aircraft carriers and the supporting force structure of large flattops capable of launching aircraft armed with nuclear weapons. The Air Force's B-36 emerged from the hearings unscathed, as did the force's strategy of nuclear attack against Soviet cities. Despite these setbacks, the Navy's preferred Cold War strategy to strike from the sea and the large aircraft carrier survived Johnson's tenure, the service life of the B-36, and the general ire of the other services. The USS *United States,* the first of the Navy's planned "supercarriers," would be scrapped, but its successor, the *Forrestal* class of four supercarriers, survived determined Air Force opposition and eventually joined the fleet in the late 1950s after carrier operations against North Korea convinced the Truman administration of the utility of the large carrier.[56] Johnson, who did not get along well with Congress, became a political liability over his assertions that his military budget cuts could sustain readiness, a claim largely disproved by the rapid success of the initial North Korean attack.[57] Gen. George C. Marshall replaced him as defense secretary in September 1950.

Not all of Johnson's personnel changes proved detrimental to naval interests. His appointment of Admiral Sherman to replace Denfeld as CNO and of Admiral Radford as commander in chief of the Pacific Fleet ensured that the Navy's preferred strategy would remain viable. As CNO, Sherman continued to refine Navy strategic concepts and plans to use naval forces in support of both strategic air and ground forces in Europe and the broader Eurasian littoral. The creation of the North Atlantic Treaty Organization (NATO) in April 1949 and the Korean War resurrected the concept of a robust U.S. military capability in the post–World War II era. The Truman administration's muscular concept of containment as embodied in the 1950 policy document NSC-68 effectively militarized the Cold War and brought about renewed growth and strength for the Army, whose leaders, Gen. Bradley and Gen. Eisenhower, focused on northwestern Europe as the main theater of future conflict with the Soviet Union.[58]

The Navy had to fight the rest of the defense establishment to pay equal attention to the Mediterranean and the Middle East, noting the United States' assumption of what historian Michael Palmer called "Great Britain's World War II role" and the importance of "peripheral operations in dispersing enemy forces before a decisive campaign," presumably in northwestern Europe, could begin.[59] In July 1951 Sherman died suddenly of a heart attack while touring the Mediterranean, but his strategic concepts would endure into the next presidential administration, and his successor, Adm. William M. Fechteler, adopted his policies. Fechteler was well supported by the newly promoted Rear Admiral Burke, who as head of the Navy's Strategic Plans Division (OP-30) further refined Sherman's strategic concepts and developed operational plans for carrier task forces and submarines to "operate offensively against enemy bases and thus force the dispersion of his land and air strength."[60]

The war in Korea also confirmed the need for an effective, mobile non-nuclear aviation capability. Although only one carrier, the USS *Valley Forge*, had been on duty in the Western Pacific with the Seventh Fleet at the time of North Korea's attack in June 1950, eleven large carriers and six smaller escort carriers would eventually serve in the conflict.[61] On the last day of combat alone, four carriers with twenty-one aviation squadrons among them engaged in combat operations on the Korean Peninsula.[62] The Air Force had been more focused on its strategic bombing mission from 1945 to 1950 and had dedicated few resources to the close air support needed by Allied ground forces fighting in Korea.[63] The Navy, by contrast, had maintained this capability, which had been created for opposed landings in the Pacific during World War II.[64] Between the testimony of naval leaders during the Revolt of the Admirals and combat experience in Korea, the U.S. Navy succeeded in convincing members of Congress of the usefulness of naval aviation and its strategy for transoceanic warfare. This strategy and its advocates, including Radford and Burke, were well positioned to support it as the nation changed administrations and containment concepts in 1953.

The contest over unification and the fielding of nuclear weapons among the services continued throughout the Cold War, and the battles created lasting suspicions among the services that persisted beyond the fall of communism. The Base Force concept of Gen. Colin Powell, while serving as JCS chairman, seemed to some naval observers to represent the ultimate victory of the Army's vision of service unification. According to naval historian George Baer, "Administratively during the 1980s the Navy lost a battle against greater Defense Department Centralization. The Goldwater-Nichols Department of Defense Reorganization Act of 1986 marked the triumph of vertical organization. It gave the Chairman of the Joint Chiefs the power to communicate his own opinion to the President via the Secretary of Defense.

Previously the Chairman had to report differing views held by the service chiefs."[65] The authority Powell derived from Goldwater-Nichols allowed him to dictate the size of the fleet without Navy input. Powell later described his dealings with the service chiefs over force structures as "muggings" because they would not willingly reduce force structure, as he demanded.[66] Powell's forced reductions in the Navy's size as formalized in the Base Force helped to drive changes in Navy strategy in the early 1990s.

NAVAL STRATEGY AND THE NEW LOOK

The election of Dwight Eisenhower as president in 1952 ended the first phase of containment. The period 1945 to 1953 brought significant changes in that the United States' Soviet ally became its most feared international opponent. How the nation and the Navy in particular planned and executed military strategy had to be significantly altered from the prewar years. That said, the forces of the United States' potential enemies did not have as great an impact on strategy as did the advent of atomic weapons, the introduction of force unification and the resultant organization of the Department of Defense, permanent JCS, an independent Air Force, and the creation of NATO.

As noted, unification put service priorities in direct competition for scarce financial resources. The JCS organization was pressed into service as an operational advisory body in a peacetime environment, a mission that it was not really designed to undertake. Robert Murray, a former under secretary of the Navy, described the post–World War II JCS system as one developed more for World War III than for limited engagements.[67] This mismatch of organization to operational responsibilities would affect naval strategy development throughout the Cold War. Unified JCS decisions were also made difficult by tensions that individual JCS members felt in representing national security requirements versus service needs in the course of their duties.[68] The creation of an independent Air Force raised the stakes of the contest to higher levels by further dividing the service resource pool among branches desperate to replace worn-out wartime equipment. The advent of atomic weapons heightened the ferocity of the competition as the services fought for a share in the employment of the ultimate weapon. The need to provide significant support to the nascent NATO alliance also complicated the situation. It further taxed national resources, required new force requirements to be deployed overseas in peacetime, and raised questions regarding the use of atomic weapons in support of alliance and U.S. national security requirements. Many of the factors that influenced the start of the Cold War would return at its end to complicate planning for the post–Cold War era.

The Eisenhower administration settled on a method of containment that generally favored the naval strategic concepts developed by Admirals Sherman, Radford, and Burke. It also, however, decided on another round of defense reorganization that was incompatible with the Navy's concepts of strategy and command of naval forces. Eisenhower assumed the presidency convinced that the nation needed a major shift in its application of the containment strategy. Truman's military buildup from $13 billion to about $40 billion to implement containment as articulated in NSC-68 and for the Korean War had strained the postwar U.S. economy and contributed to a rise of inflation. The military historian David Jablonsky suggests that Eisenhower sought a balance of affordable containment that could be maintained over decades as a substitute for perpetually large defense budgets.[69] If the cost of maintaining containment became too high, Eisenhower felt that the American public would return to favoring a policy of isolationism, a position neither the United States nor its Cold War allies saw as an option in an age of atomic weapons.[70] Estimates suggesting a small Soviet stockpile of nuclear weapons and the conventional armaments called for in NSC-68 convinced the new Eisenhower administration that a policy of deterrence could be had for a reasonable price.[71] While outgoing Truman administration officials believed that military expenditures for fiscal year 1946 would total upwards of $46.3 billion, Eisenhower set an upper limit of $41.1 billion and got to work on the mechanics of a new strategy with an eventual goal of decreasing the amount to $33 million or $34 million by 1957.[72] In a 1954 speech at the Council on Foreign Relations, Secretary of State John Foster Dulles expounded on the traits of the new doctrine of "massive retaliation." He stated that it provided "maximum deterrent at a bearable cost" and that it gave the United States and its allies flexibility and security in the face of a threat of a devastating nuclear attack.[73] This option would check Soviet aggression and allow the Western powers to choose how and where to respond to Soviet aggression rather than letting the Soviets choose the venue for confrontation. Massive retaliation was part of Dulles and Eisenhower's broader New Look policy to deter the aggressive use of communist land power. Dulles theorized that Soviet land-based forces would overrun Western forces and that no alternative other than the threat of nuclear retaliation could check such a determined Soviet effort.

Also in terms of strategy, Eisenhower did not approve of contesting what he called "local" conflicts. He saw "no sense in wasting manpower in small costly wars that could not achieve decisive results under the political and military circumstances then existing."[74] Eisenhower felt that small confrontations only strengthened U.S. adversaries like the Soviet Union and China, allowing them, rather than the United States, to dictate the terms of the conflict. Only by working with local allies to police trouble spots and threatening communist sponsors with nuclear attack would the United States avoid expensive "brush fires."[75] Under Eisenhower's reorganization for the New Look, the United States could still fight conventional conflicts if required, but it would rely on those forces already deployed overseas and supported by air power. Admiral Radford, Eisenhower's first JCS chairman, noted in his memoirs that "the organization that would evolve would be heavy in air power (both Air Force and Navy), and that the other services . . . would have to adjust to organizations that could be fleshed out rapidly in case of emergency."[76]

The 1950s heralded a smaller naval fleet in line with Eisenhower's emphasis on air-delivered strategic nuclear weapons as the cornerstone of U.S. defense strategy. The Navy prospered over the course of the decade despite further reductions in ships and personnel. Contrary to the president's new strategy of staying out of small conflicts, the Navy's experience in the Korean War suggested that the service should prepare to fight them in any case. Eisenhower would later decry the emerging "warfare state" as the "military-industrial complex," but the Navy embraced the infusion of science, technology, and associated funding that would ensure the next generation of naval weapons. The problem of defense organization, however, ended the decade on a negative note for the Navy as Eisenhower sought more restrictive Executive Branch oversight of the military services. The president's 1958 reforms would lay the seeds for another twenty-five years of defense reorganization battles, which would significantly affect the Navy's strategic concepts during the latter half of the Cold War.

According to the political scientist Samuel Huntington, "Admiral Radford probably played a more important role in shaping military strategy than any other military man in military office between 1946 and 1960."[77] Radford, an early convert to the New Look policy, was a trusted Eisenhower adviser, but he was also able to emphasize the utility of naval units in accordance with the Navy's postwar strategy. Eisenhower had earlier been impressed with Radford's "distinguished war record and grasp of global politics," leading him to select Radford to succeed General Bradley, whose term as JCS chairman expired in 1953.[78]

In February 1954, as the position of French forces in the beleaguered Dien Bien Phu outpost in Vietnam became more desperate, Radford kept aircraft carriers in the Pacific ready to conduct conventional and nuclear air strikes against Vietminh positions if Eisenhower decided to intervene.[79] When the 1954 Geneva Accords divided Vietnam at the 17th parallel, the U.S. Navy was in position to provide a humanitarian sealift, Operation Passage to Freedom, which moved 311,000 Vietnamese, who migrated to South Vietnam in the wake of the agreement. U.S. naval forces also supported Nationalist Chinese efforts to retain control of key South China Sea outposts. The U.S. Seventh Fleet evacuated some 27,000 Nationalist Chinese troops from the disputed Tachen Islands in just eighty-five hours in January 1955.[80] In August 1958 the Seventh Fleet provided a significant show of force in the Taiwan Strait, causing Communist Chinese forces to back down from a similar attempt to intimidate Nationalist Chinese into surrendering the island of Quemoy.[81]

These deployments placed a severe strain on the fleet, in particular its Pacific elements. Training and maintenance deficiencies on board four aircraft carriers and their associated air wings caused the acting CNO, Adm. Donald Duncan, to write Radford in 1954, stating, "'The deployment of four CVA's (large, attack carriers) to the Far Eastern Command is the most difficult commitment to maintain," and adding, "One entire (carrier) unit pressed through an abbreviated training period which has proved unsuitable to prepare the ship for its intended duty."[82] This new pattern of extended deployments by naval forces to overseas locations in support of national interests was rapidly becoming the hallmark of post–World War II U.S. Navy operations. It was, however, fully in line with the strategic planning carried out by Sherman and

Radford nearly a decade earlier. While Eisenhower ultimately shrank from the combat employment of naval units, the CNO after 1955, Admiral Burke, sought to prepare the service for this eventuality, at one point observing that "because major nations shrank from wreaking nuclear destruction on one another, the probability of limited war had increased."[83] The Navy's postwar strategy would fully embrace this idea in the 1960s.

Eisenhower's focus on strategic nuclear weapons and their associated technology as the primary enablers of his New Look strategy proved to be a significant boon to the Navy. It provided funding and access to scientists and engineers who would produce a new generation of naval platforms, weapons, communications equipment, and new strategic missions for the Navy over the course of the Eisenhower presidency and beyond, to the present. In 1948 Secretary of Defense Forrestal had recognized the importance of new technology to the Navy's postwar success when he said, "It is apparent that radical revisions of combat tactics and concepts are necessary, and the Navy is preparing itself in accordance with these developments."[84] Prior to that, as Secretary of the Navy, Forrestal had arranged for more than forty-five schools and industrial firms to support research in "electronics, nuclear physics, chemistry, metallurgy, and guided missiles," which would eventually make his radical revisions possible.[85]

Advancements in all these fields helped to maintain the Navy's global strategy of carrier and submarine operations against the Soviet Union and other opponents. The development of missiles, both as offensive and defensive weapons, ensured the protection of the aircraft carrier against aerial threats at sea and allowed its aircraft to attack targets at greater range. Advancements in electronics spawned a new field of network communications among ships and aircraft that enabled naval forces to disperse more widely at sea in avoidance of attack yet concentrate their offensive efforts over great distances. Meanwhile, advancements in nuclear technology gave the Navy a new platform and a new strategic mission that put it on equal footing with the Air Force in nuclear weapons delivery. It also gave the service a hard-nosed engineer bureaucrat, Hyman G. Rickover, whose management of the nuclear navy brought both success and challenges to the business of naval strategy.

In response to Soviet developments in missile technology, Eisenhower demanded that the United States produce reliable long-range nuclear-armed missiles. He announced to a December 1955 meeting of the National Security Council that he would run such a project himself if required.[86] CNO Burke responded with the Polaris ballistic missile project, a program that in less than four years produced a weapon and its attendant platform, the USS *George Washington,* a ballistic missile submarine. Rear Adm. William "Red" Raborn led the program and had implicit authority from Burke to lay claim to all the resources necessary to ensure its successful completion. The submarine-launched Polaris had a range of 1,500 miles, and the *George Washington* could carry sixteen such weapons. The program received support from the network of scientists and industrialists cultivated by Forrestal a decade earlier, including the physicist Edward Teller, the Lockheed Corporation, the Electric Boat Corporation, and General Electric.[87] The addition of the submarine-launched ballistic missile finally gave the U.S. Navy a significant role in the nation's nuclear deterrence force.

This advance in strategic weaponry and the new strategic mission for the Navy would not have happened without the development of the nuclear-propelled submarine, which was made possible thanks to the tireless and sometimes tyrannical efforts of Rear Adm. Hyman G. Rickover, the engineering duty officer who became the "father of the nuclear navy" in the early 1950s. Reporting to the Oak Ridge Nuclear Facility, Tennessee, in June 1946 after World War II assignments in ship repair and supply efficiency, Rickover focused his engineering and electrical skills on the translating the awesome power of atomic weapons to ship and submarine propulsion.[88] By 1949 Rickover was running the Navy's nuclear reactors program and actively planning a nuclear-powered submarine. On 30 September 1954, the nuclear-powered USS *Nautilus* was commissioned and quickly set new standards in speed and range for submarine operations.

Rickover's efforts attracted positive attention from Oak Ridge scientists and the Joint Congressional Committee on Atomic Energy. When Rickover faced mandatory retirement as a senior captain in late 1952, his supporters lobbied Congress to promote the unorthodox Rickover to flag rank, despite there being no specific billet for him to occupy. Thus, in 1953 Rickover was promoted to rear admiral thanks to support from key members of Congress interested in nuclear power, including Sen. Henry "Scoop" Jackson from

Washington and Rep. Melvin Price from Illinois, and despite the possibility of a congressional investigation into Navy promotion procedures.[89]

Senior officers and subordinates alike found Rickover's personality difficult. Vice Adm. Eli T. Reich, who had been a submarine force commander in World War II, called him the "Navy's evil genius."[90] He would be the bane of many future commanders, among them CNO Adm. Elmo Zumwalt and Lt. Jimmy Carter, a future U.S. president, for his withering nuclear interview, a personal audience with Rickover that according to some of the recipients hoping to work with him had the hallmarks of the Spanish Inquisition. Carter later professed only positive views of Rickover, but Zumwalt described his interview as "something akin to the hazing process from plebe year at the Naval Academy."[91]

Rickover often went beyond his purview of nuclear propulsion, leading to duels with senior military and civilian officials over the manning and employment of nuclear-powered surface warships and submarines. He made a host of enemies in the process. Rickover opposed other forms of naval propulsion, such as gas turbines, despite their efficiency, low weight, and easy maintenance, fearing that they might compete with his nuclear propulsion system.[92] The man who ultimately succeeded in retiring Rickover in January 1982, Secretary of the Navy John Lehman, had been unhappy with Rickover's failure to embrace automation and the reduced costs it could bring to the submarine fleet. Lehman also disliked the tyrannical personnel and training system that Rickover had created, describing it as a cult-like religious group.[93] Despite this, the Navy's exceptional record of nuclear-powered warship operations and safety remain a testament to Rickover's dedication and devotion to duty over several decades of service.[94] The marriage of nuclear power, submarines, and nuclear weapons made possible by Rickover's efforts in the 1950s restored the Navy's presence in the front rank of the U.S. nuclear deterrence force. This position also strengthened the Navy's general Cold War strategy of offensive operations from aircraft carrier battle groups and submarines.

EISENHOWER'S DEFENSE ORGANIZATION REFORMS: LIMITING NAVAL FREEDOM OF ACTION

President Eisenhower endorsed Navy efforts to implement a global, naval component to the New Look strategy and was supportive of the Navy's quest for new technology in furtherance of that goal. His experience of joint command in Europe during and after World War II, however, predisposed him to strict command unity behind a single commander. In 1948 he wrote, "Statesmen, generals, admirals, air marshals and even populations must develop confidence in the concept of single command and in the leader by which single command is exercised."[95] Although the JCS by law served as the principal adviser to the president and secretary of defense, Eisenhower felt that the chiefs' loyalty and primary responsibilities were so closely aligned with their services that it threatened their objectivity.[96] His program of ongoing defense unification and organizational reform emphasized a direct chain of command from the president to commanders in the field, divorcing the chiefs from direct command of their services, as the Army had done earlier in the twentieth century under the Root reforms. His outlook put him at odds with senior naval officers, who had traditionally commanded and administered the fleet through the CNO, which unlike the Army chief of staff, retained active command of naval forces.

Military historian David Jablonsky suggests that Eisenhower long believed that the JCS organization had needed greater reform and unification than provided it in 1947 and 1949.[97] Military historian Allan Millett has suggested that Eisenhower's experience as a "skilled staff officer and a wartime allied theater commander" predisposed him to a "more structured approach to defense decision-making."[98] This contrasted starkly to the perspective of senior naval officers such as Admiral Burke, who were used to independent operations far from the observation and control of immediate superiors. Of most significance, Eisenhower and the admirals differed on the nature of war at the century's middle decade. In testimony before Congress during the defense unification hearings in 1945, Eisenhower had stated, "There is no such thing as separate land, sea and air war, and we must all recognize this fact."[99] He spoke these words even before the Soviet Union emerged as the United States' Cold War opponent, and his belief in them remained with him as president.

By contrast, Burke disagreed that modern warfare was a unified venture. The business of operating a navy, he believed, was fundamentally different from that of overseeing ground forces. In the 1980s, Burke's biographer wrote, "He was reluctant to see the operational command of the U.S. Navy removed from the control of the Chief of Naval Operations. Only naval officers, he believed, were familiar enough with the unique requirements of operations at sea to direct them with the dispatch that was needed in far-flung crisis situations. He was deeply worried about the prospect of a unified military service, in which the command of a naval force might fall to an Army or Air Force officer who knew nothing about seafaring."[100] Holding such an opinion obviously stood to land Burke in a conflict with Eisenhower. The president was determined to pursue his reorganization agenda, and to that end he formed a commission in February 1953 led by Nelson Rockefeller, head of the President's Advisory Committee on Government Organization.[101]

Eisenhower received the committee's recommendations in April and swiftly acted on them to issue Reorganization Plan 6 to reform the Department of Defense through congressional approval. The plan was so-named because it was the sixth in a series of such reports drafted by the committee. In short, Reorganization Plan 6 clarified that JCS members were not a military command group, but advisers to the president and secretary of defense. Eisenhower also wanted to transfer authority over the unified commands from the JCS to the secretary of defense, who would then designate a military department and its secretary as the executive agent, making the secretary rather than the JCS in charge of assigning executive agency.[102] The plan also included additional authority for the JCS chairman to direct the Joint Staff supporting the chiefs and called for six more assistant secretaries of defense, to relieve the uniformed services of some of their responsibilities and allow the civilian secretary to oversee the department. Eisenhower was more direct in his memoir, stating that his intent had been the forcible removal of JCS members from their respective services in order to give the body a less parochial outlook in considering the best course for the nation's defense.[103]

Unlike in the reorganization battles in 1947 and 1949, Congress and the military services strongly opposed Eisenhower's concepts of reform. Members of the House of Representatives continued to dislike adopting anything resembling the "Prussian-like" general staff system so prominently associated with the defeated German Empire and Adolf Hitler's Nazi state. Representative Clare Hoffman (R-Mich.), chair of the House Government Operations Committee, charged that Eisenhower was attempting to turn the JCS chairman into a powerful figure capable of becoming a military dictator if the officer felt the need to usurp civilian authority. Eisenhower rejected claims that he was creating a potential dictator, or "man on horseback," to which Hoffman replied that the figure was indeed "on the road and riding fast."[104] Congress eventually approved much of Reorganization Plan 6, but rejected the provisions empowering the JCS chairman.

The Navy responded to Reorganization Plan 6 by doing its own study to examine its organization in light of Eisenhower's changes. Secretary of the Navy Robert Anderson appointed Under Secretary Thomas S. Gates to head a review on how to manage the growing power of the Secretary of the Navy and his staff with that of the CNO. The biggest problem, according to naval historian Thomas Hone was managing the CNO and the secretary's access to the president individually and as a naval team. The Gates Committee sought to encourage consensus between the two centers of naval power by establishing joint administrative boards where the two stakeholders could reach agreement on issues.[105] These efforts were not successful in the short term, and Eisenhower soon took matters into his own hands in response to his unhappiness with the functioning of the JCS and the service secretaries.

None of the service chiefs liked that Eisenhower had placed their civilian service secretary between them and the defense secretary and the president. Eisenhower was equally disappointed in their lack of faith and decided to replace them en masse. Admiral Radford was appointed JCS chairman and Adm. Robert Carney CNO. One of Carney's chief contributions to the further development of naval strategy was the creation of the OP-06 office (Plans, Policy, and Operations) within the CNO's staff. Carney intended the office to serve as the CNO's dedicated office to manage military planning and policy at the JCS level.[106] OP-60 (Strategic Plans and Policy) and its satellite offices would go on to become the Navy's most important strategic planning organ during the Cold War.

Carney incurred Eisenhower's wrath, however, when he balked at swiftly carrying out Navy budget cuts for fiscal year 1956 and for his dour reports on the fate of U.S forces if they engaged in battle with China in the Taiwan Strait crisis of 1955.[107] Burke succeeded him in mid-1955, after two years in the post.[108] Secretary of the Navy Charles Thomas perceived Burke as more youthful and was impressed by his strong technical background and excellent leadership record.[109] Burke was also supposed to be less resisting to defense unification than was his predecessor.[110] The prospective CNO told the Senate Arms Services Committee at his confirmation hearing that he had in no way changed his opinion on defense unification, which he had forcefully opposed in 1949 while the head of OP-23 (Organization Research and Policy Division).[111]

Burke did not hesitate to directly engage Eisenhower on issues of importance to the Navy on which Eisenhower had a different opinion. Burke secured an Oval Office meeting with the president in 1955 to explain the importance of the military draft in meeting Navy manpower requirements. Eisenhower had previously decided not to reinstitute conscription but changed his mind after Burke's presentation. He cautioned Burke, however, "never again to put his commander-in-chief in such an embarrassing position."[112] The two men also remained at odds throughout Eisenhower's second term on the value of defense reorganization, but the president learned to appreciate Burke's value, came to regard him as a member of his team, and appointed him CNO an unprecedented three times. The two men developed a strong friendship during their terms in office. Burke biographer David Alan Rosenberg related one example of this when the president sent the CNO a bottle of scotch whiskey to congratulate him on the successful launch of a Vanguard satellite in February 1959. Burke, in a thank you note, misspelled a number of words, feigning intoxication from the gift.[113]

Despite differences with Eisenhower on some issues, Burke worked well with his Secretary of the Navy, Gates, who had replaced Thomas in 1957. The two would become effective allies in mitigating the more draconian measures of Eisenhower's 1958 defense reorganization effort. They managed to retain CNO control over most operational naval forces through Gates' appointment as the civilian secretarial agent for the principal naval commands in the Atlantic (CINCLANT), Pacific (CINCPAC), and the Middle East (CINCNELM).[114] This preserved a "bilinear" concept of naval command that had been in place since World War II. Hoover Institute historian Paul Ryan described Burke's approach as one where "the CNO was able to alert his fleet commanders to potential emergencies and position ships in areas of potential trouble," while at the same time "keeping the president, defense secretary and the JCS informed of his actions."[115] This system worked well during the Tachen Island evacuation, the 1956 Suez crisis, and the 1958 U.S. Marine Corps landings and peacekeeping operations in Lebanon.

Burke was also a consistent advocate for advanced warfighting technology. In addition to his efforts supporting submarine launched ballistic missiles, he convened the Libby Board in early 1957, led by Rear Adm. Ruthven Libby, to examine naval organization as it pertained to the advocacy for and promotion of advanced naval technology.[116] Burke was concerned that the development of naval surface-to-air missile systems, as embodied in the "three Ts" program—for the Talos, Tartar, and Terrier missiles—was slow and the weapons ineffective. The Navy intended to build a layered system of missile-shooting warships around the aircraft carrier for its defense, a vital element of its preferred strategy. The Libby Board placed responsibility for new weapons development within the Office of the Chief of Naval Operations (OPNAV) and allowed Burke to strengthen his own position at a time when the president was looking to reduce the overall power of the service chiefs.

Despite these successes, the powers Burke and the other service chiefs exercised were further reduced by Eisenhower's second round of defense reforms, in 1958. Eisenhower was increasingly dissatisfied with his 1953 reform package, especially its failure to eliminate interservice budget rivalry and the battle over responsibility for the development of intermediate-range ballistic missiles.[117] Eisenhower's 1958 reorganization plan called for a further reduction of the service chiefs' powers by formally removing them from the operational chain of command, while allowing them to issue operational orders in the name of the secretary of defense. The organization of the JCS around joint committees would be replaced by a conventional service staff organization, with the prefix "J" designating the Joint Staff and the adoption of traditional staff numbers, two for intelligence and three for operations. The Joint Staff would be strengthened, as would the position of the chairman, who was to be given the authority to select the director of the Joint Staff and manage it "in the name of the Joint Chiefs of Staff."[118]

Despite significant opposition, this time led by House Armed Services Committee Chairman Carl Vinson (D-Ga.), Eisenhower again achieved most of his goals. In terms of those that eluded his grasp, Congress, still frightened by the specter of a Prussian General Staff, limited the Joint Staff to 400 members and limited reappointments to avoid the creation of a dedicated, long-serving Joint Staff cadre. The president would not be allowed to transfer specific warfare functions between the services, as Eisenhower had desired, without first informing Congress. A bilinear chain of command persisted in that while unified commanders were truly joint in composition and operational authority, their staffs continued to be selected by the component services, and the services still maintained an administrative chain of command with deployed units for the purposes of regular administration.

While Eisenhower had faced opposition in 1953 and 1958 from all of the services, it was the Navy, as in 1947 and 1949, that most directly opposed the president's reorganization plans. The Navy's concept of postwar strategy and associated operations were the ones most directly affected by the president's actions, which had now nearly accomplished the divestment of command that Burke feared. The CNO stated his fears over this change in 1958, bluntly stating in a letter to Rear Adm. Walter Schindler, "We believe in command and not staff. We believe in having 'real things to do.' We decentralize and capitalize on the capabilities of our individual people, rather than centralize and make automatons of them."[119] Burke always saw the JCS as more of a political organization than a military outfit and an arena where the services fought their battles over resources.[120] He also feared the new powers given to the secretary of defense and the Army Staff–like organization imposed on the Joint Staff. The secretary could now control service functions and their acquisition programs and delegate that authority to a growing number of subordinates. In Burke's opinion, the new Joint Staff was "alien" to naval officers, and this led to the Navy not dispatching its "best and brightest" officers to assignments there.[121] This practice would later put the Navy at odds with the Department of Defense after the Goldwater-Nichols Act required that the services assign quality personnel to the Joint Staff.

Burke had, according to Hone, generally shielded the Navy from many of Eisenhower's defense reorganization reforms.[122] He also preserved the Navy's component of the strategic nuclear deterrent during negotiations that led to JCS approval of the first National Strategic Target List and Single Integrated Operations Plan (SIOP) for the employment of strategic nuclear weapons on 2 December 1960.[123] Once again, Eisenhower was angry that the JCS had not done a better job in the effort, especially as he believed that the Strategic Air Command should have been given these tasks instead of the service chiefs.[124]

Expressing his anger about the defense organization in general, Eisenhower remarked, "The original mistake in this whole business was our failure to create one single service in 1947."[125]

Despite presidential diatribes, Burke in his efforts not only preserved the addition of the Polaris, but also successfully promoted it as the least vulnerable of the strategic triad elements.[126] Burke's successors would not be as successful in fulfilling the Navy's desires as he had been. The next three presidential administrations would make the most of Eisenhower's defense reforms and often not in ways favorable to the Navy, its concept of Cold War strategy, or its preferred force structure to implement its requirements. The magnitude of the organizational restructuring and related shifts in power was so significant that Burke's biographer calls him "the last CNO."

The policies of the Kennedy, Johnson, and Nixon administrations, from 1961 to 1974, provided multiple opportunities for the Navy to demonstrate its preferred Cold War strategy through active military operations in Southeast Asia. The long-lasting conflicts in Vietnam and adjacent Southeast Asian nations, however, sapped funds from the defense budget necessary to replace aging, World War II–era ships. These platforms were rapidly becoming outmoded in the era of missiles, electronic warfare, and networked data communications at sea. The Navy adapted well to these technological and operational shifts, but faced a horizon darkened and confused by the Eisenhower reforms in defense organization.

The reforms of 1953 and 1958 brought about significant growth and potential for continued expansion in the Department of Defense's civilian workforce. This process, referred to by Allan Millett as the "hypertrophy of civilian control of the military," prompted a "similar erosion of uniformed armed forces autonomy over military operations, the *sine qua non* of military professionalism."[127] Presidential administrations into the mid-1970s would make full use of the increased civilian control of the military enabled by Eisenhower and further expand their authority to the detriment of both the Navy and perhaps the nation. The period ended on an optimistic note for the Navy, however, with a renewed emphasis on naval strategy consequent to the rise of a more powerful Soviet Navy and leading to the most successful U.S. naval strategy since War Plan Orange was adopted in 1924.

NAVAL STRATEGY AND THE FLEXIBLE RESPONSE DOCTRINE

As noted above, President Eisenhower eschewed small wars on the periphery of Eurasia and hoped that the threat of nuclear weapons as embodied in his New Look policy would be enough to deter war with the Soviet Union and any other actors that might threaten regional peace. Many senior service leaders, especially in the Army, rejected Eisenhower's dismissal of ground forces as a central component of U.S. military efforts. Improvements in the Soviet's nuclear capability throughout the 1950s raised questions about the efficacy of the New Look going into the 1960s. Nikita Khrushchev's rise to power brought with it a new Soviet policy of supporting revolutionary wars of national liberation, such as that fought by the Vietminh against the French in Indochina in the early 1950s. Eisenhower's youthful successor, John F. Kennedy, and his group of relatively young advisers sought to develop a new, more flexible form of containment to contend with the wars on the Eurasian periphery that Eisenhower had been determined to prevent through non-military action or to delegate to proxies to fight. At the center of Kennedy's new doctrine, Flexible Response, stood Robert S. McNamara, his secretary of defense.

A former Army Air Forces operations analyst and Ford Motor company executive, McNamara's concepts of systems analysis and corporate management would play a significant role in articulating the Kennedy administration's containment policy. McNamara entered office with the specific goals of "redesigning the military strategy and Armed Forces of the United States to achieve greater flexibility and effectiveness" and "to install new methods of analysis and decision-making in the areas of planning, management and acquisition."[128] Kennedy wanted a "more robust military force posture," and McNamara intended to deliver it through five-year plans that included dividing the military into functional areas in compiling budgetary suggestions in the form of Draft Presidential Memoranda.[129]

The Planning, Programming, and Budgeting System (PPBS) became the principal tool for implementing McNamara's reforms. The purpose of PPBS was, in the words of one of its architects, the economist Alain Enthoven, to develop "decision-making based on explicit criteria of the national interest in defense programs, as opposed to decision making by compromise among various institutional, parochial, or other vested interests in the Defense Department."[130] In other words, PPBS would produce "explicit criteria, openly and thoroughly debated by all interested parties, that could be used by the Secretary of Defense, the President, and the Congress as measures of the need for and adequacy of defense programs."[131] These criteria involved systems analysis developed by a coterie of civilians responsible for implementing PPBS and whom their critics derisively dubbed the "Whiz Kids."

The core members of McNamara's new legion of analysts determined to alter defense planning were Department of Defense General Counsel John McNaughton, McNamara aide Adam Yarmolinsky, and former president of the University of California Charles Hitch.[132] They all hailed from Ivy League schools and were often contemptuous of military experience in the determination of strategy. Their approach put them at odds with senior military officers from the start: They sought to examine military programs "from a broader perspective than that of the organization proposing them, choose among real alternatives, and ascertain at what point further spending on a given military program results in incremental gains so small that it is no longer justified."[133] The Whiz Kids would play significant roles in the implementation of the nuclear and conventional aspects of the Flexible Response doctrine.

McNamara described Flexible Response in a 1962 speech at the University of Michigan as a "credible deterrent for the kind of conflict proposed by Khrushchev" and consisting of nuclear and conventional elements.[134] The nuclear component was straightforward in that the United States would, McNamara said, "maintain our nuclear strike power as a realistic, effective deterrent against Soviet initiation of long wars." The conventional component, however, stemmed from a potential gap in Eisenhower's New Look policy. McNamara suggested in 1962 that a limited conventional force would "invite the Soviets to practice the 'salami slice' technique" of "piecemeal military conquest," to which "we had no suitably scaled and obviously credible countermeasures." The Kennedy administration would therefore develop a "military force tailored to the particular challenge."[135]

The Navy had few complaints about Kennedy's containment concept. CNO Burke believed that the United States and its allies would be "well advised to prepare for a broader set of military contingencies" and that "what is more apt to occur [than a general war with the Soviet Union] are local wars, which both the Free World and the USSR will take great pains to prevent expanding into general war."[136] Burke would also later point out that the service's force structure through the 1970s had been composed primarily of forty ballistic missile submarines, representing the Navy's contribution to the nation's nuclear deterrent, and fifteen large aircraft carriers, the service's "primary cutting tool" to forestall or fight limited conflicts.[137]

The Kennedy and Johnson administrations were generally supportive of this strategy and associated force structure. Kennedy approved one of Eisenhower's final strategic initiatives, SIOP, in 1961. It allowed for the substantial force of ballistic missile submarines recommended by Burke and left the Air Force complaining that the Navy had completed a "strategic power grab" with the acquisition of its own, unique nuclear deterrent arm.[138] Implementation of the conventional elements of the Flexible Response doctrine, however, proved more troublesome. Kennedy had largely excluded the JCS from the planning process that produced the failed Bay of Pigs operation in April 1961. Burke, among all the Joint Chiefs, was most in favor of military action against Fidel Castro in Cuba and suggested covert action as one possible means of eliminating his communist government. Burke had been present at a 16 March 1960 conference where Eisenhower approved the Central Intelligence Agency's plan for a covert operation to remove Castro from power.[139] While the CIA was hopeful of success, the Joint Staff assessed that the plan had only a one in three chance of success; Burke told Kennedy that by his estimate it had a 50 percent chance.[140]

According to the historian Paul Ryan, Burke said that the Joint Chiefs should have been more forceful in demanding a role in the planning, or at least in being provided more information. The chiefs' reticence had been rooted in their past military-like relationship with Eisenhower, who brooked no dissension in the ranks once he had rendered a decision. Burke concluded that the Bay of Pigs operation was "a military operation which was conducted by amateurs all, from top to bottom, and it was a horrible fiasco."[141] Kennedy had actually wanted more advice from the chiefs and was disappointed in their lack of opinion regarding the Bay of Pigs operation. Kennedy would later say, "The first advice I'm going to give my successor is to watch the generals and to avoid feeling that just because they are military men their opinions on military matters are worth a damn."[142] Whether the chiefs had overestimated the chances of success or the Kennedy administration had not asked the right questions, the overall effect was a noticeable chill in relations between the military chiefs and the chief executive that would continue throughout the Kennedy and Johnson administrations. This lack of communication would later be cited by U.S. Army officer H. R. McMaster in *Dereliction of Duty* as one of the factors leading to President Lyndon Johnson's decision to enter the Vietnam War without seeking proper military advice.[143]

The Kennedy administration had supported further construction and operation of large aircraft carriers, but in February 1963 Secretary of Defense McNamara "directed that the Navy justify its operation of 15 attack carriers, as well as requests for new construction."[144] Caught off guard by McNamara's request, the Navy struggled to justify its large carrier force in two studies that McNamara would reject as insufficiently detailed. In October 1963 McNamara backtracked to a degree, and while he rejected nuclear propulsion for what would be christened the USS *John F. Kennedy* (CVA 67), he approved the carrier's construction.[145] McNamara's decision to forgo nuclear propulsion caused a firestorm within the Navy and resulted in the resignation, in protest, of Secretary of the Navy Fred Korth.[146] Congress became involved, and the Joint Congressional Committee on Atomic Energy held hearings on the matter. McNamara was resolute in his decision and suggested that his analysis had determined that an even smaller force of 9–11 flattops would be the right number of carriers. He cited his own analysis that the carrier's potential as a strategic platform had been reduced by the larger number of submarine-launched nuclear weapons that had become available and by improvements in land-based aircraft. The congressional committee rebuked McNamara in its November 1963 findings, stating that the defense secretary's arguments were "misleading, misinformed and incorrect."[147]

Congress had rescued the Navy's premier system for flexible response and its nascent surface ship nuclear power program, but the persistent McNamara found other venues in which to chip away at the naval service's operational strength. The defense secretary had been a persistent presence at the Office of Naval Intelligence (ONI) Operations Plot on 23–24 October 1962 at the height of the Cuban Missile Crisis. While some historians have suggested an argument took place between McNamara and Burke's successor as CNO, Adm. George Anderson, according to Capt. William Manthorpe, a retired Naval Intelligence officer, there had been no heated debate. McNamara was, however, cheated out of the honor of telling Kennedy that Soviet ships had been turned back by the blockade; officials of the National Security Agency (NSA) and ONI beat him to it. Of course, these negative encounters between the Navy and McNamara did nothing to improve relations between the sea service and the Department of Defense.

Kennedy's assassination in Dallas in November 1963 represented a great blow to the naval service. In spite of antagonisms with members of Kennedy's administration, the Navy had good relations with the president, a decorated World War II Navy Reserve officer. Relations with his successor, Johnson, were not so cordial. Kennedy had refrained from significant, active military engagement in Southeast Asia, but as president, Johnson felt compelled to continue and expand U.S. efforts against communist aggression.[148] Johnson largely retained Kennedy's national security team, including Secretary McNamara.

The period of active U.S. combat in Vietnam, from 1965 to 1973, proved to be a full-scale test of Flexible Response. The Navy, for its part, displayed its aircraft carrier strike capabilities and the ability of its riverine and coastal combat forces. The fleet continued to develop new communications and data exchange operations, and additional nuclear-powered submarines and surface ships entered the active Navy. All this, however, came at the price of a war that cost upward of $150 billion and sapped the Navy's desire to recapitalize a largely World War II–era fleet facing block obsolescence.[149] During the conflict, civilian authorities continued their usurpation of traditional military roles. The effects of the Vietnam War, both in budget shortfalls and conflicts with civilian defense authorities, left the Navy ill prepared to modify its Cold War strategy to meet the threat of a rising Soviet fleet. The Navy's youngest-ever CNO, Zumwalt, however, would begin the process of reversing that trend and initiate a strategic revolution that would put the Navy at the forefront of national strategy by the end of the Cold War.

Naval Strategy and Vietnam War Gradualism

President Johnson determined that the best way to fight the Vietnam War was through a strategy of gradualism. This involved periods of increasing military pressure interrupted by periods of pause for an opponent to evaluate their decisions and then, theoretically, to persuade the political leadership to seek a negotiated settlement. It was believed that such an approach would be an effective tool for keeping wars limited in both cost and scope.[150] Thus, in the Vietnam War, periods of intense U.S. military action were followed by palpable lulls during which the North Vietnamese and National Liberation Front (Vietcong) were meant to reconsider their actions against the South Vietnamese state.

The verified naval action in the Gulf of Tonkin on 1 August 1964 between the destroyer USS *Maddox* and North Vietnamese torpedo boats and the subsequent probable non-action on 4 August, which also involved the USS *Turner Joy*, began a significant naval combat effort in the rivers and littoral waters of North and South Vietnam. President Kennedy had approved the assignment of U.S. Navy advisers to train the South Vietnamese Navy as early as April 1961, and the Desoto radar direction patrols that brought *Maddox* and *Turner Joy* into direct combat with the North Vietnamese were only the latest in such direct missions in support of the South Vietnamese. The U.S. Navy and Coast Guard ultimately would bring to bear more than 38,000 personnel in riverine combat operations to form the largest, active "brown water" force since the U.S. Civil War.[151] Thousands of others served in an array of vessels, ranging from recommissioned battleships to modern guided missile destroyers and frigates, conducting naval gunfire support and interdiction operations against North Vietnamese supply efforts. Many of the Navy's future writers on maritime strategy began their careers in Vietnam.

The riverine, interdiction, and gunfire support missions were largely controlled by U.S. military leaders on the ground in South Vietnam. Leaders in Washington, however, more directly influenced carrier airstrike operations against targets in the north and south of the embattled Southeast Asian state. The Navy benefited from the process to a degree in that its carrier-based aviation forces played a significant role in bombing targets in North Vietnam. While these operations were useful to the overall military effort in Vietnam, they conflicted with the Navy's concepts of strategy, including those shaped by Flexible Response. Carrier operations against Vietnamese targets would achieve success only to be suddenly stopped by orders from President Johnson or Secretary McNamara to allow the appropriate pause. Naval leaders often saw this "stop and go" war as unproductive in that they had no control over its course when inundated by daily changes in the campaign's direction from Washington.[152] Adm. Ulysses Grant Sharp, CINCPAC commander in chief and operational commander of the first Operation Rolling Thunder air campaign in 1965, argued that greater pressure, rather than gradualism, was the approach needed to force North Vietnam to the negotiating table.[153] Johnson's pausing of air campaigns and non-combat patrols by U.S. warships off the coast of North Vietnam mystified naval leaders. They had prepared for limited war in the wake of the Korean War, but at the least expected to carry out most, if not all, of the military measures they recommended. Admiral Sharp would later criticize his own meekness in representing his views to elected leaders, stating, "I should have perhaps interjected myself, early on and more than once into the Washington arena with personal briefings of the sort I gave to Secretary McNamara in Saigon in mid-1967 [that recommended the mining of North Vietnamese harbors]."[154]

The approaching block obsolescence of a large part of the fleet was also of great concern. Warships constructed during World War II had served the nation during the first twenty-five years of the Cold War, many in deployed locations for extended periods. Now approaching the end of their service lives, these ships urgently needed replacement. The Vietnam War had generated an enormous drain on national resources and crippled the Navy's shipbuilding budget. By 1968, only $800 million of the Navy's total budget of $26.7 billion was earmarked for new warship construction.[155]

In the latter part of the 1960s, the Navy faced a significant challenge getting new construction funds in the face of competition for funding for the Vietnam conflict and Johnson's Great Society programs to address poverty at home. It also faced new challenges from within the Department of Defense for such requests. The root of the problem was perhaps due to the increasing level of civilian influence and outright control of strategic processes that had once been the province of uniformed officers. Attacks by McNamara and his close advisers on the big-deck aircraft carrier and the preferred means of waging war in Vietnam reflected the progressive loss of uniformed military influence over general national security affairs. Allan Millett suggests two reasons for this development: first, civilian leaders in the post–World War II era asking the JCS to advise and comment on situations beyond their military operational expertise, and second, a growing civilian assumption that the "risks of escalation [in conventional or nuclear conflict] require operational decisions by the political elite" since the JCS, as designed, did not provide answers at the speed desired by civilian leaders.[156]

The Navy viewed strategy as the product of professional military judgment.[157] It saw McNamara's vision of qualitative policy analysis as one that "devalued and eviscerated strategy and intellectual audacity."[158] The core of McNamara's concept of analysis for national defense spending had been "how much is enough," as articulated in the seminal book bearing that title by McNamara Whiz Kid Enthoven. The Navy's view, as articulated by three of its secretaries in the 1970s and 1980s, was that such a question was irrelevant to the sea service. Analysts had to make a number of assumptions in building scenarios to support their conclusions on the number of ships to build and what weapons to acquire. Naval strategists, on the other hand, who relied on much broader historical experiences over time, held flexibility as essential to naval success. They viewed the products of McNamara's systems analysts as deceptive cover for subjective judgments reached in the Office of the Secretary of Defense.

McNamara's tendency to bypass the service chiefs and the JCS collectively on operational and administrative matters and his focus on programming and analysis also served to reduce the power of the CNO's Plans, Policy, and Operations office, OP-06. With the CNO focused on the management of multiple acquisition programs, there was less time to spend on the service and on JCS strategy functions at the core of OP-06's mission. OP-06 also had to compete with OP-96 (Systems Analysis), a division the Navy had to create to meet McNamara's demand for various analyses in support of every major acquisition program. The effective retasking of the CNO from operational to programming concerns made it harder to focus on the creation of strategy in the future and represented a major change in the Navy's organizational structure and culture. Although the U.S. failure in Vietnam ultimately discredited much of McNamara's operational and tactical analysis concepts, they persisted at high levels of Department of Defense strategy development in succeeding administrations.

RISE OF THE SOVIET NAVY AND THE U.S. RESPONSE

This disagreement between the Navy and the secretary of defense over acquisition management could not have come at a worse time in the late 1960s, as it paralleled a significant rise in the size and capability of the Soviet Navy, which had been a coastal defense organization until the late 1950s. The Soviets then began retooling their navy after the development of long-range, supersonic carrier-based attack aircraft allowed U.S. and Allied carriers to remain farther offshore than previously to conduct air attacks against the Soviet homeland.[159] Their shift was further hastened by the development of the ballistic missile submarine as the new, primary nuclear weapon threat from the sea and by the negative outcomes of the 1962 Cuban Missile Crisis, which the Soviets in part determined had been due to their weak navy.[160] The Soviets responded with a shipbuilding program that emphasized anticarrier and antisubmarine platforms and further extended their maritime defense zones.[161] The Soviet Navy's commander, Admiral Sergey Gorshkov, wrote a series of eleven articles during 1972–73 suggesting that the Soviet Union, traditionally a land power, had become a "mighty seapower" and asserting that navies were a powerful means of achieving the "political goals" in an armed struggle.[162] Gorshkov also said the Soviet Navy's primary missions were defensive in nature and focused on preserving the deterrent value of Soviet ballistic missile submarines.[163] Finally, Gorshkov suggested that the expanded and empowered Soviet Navy could serve to "withstand the ocean strategy of imperialism."[164]

The Soviet shipbuilding and naval exercise program of the 1960s had followed Gorshkov's concepts. In 1968 the Soviet Navy had 790 major ships, and by 1972, it possessed 820 such vessels.[165] Meanwhile, the U.S. Navy had continued to shrink, as aging World War II–era warships were retired without replacement due to the costs of the Vietnam War and Great Society programs. In 1968 the U.S. Navy had 574 major combatant ships, and in 1972 the figure had shrunk to 447.[166] The Soviet Union had also surpassed the United States in the overall number of nuclear submarines built and under construction in 1971.[167] The Soviets' naval efforts culminated in the first half of the 1970s with two global naval exercises, Ocean 70 and Ocean 75, and aggressive actions during the 1973 Arab-Israeli War, when their surface and submarine forces closely trailed their NATO rivals and appeared ready to intervene in the conflict.[168] At that point, the Soviet Navy clearly presented the most significant challenge to the U.S. Navy and its transoceanic strategy since the Axis navies in World War II.

McNamara's departure in 1968 allowed the Navy a pause from management through analysis and gave the service some freedom to manage its shrinking budget. McNamara's immediate successor in the Johnson administration, Clark Clifford, retained his predecessor's organization and methods, but President Richard Nixon's first defense secretary, Melvin Laird, implemented a system of "participatory management." According to his deputy Lawrence Korb, "Laird looked primarily to the military services and the service chiefs for the design of the force structure."[169] His successors in the Nixon and Ford administrations, Elliot Richardson, James Schlesinger, and Donald Rumsfeld followed similar policies in the short term, but congressional budget limitations prohibited them from restoring the Navy to its pre–Vietnam War strength. The Navy's budget grew during the Nixon and Ford administrations from $222.4 billion in 1970 to $315 billion by the end of Ford's presidency in 1977, but the overall number of Navy ships sank from 743 to 559 for the same period.[170]

The reduction in numbers of ships, as well as the rise of the Soviet Navy, precipitated what John Hattendorf called a "renaissance in U.S. naval strategic thinking." A new naval leadership in the 1970s began to refine the purely transoceanic strategy of the 1950s and 1960s into one that emphasized sea control and direct combat with the Soviet Navy. Elements of this change included enhancing naval intelligence to determine Soviet intentions and revitalizing strategy development efforts within the CNO's staff, the U.S. Naval War College (NWC), and organizations specifically assembled and tasked with strategy development. This shift in focus began with the appointment of Admiral Zumwalt as CNO in 1970, who would become known not only for his social reforms within naval regulations, but also for rebuilding the Navy's strategic culture and modernizing its force structure in the wake of budget cuts and the operational strain from the Vietnam War.

Zumwalt was frequently criticized by other senior naval officers for his changes to naval culture and leadership through his ubiquitous "Z-grams."[171] He was a relatively junior flag officer when appointed, had never commanded one of the Navy's numbered fleets, and perhaps, as Hone suggests, did not have the same "image as an independent Navy man" as his predecessors, such as Admiral Burke.[172] Despite these perceived limitations, Zumwalt managed to reintroduce strategic thinking to the OPNAV staff and the Navy as a whole and alert it to the rising Soviet threat. Naval Intelligence began providing assessments on how the Soviets intended to use their new naval force, and Zumwalt put the information to good use within the naval strategic community to build an effective response. He also attempted to recapitalize an aging fleet by replacing obsolete ships with modern units. Although many within and outside the Navy frequently opposed him, his efforts in the early 1970s would enable the creation of the Maritime Strategy beginning later in the decade.[173]

Zumwalt believed that the Nixon Doctrine's treaty and nuclear deterrence measures articulated by the president and Henry Kissinger, his national security adviser, "offered a rationale for a maritime-oriented national strategy" that emphasized a "lower profile, land-based presence overseas."[174] In September 1970 Zumwalt defined that maritime strategy in a capstone document, "Project Sixty," which Capt. Stansfield Turner drafted, charting the efforts Zumwalt intended to undertake as CNO. This task list of immediate actions would be Zumwalt's most important contribution to what would emerge in the 1980s as the Maritime Strategy. This initial effort would in 1974 also spawn Project 2000—an attempt to move beyond the rigid programmatic regime of defense planning imposed by McNamara—as well as the Future Maritime Strategy Study and "U.S. Strategy for the Pacific and Indian Ocean Areas for the 1970s," released in 1974. Later, as NWC president, Vice Admiral Turner lent the support of his institution to advance Zumwalt's strategic objectives, most notably in his drafting "Missions of the Navy" (1973).[175]

The laundry list presented in "Project Sixty" ranged from the strategic to the operational and administrative and laid out four naval capabilities that needed to be preserved and reassessed in response to the growing Soviet fleet: assured second strike, control of sea lines and operational areas, projection of power ashore, and overseas presence in peacetime.[176] As Zumwalt saw it, the growth of the Soviet Navy and its global deployment meant that the U.S. Navy "must be based on the two ocean concept. We cannot concentrate forces in one ocean unless we are prepared to accept the loss in war of control of the other oceans, and thus the destruction of the Free World Alliance."[177] His solution was to recapitalize Navy units, especially in the surface fleet, and to build low-cost platforms designed to make the most of the Navy's post-Vietnam budget. Zumwalt also sought to determine the correct mix of high- and low-cost platforms to confront the Soviet Union globally.

Turner wrote the sixteen-page "Missions of the Navy" in support of Zumwalt's four "capabilities" from "Project Sixty" near the end of the controversial CNO's tour. Turner's goal was to "get USN officers to think deeply about their service . . . understand what is best for the whole organization, not just their own platforms or programs [and] focus the Navy on cross-cutting *outputs* (missions) vice parochial *inputs* (platforms, unions)."[178] Turner was also concerned about civilian control and influence over military and naval strategy, which grew throughout the Cold War era. Turner criticized the Navy for "our increasing reliance on civilians and on think tanks to do our thinking for us."[179] While "Missions of the Navy" focused on the missions from "Project Sixty" and the Soviet Union as the United States' principal antagonist, it also represented a return of the NWC to the business of developing naval strategy.

Over the course of the 1950s and 1960s, a number of NWC faulty members, including Rear Admirals Henry Eccles and Joseph Wylie, and Herbert Rosinski, had sought to develop what Hattendorf calls a "thoroughly modern synthesis of major strategic ideas for wartime."[180] Of these, only Wylie's efforts had much lasting appeal; his *Military Strategy* was one of the few readily available resources for OPNAV strategic planning in the 1970s.[181] Turner's efforts served to link the work of strategic thinkers from the NWC, like Wylie, to the broader naval profession in terms of what the Navy was expected to do in peace and war. Turner called his missions "outputs" and viewed them as more important to harnessing public support for the service than were reports on numbers of ships, aircraft, submarines, and personnel.[182]

Zumwalt and Turner's efforts met with a great deal of criticism. The two of them emphasized the sea control mission of the Navy, which other naval officers, notably from the carrier aviation ranks, saw as a purely defensive mission undeserving of primary focus. Critics said that both "Project Sixty" and "Missions of the Navy" ignored non-Soviet threats, irregular warfare, and Allied contributions.[183] Most notably, they argued that any strategy that failed to center on offensive operations would "lose the fleet and lose the war."[184] Zumwalt's desire to build more numerous, less capable warships—especially the Sea Control Ship, a small aircraft carrier—in order to prevent Soviet naval forces from cutting sea lines of communication between the U.S. and Eurasia earned him the hatred of naval aviators, who saw such ships as too vulnerable to be of offensive use. Zumwalt specifically rejected intelligence chronicled in *Soviet Naval Strategy,* the 1968 book by the analyst Robert Herrick that held that the Soviets were only interested in maritime defense. Herrick's claims would ultimately be upheld in the late 1970s by intelligence gathering operations.

Both Zumwalt and Turner had once headed OP-96 and advocated naval acceptance of McNamara's PPBS. Zumwalt conducted a significant reorganization of the CNO's staff that emphasized the increasing importance of analysis in Navy program management and strategy. He restricted OP-96 along lines recommended in Turner's "Missions of the Navy" and gave it greater authority over net assessment and extended planning.[185] This division and OP-06, where naval strategists had been housed up to that point during the Cold War, began to compete for influence within the Navy staff. In contrast to OP-96's expanding domain, OP-06 lost influence in long-range planning. Its Strategic Objectives Plans branch, OP-605, was redesignated as Mid and Long Range Plans and Policy.[186] The strategy office also had to share long-range planning efforts with the newly created CNO Civilian Executive Panel and the Navy staff (OP-00K) office, which served as the CNO's personal think tank for elements of long-range planning.

Zumwalt made use of OP-06 to carry out extensive analysis, such as the "U.S. Strategy for the Pacific and Indian Ocean Areas for the 1970s," produced by Capt. William Cockell. He also gave OP-96 significant control to generate the CNO's Policy and Planning Guidance, a companion to the Pentagon's PPBS to bring naval programming more in line with Department of Defense organization. Navy strategist Peter Swartz suggests this change marginalized

OP-06 in drafting the most important planning and strategy documents throughout the 1970s.[187]

EARLY ORIGINS OF THE 1980s MARITIME STRATEGY

Zumwalt's tenure as CNO served to prepare the fleet for the task of producing workable strategies to combat the rising Soviet fleet, despite internal Navy conflict over what constituted naval missions, the issue of offensive carrier aviation versus sea control exercised by the surface navy, and dissatisfaction in the senior ranks over personnel policy changes. Competition as well as cooperation among OP-06, OP-96, and OP-00K (Civilian Executive Panel) served to test and validate or reject concepts Zumwalt wanted to evaluate. The interaction among these offices stood at the center of naval strategic development throughout the 1970s.

Adm. James Holloway III, an aviator with nuclear power training, succeeded Zumwalt as CNO in June 1974. Holloway's term was unique in that it overlapped that of three occupants of the White House. This was a period of significant turmoil as the nation left the Vietnam conflict behind and struggled through Nixon's resignation. Holloway, like Zumwalt, began his CNO service under Nixon's White House, but amid the final throes of the Watergate scandal, it provided him no immediate direction. President Gerald Ford, a World War II naval officer, was generally supportive of a recapitalized and revitalized Navy. In 1976 Ford declared, "We cannot and will not let any nation dominate the world seas. The United States must and it will."[188] Regardless, Ford had neither the time in office nor the financial support of Congress for renewed spending for defense budgets. Of note, Congress failed to authorize $1.7 billion in naval spending for fiscal year 1977, part of which was intended to cover nuclear strike cruisers and the first Aegis destroyer.[189] Ford pledged additional support to the Navy but lost the 1976 presidential election to Georgia governor Jimmy Carter. Although Carter had been a naval officer and one of Admiral Rickover's nuclear-trained experts, he was generally unsympathetic toward naval budgets and the force structures they supported, especially carrier aviation.

Holloway, who like many naval aviators had been critical of Zumwalt's focus on sea control rather than power projection, set out to return the Navy to its primary focus on influencing events ashore. He completed a revised strategic concept by the end of his CNO assignment, which like Zumwalt's was bookended by two strategic documents. "Naval Warfare Publication-1" (NWP-1), released in 1975, represented Holloway's answer to "Project Sixty." It was divided into two main parts: naval force requirements and operational reorganization of the fleet from one based on ship types to one centered on unified battle groups.[190] NWP-1 reflected Holloway's concerns that Zumwalt and Turner had misinterpreted the concept of "missions," which in the new CNO's opinion reflected warfare areas. He instead proposed the term "functions" and reduced them to two: sea control and power projection.[191] NWP-1 was updated in 1976 and 1978 and finally canceled in 1993.[192] Holloway's focus on specific warfare areas, for example, antiair and antisubmarine warfare, and on the carrier battle group as the core organization of the U.S. Navy at sea represented a return to offensive power projection as the service's principal function.

Holloway completed the second of his documents, "Sea Plan 2000," at the end of his tenure, in 1978. The effort originated with the Navy Secretariat, not Holloway's office, but his staff played a significant role in its research and completion. "Sea Plan 2000" explored "what policy makers could expect of naval forces" and those forces' capabilities in carrying out current missions as well as those to come.[193] The document proved useful for the Navy during the Carter administration, as it was a rare positive view of the sea service in an otherwise dismal period. Carter's presidency proved a disappointment for many Navy leaders, who had thought that a Naval Academy graduate would be sympathetic to their concerns. Carter, however, was more interested in domestic policy and arms limitations than in military spending, where he focused on the land-based defense of the NATO central region in Germany.[194]

Carter's selection of Harold Brown, the first scientist to occupy the position of defense secretary and a McNamara Whiz Kid, brought the return of more directive management coupled with fresh analysis demands to the military services. While Brown was not directly hostile toward the Navy, some of his fellow administration members and subordinates were more combative. The director of the Office of Management and Budget, Randy Jayne, excoriated the Navy in a 1978 speech for its "incoherence" on strategy.[195] Robert Komer, Carter's principal NATO adviser and later under secretary of defense, favored sea control, but only as far as it supported the "classic maritime mission of protecting sea lines of communication to permit vital trade and overseas reinforcement."[196] Komer further stated that Brown's policy of the selective use of carriers demanded only twelve of the large flattops at best, not the fifteen that advocates of a larger fleet recommended. Although the Carter administration was not popular among supporters of a more aggressive naval strategy, its opposition to a larger fleet nonetheless stimulated discussion about how the Navy might regain the initiative in its contribution to Cold War strategy. As Capt. Peter M. Swartz, an eventual Maritime Strategy author, recalled, "Carter got us mad but made us think."[197]

"Sea Plan 2000" at least reinforced six hundred ships, articulated by both Zumwalt and Holloway while CNOs, as the most economical, minimum number of units to meet the naval peacetime presence and wartime combat requirements. Studies, including work done by John Lehman, a CNO consultant and future Secretary of the Navy, were conducted for fleets ranging from eight hundred to as few as five hundred ships as appropriate for carrying out the Navy's global requirements.[198] A briefing that analyzed these respective fleet sizes in March 1975 recommended six hundred ships as the best fit, as it corresponded to the current five-year projection by the Department of Defense, which cited a 588-ship fleet (based on expected growth) by 1983.[199] Holloway began to focus on the goal of a six-hundred-ship Navy as a result of these analytical efforts.[200]

While "Sea Plan 2000" and NWP-1 were like Project Sixty in that they sought to look beyond the five-year planning cycle, they were different in that they constituted a combined effort by analysis groups like OP-96, the traditional strategists in OP-06, small personal staffs like OP-00K, and academics from NWC.[201] Holloway's tenure as CNO also marked the return of the OP-06 office to a greater level of influence than during Zumwalt's tenure. Led by post–fleet command flag officers with significant influence, OP-06 boasted an elite staff from which would come nearly two-dozen flag officers from the late 1970s into the early 1990s. Holloway transferred responsibility for war-gaming analysis from OP-090 (director of Program Planning), within OP-96, to OP-06.[202] The deputy chief of Naval Operations for Plans, Policy, and Operations, Vice Adm. William Crowe, was approved to create a new strategies and concepts division within OP-06. This office, OP-603 (Strategic Concepts), became the home of the successive naval strategy experts who would play an outsized role in the creation of the 1980s-era Maritime Strategy and subsequent strategic documents.[203]

OP-96, the Systems Analysis division, had also seen its share of high-profile leaders, including future CNO Zumwalt and future NWC President Turner. Its structured analysis superseded that of the politico-military OP-06 as the basis of force programming, and it had a brief renaissance during the Carter administration when formal analysis products like those of the McNamara era were again in demand. It would be weakened and banished to less authoritative status within OPNAV in the 1980s but return in the 1990s as a force of significant strategic change. The cooperation and conflict among these differing orders of strategy experts continues to drive strategic change in the Navy to this day.

The last CNO of the 1970s was Adm. Thomas Hayward, a carrier aviator who reported to the CNO position from command of the Pacific Fleet in Pearl Harbor. After taking command of the Pacific Fleet in 1977, Hayward discovered that his unit's only war plan was SIOP, the plan for nuclear war signed by President Eisenhower in 1960.[204] He also learned that as part of the "swing strategy," most of his Pacific forces had been designated to transfer to the Atlantic in the event of war following the execution of their part of SIOP, the overall plan for nuclear war, primarily against the Soviet Union, calling for aircraft carriers to conduct nuclear-armed airstrikes.[205] Hayward took Holloway's concept of the carrier battle group and redeveloped them for multicarrier operations against Soviet bases in the Pacific.[206] Sea Strike, Hayward's concept, involved a change from defensive naval operations to an aggressive strike by carrier-based aircraft on Soviet Pacific bases like Vladivostok, Petropavlovsk, and the Kurile Islands with upwards of four carrier battle groups deployed as a single battle force. Hayward and his Pacific Fleet staff believed that the threat of such a significant strike on the Soviets' Pacific bases might prevent them from moving upwards of 100,000 troops from these bases to the European theater.[207] Hayward's experience in developing Sea Strike would play a significant role is his crafting a similar, global offensive effort in the form of the 1980s Maritime Strategy.

Hayward, like his 1970s predecessors, advocated a unified Navy effort in support of an operational concept. Rather than concentrate on budgets or force structure, however, Hayward decided to focus on the development of a war-winning strategy as the means for creating a capable Navy ready for combat with the Soviet Union on a battlefield much greater than the central front of Europe alone. The Navy's focus on budget and force structure, in Hayward's opinion, had allowed "academics and others to say the Navy has no strategy."[208] Hayward also devised his own capstone document, "CNO's Strategic Concepts," with the aid of his executive assistant, Captain Cockell, an OP-06 alumnus. It listed seventeen points to suggest that a carefully considered worldwide deployment of the fleet would be vital to a conventional forces victory over the Soviet Union. It was aimed at influencing Congress and the Carter administration on force structure and strategy, especially in its advocacy of global, offensive operations as opposed to the mission of protecting sea lines of communication as envisioned for the Navy by Carter administration officials, among them Komer.[209] The administration believed that any war with the Soviet Union would be short, sharp, and rapidly descend into a nuclear conflict, but most of the naval leadership believed in preparing for a longer war that could be maintained conventionally without reliance on potentially devastating nuclear weapons.[210]

The administration's focus on naval logistics support to NATO ground efforts in Europe was accompanied by skepticism about the usefulness of the large aircraft carrier, the signature force structure component of Hayward's strategic concepts. A 1978 Congressional Budget Office document stated that the growth in capability of the Soviet naval force had "ended the carrier's previous status as a safe haven" from which U.S. power could be projected.[211] In response, Carter and administration officials attempted to prevent the construction of additional large carriers. Thus, Carter vetoed the 1979 National Defense Appropriation Act because it included authorization of an expensive nuclear-powered flattop, the USS *Theodore Roosevelt*, in August 1978.[212] Congress failed to override Carter's veto, but the large carrier returned in the 1980 budget, thanks in part to the efforts of a Navy Office of Legislative Affairs captain, the future senator John S. McCain III.[213]

Several developments and studies successfully blocked the effort to move toward smaller and less-capable carriers. Among them was one that emerged from research to improve fleet air defense in the mid-1960s. This effort, involving the design of an advanced surface missile system, evolved into the Aegis weapons system program in 1969 and an official naval acquisition requirement in 1972, when CNO Zumwalt requested a "new highly capable, but affordable, single-purpose battle group Antiair Warfare escort ship class."[214] Zumwalt said he would cancel the requirement if the system did not fit in a five-thousand-ton warship and if it cost more than $100 million.[215] Although the system was originally intended for a larger, traditional cruiser-sized warship, naval engineers led by Capt. Wayne Meyer were able to meet Zumwalt's requirements, and Congress authorized the first Aegis-equipped warship, a modification of the *Spruance*-class destroyer hull, in the 1978 fiscal year budget.[216] The development of Aegis did much to blunt carrier critics' assertions that that flattop was vulnerable to Soviet cruise missiles. The unclassified executive summary of "Sea Plan 2000" stated, "Technology has not made the U.S. surface forces the 'horse cavalry' of the 1980s. This trend is due to the development of fighter aircraft protection, and point antimissile defenses (especially the new AEGIS air defense system) electronic warfare and cover and deception tactics."[217]

In addition to technological developments, analysis from outside the fleet bolstered the case for the larger carrier. John Lehman's *Aircraft Carriers: The Real Choices* explored concepts for large, medium and small carriers without judgment, but discovered that larger carriers were more economical to operate, generated larger numbers of aircraft sorties than groups of smaller carriers, were less prone to accidents than smaller flattops, and tended to be more survivable than their smaller counterparts.[218] The Sea-Based Air Platform Study of 1978 further reinforced the preference for the large carrier. This analysis, which examined the large nuclear carrier (CVN), the large conventional type (CV), and a smaller conventional flattop (CVV), stated that the thirty-year cost of the larger nuclear carrier would only be slightly more than a smaller conventional one. The larger ships also had a significant advantage in overall number of aircraft carried for the same system cost.[219]

Studies such as these helped to solidify the place of the large aircraft carrier as the centerpiece of naval strike capability. The demise of the Carter administration in 1980 with the election of Ronald Reagan would mark a fundamental turning point in U.S. naval strategy. Much like the advent of Eisenhower's New Look and the Kennedy's Flexible Response, the Reagan administration's turn toward a more confrontational approach to relations with the Soviet Union would empower and extend Admiral Hayward's strategic concepts to a wider and more influential audience. After the 1979 Soviet invasion of Afghanistan, the Carter administration had begun to return to a more aggressive approach toward Moscow. In terms of naval force structure, it accepted, perhaps with reluctance, the idea of an almost-six-hundred-ship Navy, first identified by its own naval secretariat as the ideal size of the fleet. Furthermore, the analyst community, which had never been warm to the large aircraft carrier, had largely confirmed the economic and operational superiority of the big flattop over smaller, non-nuclear-propelled versions. These conclusions would be put into overdrive by the incoming Reagan administration and before the end of the 1980s boost the Navy within reach of the force structure and capability goals of the 1970s.

The 1970s and the 1980s represented the coming of age of a new and dynamic group of naval strategists and analysts who would create the 1980s Maritime Strategy, make it operationally viable, and wield it against the Soviet Union as a powerful Cold War tool. These officers came from two distinctly different disciplines: Some were traditional political-military analysts seeking big-picture solutions based on history, geography, and their professional naval service at home and abroad to fashion a strategic tool for potential combat against the Soviet Union. They had their origins in the CNO staffs of Admiral Nimitz and Admiral Sherman early in the Cold War, but also in the planning offices that produced the pre–World War II War Plan Orange, the foundation for the defeat of Japan in the Pacific during the war. Some had risen to flag rank by the late 1970s, including Crowe, a future JCS chairman. Largely occupying OP-06 and OP-603 of the CNO's staff, they had been the authors or coauthors of various strategic documents throughout the 1970s.

Their sometime collaborators and opponents had more recent origins in analysis of the strategic bombing campaigns of World War II and in the emerging science of systems analysis. They got their own CNO office, OP-96, in 1965 during the Pentagon's golden age of systems analysis under Secretary of Defense McNamara. This staff contingent soon also had flag representation in the form of Admiral Zumwalt, its first director and later CNO, and his right hand, Admiral Turner, who would be a Maritime Strategy critic. The office was the center of a great deal of activity in the late 1960s. As Capt. Wayne

Hughes, USN (Ret.), an OP-96 alumnus and future naval tactics expert, wrote, "We were on center stage, as decisions were going to be made by analysis."[220]

The interaction among these groups became the foundation of the production and evolution of the Maritime Strategy. While political leaders sanctioned its development, these officers made it work at all levels of the chain of command, from the Pentagon down to individual ships, submarines, and squadron commands at sea. Then, in the 1990s, when the Soviet Union collapsed and deprived the Maritime Strategy of its reason for existence, the Navy again turned to these officers to develop and implement its successors. Many remain active in naval strategy development in the second decade of the twenty-first century.

The evolution of U.S. naval strategy from 1945 to 1980 was to a great degree shaped by four factors: geopolitical changes, lessons learned from conflict, defense reorganization, and advances in military technology. The demise of old geopolitical systems and their replacement by new ones in the wake of World War II was the dominant reason for changes in U.S. naval strategy, but other factors significantly shaped how that process unfolded. The lessons drawn from conflict, such as those from the Korean and Vietnam Wars regarding the use of carrier aviation, played a role in what strategy and force structure followed a conflict's conclusion. Defense reorganization reform throughout the Cold War shaped how and in what service structures new strategy was shaped. Finally, the elusive but enduring quest for advanced military technology, often as a means to drive down costs and enable the armed forces to do more with less, also shaped the process of making new strategy through new systems like the cruise missile and Aegis. All of these factors would play outsize roles in replacing the Maritime Strategy after the collapse of the Soviet Union and the policy's foundational geopolitical construct.

CHAPTER 2

THE 1980s

The Strategic Environment of the Early 1980s

A remarkable C-SPAN recording documents what some might consider the high-water mark of the debate surrounding the U.S. Navy's Cold War maritime strategy. On 12 March 1987, the Senate Armed Services Committee held hearings on the proposed accelerated allocation of funding for two aircraft carriers in the fiscal year 1988 budget, a measure ultimately approved by Congress and resulting in the USS *John C. Stennis* (CVN 74) and USS *Harry S. Truman* (CVN 75).[1] The hearings featured many of the key players involved in discussions about the Maritime Strategy earlier in the 1980s as well as some of the legislators who would influence naval procurement for the next two decades.[2]

The members of the Senate Armed Services Committee and their staffs at the hearing represented a who's who of current and future defense leaders: the chairman, Edward M. Kennedy (D-Mass.); former Secretary of the Navy John Warner (R-Va.); future secretary of defense William Cohen (R-Maine); future vice president Dan Quayle (R-Ind.); and future presidential candidate and firebrand John McCain III (R-Ariz.). Other Senators of note included future Senate heavyweights Carl Levin (D-Mich.) and Richard Shelby (R-Ala.). Behind the members sat well-known and influential congressional staffers, of particular note the defense reformer William Lind and James Locher, architect of the Goldwater-Nichols Act of 1986.

The committee members were remarkably astute in regard to the method of carrier deployments along with their escorts, vulnerabilities, and costs. Kennedy spoke on the specifics of carrier deployment rotation and Warner on the history of the flattop since World War II and the meteoric rise of the Soviet Navy. Cohen noted the need for U.S. bases in the Middle East; Levin spoke about the effects of accelerating the carrier purchase; and McCain outlined the strategic differences between fixed and mobile air bases. Those testifying were equally a distinguished group, a "varsity" team of navalists and anti-navalists during the Cold War. The first to speak on behalf of the carrier purchase was Francis "Bing" West—former U.S. Naval War College (NWC) professor, "Sea Plan 2000" team leader, co-creator of the Global War Game simulation, and naval strategy expert. He explained the trade-offs between the global uses of naval platforms versus the more limited utility of investing in European-based air and ground units. "Uncertainty in the geopolitical world," said West, "ought to recommend that the Armed Services Committee invest in the flexibility of naval forces, especially aircraft carriers." In response, the defense expert Edward Luttwak and Robert "Blowtorch Bob" Komer, a former defense official in the Johnson and Carter administrations, criticized the operational utility of the carrier as a weapon system. Luttwak characterized the Reagan administration rearmament as one with a "navalist thrust" throughout and dependent on a carrier force that was too expensive and increasingly vulnerable to Soviet air, submarine, and land-based missiles. The ever-colorful Komer echoed some of Luttwak's criticisms and firmly emphasized ground-based forces for the defense of Europe and the Middle East. In particular, he chastised the Navy for failing to "thank him" for getting the British to lease the vital communications node of Diego Garcia to the United States during the Carter administration.

West, Luttwak, and Komer were followed closely by Vice Adm. "Hammerin' Hank" Mustin, deputy chief of Naval Operations and a former Second Fleet commander who was as colorful and outspoken as Komer. After him came Secretary of the Navy John F. Lehman Jr., perhaps the most eminent navalist of the Reagan years, making his last appearance before the committee prior to leaving office in May. While Lehman engaged in a generally positive back-and-forth with committee members and later even shook the hand of the arch anti-navalist Komer, Mustin's replies to the committee and Chairman Kennedy were much more colorful. Mustin corrected Kennedy on required carrier numbers at one point, calling the need for fifteen carrier battle groups a "peacetime" requirement while twenty such formations would be needed for active wartime operations.

The C-SPAN video is remarkable in that it is one of the last public duels of the Maritime Strategy protagonists before the collapse of Warsaw Pact governments, followed by the alliance itself and then the Soviet Union, made nearly all of the Maritime Strategy debate—a decade-long conversation on the Navy's role in a conflict with the Soviet Union—a historical footnote of the Cold War. Whether the Navy would directly attack the Soviet homeland or just escort supplies across the Atlantic was fast slipping as a meaningful point. Budget limitations and concerns about skyrocketing defense costs reported by the bipartisan Congressional Defense Budget Caucus were causing officials to rethink some of the Reagan administration's military force goals. Less than a year later, the Secretary of Defense Frank Carlucci III would recommend retiring sixteen of the Navy's oldest frigates, effectively ending the drive for a six-hundred-ship navy to support the Maritime Strategy finalized during the start of the first Reagan administration.[3] The Maritime Strategy would survive until 1990, even though less than two years after the hearings recorded by C-SPAN the prospect of a cataclysmic war with the Soviet Union seemed much less probable. The Maritime Strategy's retirement in 1990 by Admiral Frank Kelso, CNO, seemed the final signpost on the United States' road to maritime superiority, a thoroughfare that would remain relatively deserted until the rise of the Chinese Navy and the resurgence of the Russian fleet in the 2010s again cultivated concern over the size and capability of its maritime forces.

ENTER THE REAGAN ADMINISTRATION

The change in administration from Carter to Reagan in January 1981 had not brought about a significant shift in U.S. military force structure and operations, but it did portend a change in attitude and the provision of greater funding for previously approved force levels. Reagan had emphasized "peace through strength" in his campaign, which, he said, meant that "improved U.S. military abilities would check the Soviet Union's imperialist ambitions."[4] A critical element of this pledge was the military expansion program Reagan undertook at the outset of his first term. The military historian Andrew Bacevich suggests that President Jimmy Carter "seldom spoke at length about American military power" and gave the impression to some that "he took American soldiers for granted."[5] In contrast, Reagan exalted U.S. military personnel, past and present, as symbols of heroism and self-sacrifice in service of the nation. Bacevich viewed Reagan's election as the beginning of a new sense of American militarism of which the drive to a larger fleet would be a part.[6]

Carter, who took office in 1977, had been generally opposed to increasing military spending and expansion until 1979, when several events drove him to react, though slowly, in support of greater military strength.[7] To wit, the Soviet decision to place medium-range SS-20 ballistic missiles in Eastern Europe, the taking of U.S. diplomatic and military personnel as hostages by Iranians who seized the U.S. embassy in Tehran, and the 1979 Soviet invasion of Afghanistan combined to change Carter's outlook on defense cuts.[8] The Congress that convened in January 1980 after the Soviet invasion of Afghanistan was also decidedly more hawkish and committed to an agenda of a "stronger defense force," in the words of House Speaker Thomas P. "Tip" O'Neill.[9] By the end of 1979, Carter had committed to a military buildup that included a much larger fleet than proposed earlier in his administration, with new Trident ballistic missile submarines and an expanded force of maritime prepositioning ships to better support U.S. forces in remote locations.[10]

Later analysis revealed a more even pace of defense spending over the four years of the Carter administration than recognized at the time. Lawrence Korb, assistant secretary of defense for Manpower, Reserve Affairs, Installations, and Logistics during Reagan's first term, asserted that defense spending across the Carter administration was largely flat and kept pace with inflation. In addition, in 1980 Carter presented Congress with a much-increased five-year defense plan of more than $1 trillion.[11] According to Korb, Reagan had promised a 5 percent defense budget increase over Carter's, and when added to the already inflated Carter budget for 1981, the average, real increase totaled 10 percent.[12]

Korb also wrote that the 10 percent increase remained in place due to the recommendation of John Tower (R-Texas), chairman of the Senate Armed Services Committee, who advised Secretary of Defense Caspar Weinberger to make the most of such fleeting opportunities. Some critics, Korb among them, would later charge that the Reagan Pentagon, flush with resources, significantly wasted defense spending as the decade progressed, inviting congressional scrutiny and the curtailment of funding later in the decade.[13]

Areas of strategic concern to the United States expanded at the end of Carter's presidency due to the series of events cited above that changed his perspective on defense spending. In January 1980 Carter responded to the presence of Soviet forces in Afghanistan by issuing the Carter Doctrine, which made clear U.S. interest in the Middle East. It stated, "An attempt by any outside force to gain control of the Persian Gulf region will be regarded as an assault on the vital interests of the United States of America, and such an assault will be repelled by use of any means necessary, including military force."[14] The U.S. Navy was unsure of the Gulf region's potential importance in a global war in terms of how much force could be spared to retain access to the oil-producing region. "Sea Plan 2000," a study from 1978, proffered that "the Persian Gulf region cannot be ignored," but it also stated that support to Atlantic and Pacific allies across those respective oceans remained the primary fleet tasks.[15] In the early 1980s U.S. naval leaders would suggest that the Persian Gulf be abandoned, given that the Navy had too few ships to fight the Soviet Union everywhere and still prevail.[16]

Members of both the Ford and Carter administrations had determined that roughly 580 to 600 ships constituted the right fleet size in terms of global conflict with the Soviet Union, peacetime presence operations, and affordability. During the Carter administration, the Navy's budget had slowly grown before jumping from $41.7 billion in 1979 to $47 billion in 1980,[17] but despite the added spending, the overall strength of the fleet did not change. Ship strength remained at approximately 530 ships, including auxiliaries, and the Navy counted some 6,300 to 6,400 aircraft.[18]

President Reagan and the incoming Republican administration were well positioned to take advantage of the initial fleet force planning done by Carter and accelerated the process through the aforementioned additional defense funding that Carter had requested. The Republican Party platform for the 1980 election included references to maritime superiority over the Soviets and a six-hundred-ship fleet, so the Reagan administration's subsequent pursuit of these objectives came as no surprise.[19] The administration strongly favored a larger and more capable Navy from the outset. National Security Decision Directive (NSDD) 32 of 20 May 1982 emphasized the importance of sea lines of communication to Europe, oil supplies from Southwest Asia, and links to Pacific and Indian Ocean allies.[20] Of these links, the most critical was the one between Europe and North America in support of NATO's defense of Europe against Soviet attack. U.S. naval forces were specifically tasked with maintaining this link in the Maritime Strategy as follows: "In the NATO-European theater, naval and air forces have, as *first* order of business, the control of the North Atlantic SLOCs [sea line of communication]. A key role is assigned in securing the flanks of the Northern and Southern region, affecting the weight of attack the Soviets may bring to bear on the Central Front."[21] The Maritime Strategy also specifically supported defense of the links to Southwest Asia and the Indo-Pacific in accordance with the 1982 defense-planning guidance supporting NSDD 32. This emphasis on specific Reagan administration guidance well positioned the Maritime Strategy to claim the role of the maritime component of national strategy.

Reagan called for a return to U.S. maritime supremacy early in his first term.[22] Secretary of Defense Caspar Weinberger's first annual report to Congress, in February 1982, asserted a clear need for increased naval power. It stated, "The most significant force expansion proposed by the administration centers on the Navy, particularly those components of it that have offensive missions."[23] Weinberger referred to the Maritime Strategy by name in his 1987 annual report, but couched it in terms of force structure, with only brief mention of the strategy components, including "keeping key sea lanes open, supporting air and ground operations on the flanks of NATO, and elsewhere on the Eurasian littoral, and taking the initiative against weak points in the Soviet military structure."[24] The Reagan administration belatedly endorsed the Maritime Strategy in November 1986 at the commissioning of the aircraft carrier USS *Theodore Roosevelt,* at which Weinberger said, "The greatest value of President Reagan's Maritime Strategy is that it focuses on the crucial issue of how we can best use our maritime forces and those of our allies to achieve the basic goal of deterrence—and deny the adversary his preferred warfighting strategy."[25]

The perspective of European NATO members varied somewhat from the United States' in terms of the Maritime Strategy as part of an effective NATO deterrent, but the U.S. allies were generally supportive of its principles of forward defense and action on the flanks of a would-be Soviet attack on Western Europe. The British naval historian Eric Grove wrote that while the 1986 public brochure on the strategy overly emphasized "extreme war fighting scenarios," it was still a "useful rearticulation—with some significant additions—of NATO's maritime strategy dating back to the earliest days of the alliance."[26] According to Grove, despite some element of "nuclear uncertainty," conventional maritime forces could "prevent an attacker rapidly gaining his objectives on land."[27] He also asserted that the Maritime Strategy had helped to reinvigorate the British Royal Navy's discussion of forward maritime defense.

The British naval historian Geoffrey Till considered as unfair the criticisms of some European observers that the Maritime Strategy was an "independent maritime campaign that had precious little to do with the grim air/land war realities of the European Central Front and that it would jeopardize the humdrum business of the direct defense of NATO's sea lines of communication."[28] Till described the Maritime Strategy effort as one that would "improve the correlation of forces on the European central front by posing an outflanking threat to the north and threatening the Soviet Union's all-important ballistic missile submarines."[29] He also claimed that the Maritime Strategy echoed the philosophy of the American naval strategist Alfred Thayer Mahan as explained by U.S. naval historian Jon Sumida, who had written in a later work that Mahan "was concerned with wider and broader aspects of maritime power in which its function was to defend the international trading system on which the world's peace and prosperity seemed to depend."[30] A number of NATO observers remarked that the Maritime Strategy generally followed the alliance's Concept of Maritime Operations of 1980, which stated that the "containment of Soviet forces was based on forward operations, conducting defense in depth and maintaining the initiative at sea."[31] These opinions suggest a significant correlation in U.S. and European thinking on forward conventional maritime strategy in the 1980s in spite of continued fears of nuclear conflict.

The initial opposition to the Maritime Strategy and attendant six-hundred-ship fleet had emerged primarily from legislative budget-monitoring activities, such as those by the Congressional Budget Office. A 1983 report by the agency cautioned members of Congress that not only was the planned increase to six hundred ships expensive, but also risked provoking the Soviet Union to use nuclear weapons against offensive naval platforms.[32] Additional, critical reviews of both the strategy and fleet would come from former Carter administration officials and policy academics.

The Maritime Strategy and the six-hundred-ship fleet proved durable throughout the 1980s despite the various criticisms. From 1981 to 1990, three successive CNOs—Adm. Thomas Hayward, Adm. James Watkins, and Adm. Carlisle Trost—managed to execute the global strategy, which had been under research and development within the Navy since the mid-1970s. In the doctrine's development, the Naval Intelligence community, which had been collecting information on Soviet maritime intentions, had become more effectively lashed to the process of strategy creation than at any time since World War II. The NWC, approached in the past to support strategic thinking, was again enlisted, this time to form and host the Strategic Studies Group (SSG), which included rising, handpicked naval leaders directly responsive to the CNO who would develop operational and tactical support components for the Maritime Strategy. Some would go on in the next decade to develop the Maritime Strategy's successors.

The naval historian Tom Hone wrote that in appointing Lehman, who completed the shift in focus of naval planning from programs to geographic strategy, Reagan unleashed the "most aggressive and organizationally perceptive Navy Secretary since Forrestal."[33] A shift in focus had begun with the change in administration in 1968, which led to demoting Secretary of Defense Robert S. McNamara's quantitative analysts to a more subsidiary role. The Nixon administration promoted the idea of service-generated defense programs as opposed to centralized control by Pentagon civilian analysts. It achieved this through the Program Objective Memorandum (POM) of 1969, which returned control of the design and organization of forces to the services and the Joint Chiefs of Staff.[34] Freed from the program battles with the Office of the Secretary of Defense that characterized McNamara's tenure, in the 1970s service leaders were able to spend more time considering the future. The change from programmatics to strategy energized the CNO's strategic planners, who created and implemented the new Maritime Strategy at the Pentagon and at sea as commanders of the fleet, a situation not seen since Adm. Arleigh Burke's term as CNO.[35]

By the end of the 1980s the Navy had made progress toward replacing the nearly 50 percent of the surface ship fleet that faced obsolescence in the 1970s. Naval theory in terms of what constituted sea control in the nuclear age had been debated since the end of the World War II but was now coalescing around the concept that conventional warfare would continue and require large, capable forces. In addition, in the wake of the end of the Vietnam War, a resurgence in strategic thinking among all of the U.S. military services and the academic community promoted thoughtful examination of both old and new concepts.[36] The naval historian John Hattendorf viewed the period from 1979 to 1985 as a "renaissance" in U.S. naval strategic thinking that was made possible by that environment.[37]

Not all the elements of the Navy's "strategic enterprise," a term coined much later to describe the personnel engaged in Navy strategic planning, equally benefited from the renaissance in strategic thinking. The now-rejected, centralized analysis approach had spread through the services to allow them to respond to McNamara's revolution in defense organization by establishing their own separate analytical offices. The Navy's response, the CNO staff's OP-96 division, boasted an impressive series of leaders over the years, including Adm. Elmo Zumwalt along with Adm. Stansfield Turner and Adm. Carlisle Trost. Conflicts over force structure expansion in the 1980s put this office in conflict with some members of the strategy community bent on increasing the fleet to six hundred ships at a faster pace and higher cost than had been postulated in the studies that recommended that amount at the end of the 1970s. The strategists exiled the analysts from the immediate power circles around the CNO after marked conflict over the six-hundred-ship navy concept in 1982 and 1983. The analysts remained sidelined, their influence greatly diminished, for a nearly a decade. They would return, however, in the wake of the Soviet collapse and go on to dominate the strategists for more than a quarter century.

Over the course of the 1980s, developing and implementing the Maritime Strategy became the Navy's sole purpose. The service's uniformed political-military strategists crafted successive versions of it before the Navy descended into a period of strategic drift when the focus of the strategy, the Soviet Union, collapsed. The recovery took several years, during which time the U.S. strategic vision radically changed. On 2 August 1990, President George H. W. Bush delivered a speech in Aspen articulating a new, post–Cold War strategic geography where regional concerns in the Mediterranean, the Pacific, and the Persian Gulf, where Iraq had just invaded Kuwait the night before, would surpass those of Europe, and if needed, be met by (a scaled-down) U.S. military force.[38] From 1989 to 1994, the Navy would try to reforge a set of unifying principles in a period of significant strategic drift.

THE MARITIME STRATEGY: AN OVERVIEW

The story of the Maritime Strategy's formulation and presentation to the naval and civilian leadership over the course of the 1980s has been well documented by Hattendorf and Capt. Peter M. Swartz, the latter of whom drafted one of the incremental updates of the strategy in the mid-1980s. Their works provide the best overview of the strategy's development and evolution over the course of the 1980s. It is of vital importance to understand how various efforts—by CNOs Hayward and Watkins, Secretary of the Navy Lehman, Naval Intelligence, the SSG, the fleet commanders and their staffs, and the staff in the Office of the Chief of Naval Operations (OPNAV)—came together in 1982 to produce the first version. The working, staff-level commanders and captains were of particular importance in this effort, as they would go on to develop and implement " . . . From the Sea," the Navy's first post-Soviet strategy.

Adm. William Small, vice chief of Naval Operations, had commissioned what would become the Maritime Strategy in a December 1981 memo to the director of OP-90 (Program Planning) and other senior OPNAV officers in which he detailed his thoughts on program management problems.[39] Small was concerned that programs for the construction of new ships, submarines, and aircraft tended to drive strategy, whereas the opposite dynamic would be the better approach. He wanted to change this so that "serious and responsible thought about the naval part of national strategy would eventually become the basis upon which the United States built its navy for the future."[40]

Small's memo provoked action from multiple offices in OPNAV, including OP-06, OP-095 (Naval Warfare), and OP-96. There was general agreement that the Navy needed a strategy that fit Secretary Lehman's six-hundred-ship program and that supported the POM, which laid out the Navy's planned force structure acquisitions for the coming years. It was also generally agreed that the OP-06's OP-603 branch would take the lead in developing the strategy. OP-603 branch chief Captain Elizabeth Wylie assigned the work of assembling the strategic document to Lt. Cdr. Stanley Weeks, a surface warfare officer with significant academic credentials, including a PhD from American University in international relations.[41] Weeks teamed with Cdr. William Spencer Johnson, another surface warfare officer with strong academic credentials from the Fletcher School at Tufts University.[42] Johnson was at the time engaged in the OP-603 effort to expand the number of ports in the continental United States where naval vessels could be permanently assigned. He also had experience working directly with Lehman and had spent twenty-seven months assigned to the Joint Staff.[43]

Weeks and Johnson molded the force structure of their strategy by combining the force requirements from each of the unified commanders in chief (CINCs). They used the CINC's war plans as the basis for the Maritime Strategy's Atlantic, Pacific, and Mediterranean elements. Much of the inspiration for the plan came from Admiral Hayward's war planning for the Pacific when he served as commander of the Pacific Fleet, prior to his selection as CNO. Weeks used elements of Hayward's Sea Strike, which involved massing carrier groups for attacks against selected targets, as one of the core operational elements of the Maritime Strategy.[44] Control of vital island chains and landmasses above the transoceanic trade routes formed the core of the Atlantic and Pacific elements. Weeks and Johnson added Marine Corps and Air Force units to their force structure accounting to cover control of some of these areas, notably Norway, but did not notify representatives of the Air Force. Neither service would later object to their inclusion. In fact, the Air

Force was pleased that its B-52D aircraft was designated as a minelayer, which provided justification for elements of their service force structure.[45]

To obtain additional insight into the most recent intelligence on Soviet naval intentions, Weeks passed elements of his document through Capt. Bill Manthorpe, USN (Ret.), a Naval Intelligence officer who directed OP-96N (Net Assessment) in OPNAV, OP-603 alumnus Cdr. Kenneth McGruther from the CNO's SSG support staff in Newport, and Cdr. Tom Marfiak, also from OP-603 and a Fletcher School graduate.[46] Weeks' peers and superiors extensively reviewed and critiqued the strategy for accuracy and in preparation for the questions that would undoubtedly come from senior officers in response to their briefing. This process, "murder boarding," inherently created highly skilled briefers able to anticipate and be prepared to answer detailed questions. Commander Johnson made sure the strategy comported with budget guidelines and also served as "adult supervision" to the junior Weeks.[47] By the early fall of 1982 the strategy was deemed mature enough to present to forward-deployed unified commanders, who would be carrying it forward.

The strategy was to be presented at the CNO's annual CINCs conference in October 1982. Rather than hold the gathering in Washington, D.C., as usual, the new CNO, Adm. James Watkins, decided to host the conference at the NWC. As recounted by Hattendorf, Watkins wanted to emphasize the centrality of the NWC in naval strategic thinking and highlight the efforts of the CNO's SSG fellows, the second group of which was beginning its yearlong tenure in Newport that fall.[48] Watkins liked the SSG agenda prepared by director Robert S. Murray and asked him to draft a memorandum for the flag officers' gathering that would, as Hattendorf wrote, "outline the framework within which U.S. naval forces could be best utilized toward the objective of defeating Soviet strategy."[49]

The memorandum was supported by recent Naval Intelligence work suggesting that the Soviets' strategy for conducting a war against the NATO alliance was primarily defensive. It advocated a high-capability fleet force structure as the best way to launch an offensive strategy to drive the Soviet fleet from the oceans and influence the battle on land. In response to the presentation, Adm. William Crowe, commander in chief of Allied Forces Southern Europe, warned that the Mediterranean Sea would present challenges for implementing the strategy due to Soviet threats. Adm. Sylvester Foley, deputy CNO for OP-06, opined that it was arrogant to assume so much about the Soviet's intended operations.[50] Despite such criticisms, the presentation garnered enough support to press on with developing the strategy. Secretary Lehman, CNO Watkins, and the Marine Corps commandant, Gen. P. X. Kelley received and subsequently approved the first full version of the Maritime Strategy on 4 November 1982.[51]

Reduced to basics, the document presented a three-phase plan to defeat the Soviet Navy, driving it from the world's oceans, and support Allied ground forces in Europe and other locations. The doctrine it laid out made use of existing concepts, billed itself as the maritime component of a national strategy, and outlined support for NATO allies. The document did all this in a narrative style rather than a presentation of calculated analysis. In phase one, "Deterrence and/or Transition to War," the U.S. and Allied naval forces would take "positions at sea to deter Soviet forces from attack and in preparation for conflict and in direct support of Norway, Greece, Turkey and Japan."[52] Phase two, "Seizing the Initiative," described U.S. actions against Soviet forces as taking place "as far forward as possible," which included attacking Soviet nuclear ballistic missile submarines in their protected bastions in the Barents and Arctic Seas.[53] Phase three, "Carrying the Fight to the Enemy," considered strikes against the Soviet homeland as the threat from its naval aviation was eliminated.[54]

The Maritime Strategy supported a global wartime effort as constructed by Lieutenant Commander Weeks based on the various CINCs' war plans and force requirements. Although the CINC requirements called for twenty-two aircraft carrier battle groups to support global combat efforts, Weeks based the Maritime Strategy around the extant fourteen-carrier force, of which only eleven would be immediately available in the first weeks of a war.[55] The document emphasized the input of Allied forces and supported the NATO doctrine of forward defense. In addition to securing important sea lines of communication to alliance members and the Middle East oil supply, the strategy called for offensive maritime action on NATO's northern and southern flanks to divert Soviet attention from the vital battle for Central Europe. In the north, this meant securing Norway and Iceland to protect NATO's northern land flank opposite the Soviet Union and the North Atlantic sea line of communication. In the south, it entailed a variety of operations that included driving the Soviet naval presence from the Mediterranean, securing and supporting NATO allies bordering the Mediterranean, driving the Soviets from Libya, and supporting continued NATO control of the Turkish Straits to deny Soviet reentry into the Mediterranean from the Black Sea.[56]

The contributions from Hayward's Pacific carrier-based strategy, the SSG's work, recent intelligence collection efforts, and planning from the 1970s were all evident in the Maritime Strategy. The aircraft carrier in the form of multiple ship battle groups, first demonstrated in the Pacific when Hayward served as Pacific Fleet commander in the 1970s, remained the primary offensive punch in the first version of the document. Great effort went into planning how aircraft carriers could operate in a high-threat Eastern Mediterranean, a prospect the second SSG examined in detail. While the Soviets were assumed to have the capability to launch attacks on NATO sea lines of communication, the Maritime Strategy described an offensive campaign against Soviet forces that did not wait for them to transit the Greenland–Iceland–United Kingdom "gap," the traditional highway the Soviet submarine force traveled from the Barents Sea to enter the Atlantic Ocean. Instead it called for Soviet forces to be interdicted by up to four carrier battlegroups before they even entered the North Atlantic.[57] The destruction of Soviet naval forces worldwide and continued support to NATO ground forces combating their Soviet counterparts rounded out the list of requirements.

Although the Maritime Strategy supported the national military strategy, it was also written for a Navy audience. In *U.S. Naval Strategy in the 1980s*, Swartz identified the primary internal reasons behind the document:

- to disseminate to the fleet new intelligence views on a more defensive Soviet naval posture;
- to counter Secretary Lehman's claim at the outset of his term that the naval officer corps did not "do strategy";[58]
- "to educate the OPNAV staff on wider world of joint & USN intelligence, strategic plans & policy,"[59] a feature of special importance to OP-06 drafters because it emphasized their work connecting OPNAV staff to the wider Joint Staff organization.

- to vet fleet and SSG inputs that were under development, such as the SSG's work designing protective basins for aircraft carrier operations in the Eastern Mediterranean and the 1981 Ocean Venture Exercise, during which the Second Fleet, under Vice Adm. James "Ace" Lyons, conducted an extensive war game simulating naval warfare in the North Atlantic.[60]

The Maritime Strategy accomplished external and internal goals. Along with supporting the six-hundred-ship concept, a strong component of the Reagan administration's military program, its offensive character fit well with Reagan's return to the more aggressive Cold War strategy against the Soviet Union pursued during his first term in office. It also accomplished the naval and civilian leadership's intended goal of the proposed strategy becoming the maritime component of national military strategy, ultimately through the end of the decade and the Cold War. The Maritime Strategy had an effect on the Navy's POM, the most keenly felt budgetary item being the continued construction of large, nuclear-powered aircraft carriers.[61] The document served as a means of strategic communication by signaling the Navy's capabilities and intentions to the Soviet Union,[62] but most important, it provided the Navy a leading role in national strategy by giving the Navy a global, strategic role, as opposed to the more limited regional missions met by the other services.

THE MARITIME STRATEGY: TRANSLATING A VISION FROM THE 1970s

Factors ranging from technology to personnel to intelligence contributed to the environment that facilitated the creation and implementation of the Maritime Strategy.

Technological Advances and Weapons Development

Freed from the Carter administration's limited view of the Navy as a convoy escort for NATO resupply missions, CNOs Hayward and Watkins restructured the fleet's priorities by first changing the emphasis of its force structure. For the sea control mission promoted by President Nixon, CNO Zumwalt had advocated a mix of some higher-capability ships—aircraft carriers and guided missile cruisers—supplemented by a much larger contingent of smaller, less-capable warships—frigates and smaller vessels—as the best, most affordable fleet for sea control missions. Rather than perpetuating the defensive, sea control, and convoy escort mission championed by Carter, Hayward ended Zumwalt's "high/low" mix in favor of a concentration on high-capability warships best suited for combat against the Soviet Union's naval forces.

The ships that entered the fleet in the early 1980s reflected the fruition of technical efforts in the previous decade to counter Soviet cruise missile development and the overall increasing size of the Soviet Navy. Advances in naval technology helped win the Navy more supporters in Congress and the public. Many critics argued that the aircraft carrier was highly vulnerable to attack by air and especially by cruise missiles. In response to the threat of Soviet air and missile attack against carriers, the Navy touted the Aegis Combat System entering the fleet on board *Ticonderoga*-class cruisers. Aegis employed a combination of extremely accurate radars, a computerized fire-control system that could track dozens of targets, and the capacity to unleash rapid, automated fire in response to aircraft and missile attack.[63] When the Aegis system emerged in the mid-1970s, many considered it the great equalizer in the defense of carrier battle groups against Soviet air and missile attack.

Although Aegis was originally conceived from nuclear-powered large escorts, Adm. Wayne Meyer, the Aegis program manager, was able to downsize the system to fit on a smaller hull, which reduced costs, making it more affordable and thus acceptable to Congress. Aegis eventually became the cornerstone of all aspects of surface warfare battle management, not just an expensive anti-aircraft and anti-missile system.[64] While there was some resistance within the Navy to a fully integrated battle management system and questions about how Aegis would interface with the Navy's proven Naval Tactical Data System, used to manage warfare coordination for nearly two decades,[65] the systems were successfully merged, and the later addition of a vertical-launch missile system allowed a larger number of weapons to be carried and to be fired more rapidly. This gave the Navy confidence about the sustainability of an aggressive carrier-centered strategy on the borders of the Soviet Empire.[66]

Also helpful in meeting the Soviet threat at sea were improvements in antisubmarine warfare with the addition of the Light Airborne Multipurpose (LAMPS) system of the SH-60 lightweight helicopter and shipboard datalink equipment that combined the sensors and weapons of the ship and the helicopter into one system. LAMPS and new lightweight towed array sonars that could hear Soviet submarines at much greater distances also bolstered the surface navy's confidence in its antisubmarine warfare capabilities.[67]

The development of the Harpoon and Tomahawk cruise missiles in the 1970s helped to improve the ability of the surface navy to strike at targets afloat and ashore. Some surface navy flag officers, notably CNO Zumwalt, blamed the naval aviation and submarine communities for delaying the development of these weapons for the surface community when they might have been available earlier to the fleet.[68] At $255,000 a copy in 1972, Harpoon was an expensive weapon, but the price tag was designed to assure users of its reliability. One Harpoon project officer was reported as remarking, "You couldn't carry five missiles around with the hope of getting off three."[69] Some aviators saw the much-longer-range and nuclear-warhead capable Tomahawk as a threat to replace manned aircraft operations and therefore opposed them. Zumwalt's trusted subordinate Adm. Stansfield Turner, who like Zumwalt was a surface officer and not an aviator, said that he did not fear the Soviet surface fleet, as carrier aircraft were more than capable of defeating them.[70] Unfortunately, the diminishing number of carriers over the course of Zumwalt's CNO term, from 1970 to 1974, suggested to some that a carrier and its aircraft might not always be available to cover surface assets, as had happened in 1968, when North Korean surface units captured the intelligence vessel USS *Pueblo*.[71] All of the new systems served to better equip the surface navy to perform a more offensive role in the 1980s.

Staff Restructuring and the CNO's Think Tank

CNO Zumwalt had overseen a significant reorganization of the OPNAV staff in 1970 to better support the development of Navy ships and effectiveness in weapons system programming.[72] CNO Hayward also conducted a reorganization of the OPNAV staff during 1980/81, but his focus was on improving all warfare capabilities. His restructuring, unlike Zumwalt's, rejected the method of strategy following from quantitative analysis, practiced in the 1960s. The POM was a key element of the Department of Defense's Future Year Defense Program (FYDP), a component of the Planning, Programming, and Budgeting System (PPBS) that governed how the service intended to balance its allocation of resources over five years.[73] Zumwalt had made the creation of the POM the exclusive province of OP-090. Hayward, seeking a "whole of Navy" approach to programming, policy, and strategy, sought to distribute programming influence beyond OP-09. Prior to 1980, OP-095 had been the antisubmarine warfare staff office, but Hayward directed it to control all naval warfare functions, including some program spending authority.[74] In changing the composition of the directorate, Hayward had sought to produce, through the POM's input to the FYDP, a perspective presenting a more balanced and global strategic and operational level of war. Hayward increased the professional competence of the office by staffing it with officers just returning from fleet service, war game experts, and former SSG members.[75] Armed with this new authority over multiple warfare disciplines, OP-095 (Naval Warfare) superseded OP-96, as the "driver" of the Navy Program Planning Appraisals.[76]

This last change did not elicit comment or opposition from the Carter administration, which much of the time had been estranged from the Navy's uniform leadership and in some ways from its own Secretary of the Navy. Disagreements with the policies of Secretary of Defense Harold Brown had left little room for continued engagement. Secretary of the Navy W. Graham Claytor disagreed frequently with Brown, and in 1980 he wrote Brown a memorandum asserting that the administration's efforts to reduce defense spending were having a negative effect on national security.[77] Claytor also pushed ahead with the "Sea Plan 2000" analysis effort, which confirmed the figure of six hundred ships as the right size for the Navy, as first proposed during the Ford administration, and contradicting Brown's statements that a smaller number of warships would suffice.[78] Despite these disagreements, Brown valued Claytor's bluntness and willingness to speak his mind on issues of concern to the naval service and later appointed him deputy defense secretary after Carter adopted a more hawkish tone on defense expenditures.

Hayward created his own think tank of sorts at the Naval War College to assess the global and regional strategic issues resulting from the improved POM process. The SSG would play a significant role in making what became the Maritime Strategy work at the regional level. In April 1981 at the Current

Strategy Forum at the NWC, Admiral Hayward had stated, "There is no dearth of strategic thinking going on these days in your navy. What is lacking is a more useful way to capitalize on that abundant talent with more alacrity."[79] Hattendorf asserts that Hayward thrived on a diversity of viewpoints in his quest to create a global, offensive naval strategy. To this end, in July 1981 he created the Center for Naval Warfare Studies at the NWC and the SSG at its core. The two distinct purposes, as former SSG adviser John Hanley quoted Hattendorf, were "to create a core of future naval leaders who were well versed in the role of naval forces in national policy and strategy and to reestablish the Naval War College, in everyone's view, as the pinnacle for education in naval strategic thinking."[80] Bob Murray, a former under secretary of the Navy, was selected as the first moderator of the SSG, but he had little idea how the SSG or the center could best be used. Murray later told Hattendorf, "In July 1981, nobody knew what the Center for Naval Warfare Studies was to be, including me!"[81]

Murray received a fair amount of leeway in constructing the mechanics and operating method of the SSG. The CNO and the commandant of the Marine Corps personally selected the members, a group of Navy captains and commanders and Marine Corps colonels who worked as a discrete team on an operational element of naval strategy for their rotational, year-long tour with the group. Murray was soon convinced that the coherent strategy that Hayward desired could not be produced in the isolation of the NWC in Newport.[82] Given this, he wanted SSG members to travel widely and meet as a group with as many commanders as possible to ensure that everyone involved "had a stake in the issues discussed and that, most importantly, the process could spawn broad ideas that could merge narrow concepts together."[83] To this end, the SSG's budget for travel was significant.[84] The SSG was not warmly welcomed in all quarters and pursued some unconventional concepts.[85] According to Murray, several operational commanders uninterested in SSG assessments threw the group out of their office.

The SSG often included iconoclasts. In the inaugural group, Cdr. Arthur Cebrowski, a future leader of the Office of Force Transformation, was regarded as quite intelligent by his fellow SSG members but pursued some avenues of research that later "led down rabbit holes," in the words of one fellow SSG member, Cdr. Bill Owens, later an admiral.[86] In one such instance, according to Owens, "Art Cebrowski decided we should all go to Woods Hole Oceanographic Institute in order to see how gray whales communicate. This was very strange, but Cebrowski had found out that gray whales communicate at the 20 Hz range and was interested in seeing if the US Navy might communicate at similar low frequencies under the cover of animal sounds."[87] Many members of the SSG often thought that Cebrowski's ideas made sense "only after a few drinks," but this was the sort of freewheeling atmosphere that Hayward and Murray had wanted to create in the SSG.

One of Murray's personal goals for the SSG was to introduce a greater sense of operational art into the Navy through the group's investigations. Murray later recalled, "In the mid-1970s I was involved in the beginning of Air/Land Battle. I saw in that process an evolution attempt by the Army and Air Force to think themselves out of their post-Vietnam bad situation to a new strategy with a purpose. I saw in this a possibility for the Navy to also re-invent conventional strategy. This led to new ideas for ways the Navy and Marine Corps could support a potential war in Europe."[88] The first two SSGs, in 1981 and 1982, focused much of their efforts on how to operationally contend with Soviet forces in the Mediterranean and Norwegian Seas as well as the Pacific Ocean in support of this effort.

The second SSG examined a number of operational issues involved in a potential Mediterranean conflict and produced novel and potentially effective solutions. The experience of the standoff between the U.S. Sixth Fleet and the Soviet Mediterranean 5th Eskadra worried the U.S. naval leadership and provoked questions about whether the Sixth Fleet could defeat its Soviet counterpart in combat without suffering heavy losses. The SSG recommended that the Sixth Fleet not abandon the Eastern Mediterranean as its war plans suggested in the event of war with the Soviets, and instead make use of natural features and deception to maintain a vital U.S. presence. One deception, introduced by submariners in the group, according to Capt. Rene Leeds, USN, involved identifying natural "masking areas," where Sixth Fleet carriers could go and remain acoustically hidden from Soviet submarines.[89] Rear Adm. Clarence "Skip" Armstrong, another member of the second SSG, recalled that such ideas were initially met with skepticism among the Sixth Fleet leadership, but sometimes later gained currency when tested by units at sea.[90]

The SSG proved to be a remarkable tool during the 1980s for testing elements of what became the Maritime Strategy. The 1981 SSG created its own war game series to evaluate its inputs for the Global War Game, a simulation created by Capt. Hugh Nott, Cdr. Jay Hurlburt, and NWC professor Francis West in the late 1970s to evaluate elements of "Sea Plan 2000."[91] Naval leaders were not encouraged by the results. The game had assumed the withdrawal of U.S. carrier assets from the Mediterranean because of a supposed lack of survivability and a need to support sea control efforts in the North Atlantic. In a "political and military disaster," the central and eastern Mediterranean Sea became a "veritable Red [Soviet] lake," and Greece and Turkey were forced out of the NATO war against the Soviet Union.[92] The second SSG's simulated efforts in securing a carrier presence in the Eastern Mediterranean during wartime were a positive step toward resolving the problems of carrier vulnerability and were directly supportive of overall strategic efforts.

The combination of SSG concepts, war gaming, and operational experimentation by deployed commanders proved to be a significant aid in developing the details of the Maritime Strategy. None of these steps, however, would have been possible in the absence of good intelligence on potential Soviet actions. The 1970s were a period of development for operational naval intelligence as well as potential strategy and force structure. Continuing intelligence efforts would prove a major enabling force behind the core concepts of the Maritime Strategy.

Naval Intelligence Prepares the Battle Space

The expansion of the Soviet Navy in size and capability from the late 1960s through the 1970s raised considerable concern in the United States and among its NATO allies and resulted in the emergence of two differing viewpoints among Western observers on how the Soviets might employ the force in wartime. The first, articulated in the 1960s by uniformed members of the Naval Intelligence community, academics, and political leaders, assumed that the Soviet Navy's acquisition of large numbers of submarines meant another Battle of the Atlantic. This conclusion was perhaps unsurprising given that the relevant history on the subject of submarine operations concentrated on German operations against merchant convoys in both world wars. American political scientist Richard Neustadt has proffered that concerns derived from history can be prejudiced by the historical examples decision makers select to guide them in their choices.[93] The combination of a powerful Soviet submarine and naval aviation force with enhancements to the Soviet surface fleet introduced by fleet commander Admiral Sergey Gorshkov in the 1970s created the "specter of a powerful Soviet Navy leaving home waters, overwhelming U.S. and Allied defensive checkpoints and barriers, and proceeding into the open oceans to disrupt sea lines of communications."[94] This threat was perhaps enough to meet Neustadt's criteria and strongly suggest to U.S. Naval Intelligence that the Soviets intended a campaign against NATO resupply efforts, much as the Germans had conducted in past conflicts.

A remarkable group of U.S. naval analysts emerged in the late 1960s who supported a very different view of Soviet naval strategy. As early as the late 1960s, some analysts were rejecting the idea that the Soviet Navy was a mirror image of navies in the West. Robert Herrick, a Naval Intelligence officer, claimed in *Soviet Naval Strategy* (1968) that the Soviets Navy's primary purpose remained a defensive one, focusing on the prevention of nuclear attacks on the Soviet homeland from Western aircraft carriers and submarines.[95] Based on his analysis of Soviet statements and actions over five decades, Herrick cited a military leadership dominated by army generals, a lack of understanding of strategic sea power, and an unfavorable maritime geography in lacking warm-water ports as proof of a defensive Soviet ethos of sea power. Gorshkov attempted to articulate a more independent, global role for the Soviet Navy in the late 1970s and early 1980s around the publication of his book *Seapower of the State* (1979), but the Soviet defense minister, Marshal Nikolai V. Ogarkov, rebuffed him. An *Izvestiya* article in the early 1980s declared all the branches of the Soviet armed forces "symbolically equal," and Ogarkov, uninterested in an independent mission for the Soviet Navy, had apparently been successful in subordinating naval strategy to overall Soviet military strategy.[96] Other U.S. analysts, among them James McConnell at the Center for Naval Analyses (CNA), came to a conclusion similar to Herrick's in the 1970s and argued for a move away from an "American ethnocentric view of the Soviets."[97]

Human intelligence and some remarkable efforts in submarine-based intelligence collection confirmed the defensive cast of Soviet naval strategy in the late 1970s and early 1980s. Specially outfitted attack submarines were equipped with devices that enabled them to place taps on the Soviet Navy's underwater communications cables in the Sea of Okhotsk and the Barents Sea. President Carter authorized the taps in 1977, and they remained in use for the rest of the Cold War.[98] The information they collected suggested that the Soviets indeed had a defensive strategy that emphasized the protection of their submarine-based nuclear weapons deterrent above all other Soviet naval efforts. Early analysis indicated that the Soviets appeared to be turning away from far-flung naval deployments and were instead "dedicating the bulk of their ships, attack subs and planes to protecting their missile subs in safe bastions close to home."[99] Dramatic briefings on the technology involved in the collection efforts as well as the results as assessed by Rich Haver, a civilian analyst in the Office of Naval Intelligence (ONI), captured the interest of both Carter and his successor, Reagan. Additional missions in the early 1980s led to the emergence of a clearer picture of Soviet naval strategy.

One piece of this picture involved the peacetime movements of the Soviet fleet. Contrary to Western expectations, the Soviets did not conduct a global naval exercise in 1980 as they had in 1970 and 1975.[100] From 1980 to 1982, the director of Naval Intelligence, Rear Adm. Sumner Shapiro, held a series of high-level seminars that included members of ONI, the Defense Intelligence Agency, the Central Intelligence Agency, and CNA. They examined Soviet fleet movements and other aspects of Soviet naval operations. Their conclusions tended to support the idea that the Soviets intended for their navy to primarily operate in home waters in defense of the homeland and in support of nuclear-powered ballistic missile submarines (SSBNs). This had not previously been the case in Soviet SSBN operations.

Prior to the 1980s the Soviets had relied on Project 667–class ballistic missile submarines, NATO code name *Yankee*, with shorter-range nuclear missiles as their primary sea-based nuclear deterrent. These subs would have to travel past underwater detection cables, the Sound Surveillance System, or SOSUS net, in the Atlantic to reach patrol boxes from where their weapons could threaten the continental United States. The advent of longer-range ballistic missiles on the succeeding *Delta*- and later *Typhoon*-class ballistic missile subs allowed the Soviets to position their submarines in areas of the Barents

Sea and Sea of Okhotsk close to the Soviet Union. Soviet air and naval units could well protect these areas, which U.S. naval analysts called "bastions." This strategy fit well with the original assumptions of Herrick and CNA analysts and was also more cost effective for the Soviets than deployments into the Atlantic in terms of operations and maintenance.[101]

These revelations surprised naval circles in the United States and elsewhere in the West. A briefing to the CNO and fleet commanders in August 1981 generated disbelief. CNO Hayward found it unbelievable that the Soviets could operate their navy in such a manner. The deputy CIA director, Rear Adm. Bobby Inman, asked whether the analysis behind the conclusions was flawed. The officers who were confident in the intelligence assessment—notably the vice chief of Naval Operations, Admiral Small, and his executive assistant, Capt. William Studeman—set out to convince senior naval leadership of the assessment's validity. Manthorpe, from the Net Assessment Office, ably assisted them in the effort. Manthorpe's 1981 assessment of Soviet intentions largely confirmed the intelligence finding, as did the Navy's Advanced Technology Panel of senior officers. The CNO's executive assistant, Capt. William Cockell, an OP-06 veteran, recognized the implications of the intelligence and suggested that the CNO require ONI to create an office to monitor the development of Soviet strategy. War games in 1981 and 1982 tended to confirm the viability of the intelligence and suggested that an aggressive forward strategy against the Soviet fleet was possible.

Not everyone, of course, agreed with the new assessment of Soviet naval strategy. Secretary of the Navy Lehman became aware of the Navy's emerging anti-SSBN strategy in 1982 and generally approved of it as part of an overall, aggressive strategy against the Soviet Navy. He also recognized that acceptance of a defensive Soviet posture would mean less of a need for the proposed six-hundred-ship navy, a stance that would put him in conflict with OPNAV.[102] The Navy's nuclear submarine leadership was also skeptical of the new assessment of Soviet intentions. Vice CNO Small later suggested that Adm. Hyman G. Rickover had played a role in shaping the opinion of more aggressive Soviet intent, but it did not last after Rickover's retirement in 1982.

Over time, more-senior officers converted to the view that the Soviet Union did not intend to operate its navy in the tradition of the West, but instead planned to use it as another line of defense in securing the Soviet homeland and their vital SSBNs from attack. The intelligence findings that supported this change in thinking made their way into more significant documents, including being largely encapsulated in the U.S. intelligence community's 1982 National Intelligence Estimate under four priorities regarding the Soviet Navy. The two main priorities were "to deploy and provide protection for ballistic missile submarines in preparation for and conduct of strategic and theater nuclear strikes" and "to defend the USSR and its allies from strikes by enemy ballistic missile submarines and aircraft carriers."[103]

The Soviets' focus on naval operations as support for ground forces and as a defense for nuclear weapons platforms had caused surprise because it suggested that the Soviet Navy was, as one U.S. admiral described it, "no more than a deep water adjunct to ground forces."[104] It would be some time before the United States could fully evaluate the new Soviet strategy, but its focus on defensive operations played a significant role in the development of the Maritime Strategy throughout the 1980s. Over the course of the decade, the naval chief's "political military planning brain trust"—ONI, SSG, the Center for Warfare Studies, OP-95, and OP-603—would all made use of these initial findings in the Maritime Strategy's development.[105] Although some elements of the Maritime Strategy, such as a global, aggressive campaign against Soviet naval forces, had been proposed before the intelligence was fully developed, the naval historian David Rosenberg and arms control expert Christopher Ford held nonetheless that "the Navy's Operational Intelligence was vital to the analytical understanding of the Soviet Navy upon which the Maritime Strategy was based."[106]

One can in hindsight see how the inputs for developing the Maritime Strategy in the 1980s fell into place. The six-hundred-ship navy gained general acceptance as the goal for both affordable wartime operations against the Soviet fleet and for establishing a peacetime presence. The aircraft carrier, a platform hotly debated in the late 1970s, successfully weathered challenges to its position as the premier instrument of naval warfare against both land and sea-going targets: The combined warfare commander concept, for the command and control of the carrier battle group developed in the 1970s, ensured a more flexible, decentralized approach to defending the large flattops at sea.

The development of the Aegis combat system and vertical-launch missiles for surface combatants improved both the ability to defend the aircraft carrier from attack and to conduct offensive operations over those of previous warship classes. Intelligence work provided vital clues as to how the Soviets intended to use their own fleet in war.

The work of three successive CNOs over the course of the 1970s had developed many of what would become the Maritime Strategy's chief tenets. Groups of staff officers and analysts were in place to create, develop, war game, and refine strategy and operational and tactical concepts. All that was needed was a catalyst to set the apparatus in motion to produce a strategic product. Secretary Lehman emerged as that catalyst.

Lehman

A combination of strategic analysis, operational choices in the Pacific Ocean and the Mediterranean Sea, advanced technology, and operational intelligence laid the foundations for the Maritime Strategy, which in the 1980s constituted a significant shift to an offensive stance in U.S. naval strategy that would prevail for nearly a decade. All told, however, every revolution involves a person with a vision.[107] In this case, that person was John Lehman, Secretary of the Navy from 1981 to 1987, during the Reagan administration.

Lehman, a student of the noted political geographer Robert Strausz-Hupé, thought strategically along geographical and historical lines, rather than based on budgets, systems analysis, and defense organization.[108] He dropped his plans for law school and Strausz-Hupé's PhD program at the University of Pennsylvania in 1965 to spend a year abroad studying at Cambridge University. His "interests in things naval" began in England while studying the diaries of Samuel Pepys, the seventeenth-century secretary to the Admiralty Board.[109] After Cambridge, Lehman spent a year at the University of Pennsylvania's Foreign Policy Institute studying toward a doctorate in international relations. He took leave from that effort in 1968 to work for the Nixon presidential campaign, and after the election landed a job on the staff of national security adviser Henry Kissinger as his point person for dealings with Congress.[110] Lehman left the National Security Council (NSC) staff in 1974 and finished his doctoral dissertation while a visiting fellow at the Johns Hopkins University

School of Advanced International Studies.[111] He also served under President Gerald Ford as deputy director of the Arms Control and Disarmament Agency from late 1974 until the end of Ford's term, in 1977.

While working as a private policy consultant, Lehman remained interested in naval affairs and was a member of the Republican Party's policy committee. Through his work as a consultant to the chief of Naval Operations on the development of "Sea Plan 2000" in the late 1970s, he contributed to elements that became the basis of the Maritime Strategy. In *Aircraft Carriers: The Real Choices* (1978), he examined the potential effectiveness of various sizes of carriers in relation to global naval strategy. His approach to maritime strategy was in part informed by his service as a Naval Reservist intelligence officer and an aviator from 1968 into the 1980s. Unlike previous Secretaries of the Navy with experience grounded in business affairs or military service decades earlier, Lehman's status as a Navy Reserve aviator greatly enhanced his understanding of the naval issues of the day leading up to his tenure as Secretary of the Navy in the 1980s, as it had also done in the environment of the 1970s.[112]

Lehman later stated that his reasons for wanting to lead the Navy under Reagan stemmed from the problems he had observed from Nixon to Carter and from the concerns Kissinger had expressed about the decline in fleet size. Kissinger had commissioned a study on fleet size before the end of the Ford administration that recommended a fleet of six hundred ships, including fifteen aircraft carriers. Lehman had taken part in the study as an analyst and was greatly influenced by its conclusions.[113] The Carter administration's proposed cuts to naval force structure deepened his resolve to reverse them as an active participant in the next Republican administration.

Lehman joined with a number of future Reagan administration officials, defense experts, and sea power advocates in developing what he later called the "forward strategy," which greatly influenced his own push to generate greater Navy strategic thought as Navy Secretary. He and other members of this group—including Strausz-Hupé, Bing West from the NWC, Samuel Huntington of Harvard, and future Reagan administration national security adviser Richard Allen supported a larger navy that could operate globally and free of the Carter administration's swing strategy of shifting the Pacific Fleet to the Atlantic in the event of war with the Soviets.[114]

Lehman's time on Kissinger's NSC staff prepared him well for service in the Reagan administration, although his overall performance as Secretary of the Navy would receive mixed reviews. Lehman described the differences between the Nixon and Reagan administrations' policy debates, writing, "Debates over policy issues in the Reagan administration have been at times rather sporty, but are genteel indeed compared to the brawls between the Nixon administration and the Senate in the early 1970s."[115] The naval historian Thomas Hone described Lehman as the "most aggressive and organizationally perceptive Navy secretary since James Forrestal,"[116] while the political scientist John Mearsheimer called Lehman an excellent "bureaucratic warrior," but castigated him for the Maritime Strategy and the six-hundred-ship navy, calling them the "equivalent of buying pellet guns to shoot rampaging elephants," the latter referencing the Soviets' powerful land-based defenses.[117] More than a decade later, in 2003, Gen. Colin Powell would describe Lehman as the "best bureaucratic infighter in the building [the Pentagon]" and as well qualified to fight the political struggles necessary to remove obstacles to both the Maritime Strategy and its supporting pillar, the six-hundred-ship navy.[118]

Lehman as Secretary of the Navy advanced the case for a renaissance in naval strategy that had begun in the 1970s under the leadership of CNOs Zumwalt, Holloway, and Hayward. While these officers had been capable of advancing strategic concepts within the fleet, Lehman, as an influential member of the Reagan administration, was in a position to generate broad support for emerging naval strategic concepts. He served as a catalyst in moving the Maritime Strategy and accompanying six-hundred-ship navy from the realm of theory to reality. In addition to advancing the ship-building program, Lehman entered office vowing to "revitalize strategic thought in the navy as well as to establish firm links between strategy and programs."[119] He sought additional allies through regular contact with the up-and-coming uniformed and civilian leadership of the Navy, including hosting regular strategy lunches for the "Young Turks" of the Navy staff with responsibility for the creation of what would become the Maritime Strategy.

Lehman was also the vital conduit for approval of the Maritime Strategy beyond service leadership. Following the first presentation of the strategy to him on 4 November 1982, by Vice Adm. Arthur Moreau, deputy chief of

OP-60, Lehman remarked, "Bravo, you have given us a handbook that can be used in our deliberations with the third deck [Office of the Secretary of Defense], with Congress, with OMB, and the joint arena."[120] Lehman also suggested that the strategy could support development of the Navy's POM, the service's key input to future force planning. Although the six-hundred-ship navy was not originally connected to the Maritime Strategy at the outset, Lehman's associated campaign garnered support for it. A report from Rep. Charles Bennett (D-Fla.), chairman of the House Subcommittee on Seapower and Strategic and Critical Materials, to Rep. Les Aspin (D-Wisc.) stated, "The subcommittee finds that the Maritime Strategy is, in fact, a proper naval component to national level military strategy, and that the 600 ship navy, as currently described, is a reasonable and balanced approach to meeting the force structure requirements of that strategy."[121] While Bennett was favorably disposed to the Maritime Strategy, Aspin was not, a point the officer who briefed the subcommittee later suggested when he described the briefing event as one where "we took on some of our most ardent critics head to head."[122]

Lehman gave speeches and generated a stream of articles advocating that the Navy return to the "historical, global, conceptual approach to strategy brought to the Navy by Theodore Roosevelt" organized within "an integrated, coherent, intellectual framework."[123] These efforts resulted in Lehman being identified as one of the key architects of the Maritime Strategy. While often given the predominate share of the credit for its development, Lehman was but one of the strategy's many creators and promoters. Hattendorf asserts that Lehman along with CNO Watkins, who succeeded Hayward, "clearly deserve credit for their efforts in further coordinating and helping to bring the diverse segments of the navy together, focusing on the basic and continuing strategic issues."[124]

While Lehman was not the only "father" of the Maritime Strategy, his written and spoken work in its advocacy, combined with his efforts to support strategic institutions within the Navy, served to increase acceptance of the strategy both within and outside the Navy. The aggressive elements of the Maritime Strategy appealed to members of the Reagan administration who had been skeptical of the Carter administration's more defensive stance.[125]

Reagan had made a campaign pledge to restore the Navy to six hundred ships and made progress toward that goal. Lehman's experience in working with Congress as a member of Kissinger's NSC staff gave him an advantage in persuading individual members to support the strategy and the accompanying force structure. A number of historians credit Lehman with ensuring their success. According to Ronald Spector, "Lehman offered a coherent, integrated framework for naval planning and procurement" and "forged his own connections [with] key congressmen and senators" while taking "full advantage of President Reagan's commitment to a massive defense buildup."[126] Stephen Howarth is more critical of Lehman's performance as secretary, but notes his dedication to the maritime service in that "not only did he support it vigorously and coherently, he also identified with it passionately, and was responsible for its increase from 470 ships in 1980 to 516 by the end of his service as Secretary."[127]

Despite collecting various accolades for his accomplishments, Lehman of course made enemies during his service as secretary, some of his most persistent critics being in the Navy's own ranks. Lehman was especially effective at promoting the Navy staff's strategy cohort within OP-06, but often at the expense of and in direct opposition to OPNAV staff involved in systems analysis, programming, and budgeting. Lehman opposed the "institutional obsession with engineering and hard sciences" imposed on the Navy by Rickover, the nuclear program czar.[128] He also detested the "mechanistic religion of the McNamara managerial reorganization" of the Pentagon, as by 1981 it had resulted in 85 percent of the OPNAV staff being devoted to analysis, programming, and budgeting.[129]

Lehman especially opposed the level of control that analysts had over Navy strategy. He described strategy as the "logical set of allocations and priorities that guide how the Navy Department spends its money and trains its people,"[130] but successful maritime strategy by his own definition also included "enduring realities and vital interests," such as diplomatic and military alliances and commercial and energy interdependence, as building blocks.[131] The business of making logical sets of allocations and priorities, however, had been the province of the Navy's operational analysts and net assessors in OP-96 as part of a larger group of Department of Defense analysts. This organization had been in place since McNamara, whose idea of strategy formed the basis for the department's PPBS, which focused on the defense budget as the primary consideration in strategic planning. The economist Alain Enthoven, one of McNamara's principal assistants and a PPBS architect, noted that before McNamara introduced his system, defense budgeting "did not follow from decisions about strategy, military needs, and weapon systems."[132] To overcome this problem, McNamara and Enthoven established a strong systems analysis office to review strategy and force requirements in light of budgets and render advice independent of military service allegiance.[133]

Lehman agreed that the Department of Defense needed "tools of empirical analysis" that would be "useful in providing a framework in making judgments" on "quicker, thicker and slicker weapons."[134] His concern, however, was that McNamara's tool "had become the decision process" and represented a dangerous development for a naval officer corps that already had an "overwhelming engineering bent."[135] Lehman believed that an absolute focus on systems analysis would further limit traditional concepts of strategy from active consideration in the uniformed Navy. This led him to work throughout his tenure to reduce the influence of analysts within the Navy staff. OP-96 and its OP-965 (Extended Planning) branch emerged as the foci of his discontent.[136]

The systems analysts within these OPNAV staff offices based their arguments against a six-hundred-ship navy could be bought and sustained on the Extended Planning Annex (EPA), an analysis document regularly attached to the Navy's annual POM detailing the service's budget requests for the year. The EPA had been a required document since the POM's introduction as the services' primary budget tool in 1970. Admiral Turner had put OP-965 in charge of producing the annex in the early 1970s. The EPA for 1982, for the 1983 budget and assumptions for 1984, was especially controversial. Cdr. Harlan Ullman, who served in OP-965 in the early 1980s, recalled that the branch had opposed the six-hundred-ship concept, which Lehman was promoting in conjunction with the Maritime Strategy.[137] OP-965 considered the concept unsustainable in long-term costs, asserting in the 1982 EPA that realizing it required unprecedented 8 percent growth in the Navy's total obligational authority (TOA), the percentage of all allotted congressional outlays for one year. OP-965 cited 3 percent as the average annual growth rate of the Navy's TOA from 1949 to 1983.

Lehman, who felt the six-hundred-ship fleet met the strategy conclusions of the last several presidential administrations, retorted that the six-hundred-ship fleet could be maintained with the 3 percent growth as suggested by the "Sea Plan 2000" study from 1978. Lehman said the post-Vietnam era of limited defense budget growth was in fact an anomaly and that the American people supported the Reagan administration's planned defense growth. Lehman already faced considerable opposition from the Congressional Budget Office, which in a January 1981 report had bluntly stated that no plans had been made for a major naval expansion despite the victorious Republican Party's demand for a six-hundred-ship navy in its national platform for the 1980 presidential election.[138] A 1982 report issued by the agency stated, "A gross ship total, such as 600 ships, can be justifiably criticized as an inadequate indicator of naval strength."[139]

Lehman's reaction to the criticism from within the Department of the Navy is not surprising given the oppositional environment and his strong convictions regarding fleet size. Despite objections from some Navy staff, CNO Watkins and Lehman succeeded in abolishing OP-96 and with that the Extended Planning and Net Assessment branches, OP-965 and OP-96N, respectively, in 1983. These offices had dominated Navy input to the PPBS and had controlled most aspects of the U.S. defense strategy, programming, and spending since the early 1960s. OP-96 staff were transferred to OP-91 (Program Appraisal), an office with a mission similar to OP-96 and OP-965 but did not produce products that traveled outside the Department of the Navy.[140]

Some Lehman critics charged that the secretary had assumed all planning authority for the Department of the Navy, eliminating input from honest brokers.[141] Lehman disestablished the OP-96N, led by retired captain Manthorpe, whose intelligence net assessment of the Soviet submarine force had helped to advance the Maritime Strategy in 1982.[142] Some defended Lehman's positional authority to make such changes. While not a "fan" of Lehman, Manthorpe later defended his right to make the choices he did, saying, "Many of the senior uniformed leaders worked hard at modifying or changing Secretary Lehman's views. But when he gave specific direction or orders, as was often the case, they were obliged to carry them out."[143] In place of the systems analysts, Lehman tapped OP-095 (Naval Warfare) to formulate the Navy's initial PPBS inputs.[144]

The end of OP-96, and Navy systems analysis with it, gave the political-military experts in OP-06 and its branches principal authority for the creation and updates to what emerged as the Maritime Strategy in 1984. OP-06 staff drafted and were the principal briefing officers for the five classified versions of the Maritime Strategy produced in the 1980s. OP-06 also became the "primary OPNAV interlocutor with the Joint Staff at a time when the CJCS [chairman of the Joint Chiefs of Staff] and the Joint Staff were increasing in competence and influence."[145] The influence of the office and the cohesive group of uniformed political military experts who staffed it played a significant role in the successful development of the Maritime Strategy in the 1980s. On the downside, the power of OP-06 may have created an imbalance in strategic thinking that made it more difficult for the Navy to create a successor to the Maritime Strategy after the fall of the Soviet Union.

OP-06 and OP-96 constituted different intellectual traditions among the OPNAV staff. U.S. Army historian Brian McAllister Linn constructed *The Echo of Battle: The Army's Way of War* based on the premise that intellectual traditions within an armed service form that service's particular "way of war."[146] Linn observed that these service traditions sometimes overlapped, which is what occurred within the Navy staff between OP-06 and OP-96. Some officers were assigned to both offices over their careers. The CNO's executive planning office, OP-00K, also included officers from both the analysis and strategy disciplines but competition between the two groups persisted throughout the 1980s.

Carl Builder, a defense analyst and former naval officer, expressed a view of the Navy's treatment of analysis as a discipline that perhaps models the competition between the Navy's uniformed political-military strategists and its analysts:

> The Navy's attitude towards analysis is quite different again. The Navy has been at the forefront of *operational* analysis—to improve the tactical or operational use of its *existing* platforms and forces. But it has little tolerance for analysis for planning, or evaluating the Navy. Analysis of naval force requirements or effectiveness is a direct threat to the Navy's traditional institutional prerogatives. The Navy doesn't need analysis

> to define its requirements; it has always known what its requirements were. It *knows* that naval forces are effective when the Navy is left alone to use them as it sees fit.[147]

Builder's opinion on the Navy's response to analysis also suggests how the Navy's political-military strategists in OP-603 responded to the operations analysts in OP-96 and OP-965. Operations analysis is acceptable for operational and tactical use, but it fails in the kind of geopolitical thinking that dominates strategy. Navy force requirements are determined by geographic and associated operational concerns rather than by the pure analysis of means to ends, which is common to the other services. In this respect, Builder describes the Maritime Strategy as "not a concept for relating means and ends; it is an explanation of how all existing means can be related to all ends."[148] Critics of the strategy would likely agree with Builder's assessment of why the Maritime Strategy appears "unconstrained," that is, not forcing means to support ends. The naval strategist Adm. J. C. Wylie perhaps better recognized that geography rather than force structure management underpinned Navy strategic concepts in the post–World War II era. Wylie asserted, "[A] maritime strategy is one in which the world's maritime communication systems are exploited as the main avenues by which strength may be applied to establish control over one's enemies."[149] This intra-service argument was prominent in the broader interservice and academic worlds in the critical reviews of the Maritime Strategy.

In addition to internal OPNAV criticisms, the Maritime Strategy faced considerable opposition from former Carter administration officials, including Robert Komer and Adm. Stansfield Turner, and political scientists, among them John Mearsheimer, Edward Luttwak, and Barry Posen. The former Carter officials thought there should be greater emphasis on protecting the sea line of communication to Europe in support of NATO ground forces. Komer believed aircraft carriers could not survive against the air defense, surface ships, and submarines that the Soviet Union could assemble against the carrier, its air wing, and escorts.[150] Turner opposed the offensive definition of U.S. naval power and its focus on large aircraft carriers as its principal combatant, preferring a focus on sea control as he had done when helping construct Admiral Zumwalt's Project Sixty.[151]

From within the academic community, Mearsheimer couched his opinion in Cold War deterrence strategy, asserting that the Navy did not have a strong role in conventional deterrence. Offensive operations in the Barents Sea, in his opinion, would be a foolhardy errand given that Soviet naval forces would likely concurrently attack the vital sea lines of communication between Europe and North America.[152] Mearsheimer also thought that attacking the Soviet SSBNs would lead to heightened tensions in regard to the first use of nuclear weapons.[153] Luttwak cited the high costs of the aircraft carrier force designed to carry out the Maritime Strategy missions against the Soviets' navy and homeland. He wrote, "A classic strategic error has been made in devoting so much money to aircraft carriers and all that goes with them."[154]

Posen advocated the sea control strategy promoted by the Carter administration and avoidance of provocative attacks against the Soviet ballistic missile submarine force and Soviet homeland. He preferred a NATO defense line running across the Greenland–Iceland–United Kingdom "gap" and believed that any Soviet asset that crossed that line to enter the North Atlantic Ocean should be "fair game" for NATO attack.[155] Attacks by NATO, especially U.S. carrier and submarine use of force against Soviet nuclear assets and bases, Posen wrote, would create "dangerous and escalatory pressures," which the Soviets would view as aimed at degrading their nuclear retaliatory capability. This would therefore "invite a nuclear response."[156]

What the above critics said about the Maritime Strategy was well founded in terms of Cold War strategy and assumptions about Soviet military strategy, but they did not benefit from the same intelligence picture as the strategy's planners. They also tended to "mirror image" Soviet intentions from a U.S. perspective, rather than adopting a Soviet perspective. The Soviets, in retrospect, were much more interested in protecting their SSBN force than in attacking transatlantic convoys. Luttwak's concerns about the high cost of aircraft carriers and their escorts would resurface in the late 1980s, when concerns mounted over the cost of the Reagan military buildup.

MARITIME STRATEGISTS DOMINATE THE OPNAV STAFF

Of great importance to the business of making U.S. naval strategy was acceptance of the Maritime Strategy within U.S. Navy organizations, in particular among the OPNAV staff. This gave unprecedented influence to OP-06, whose OP-603 branch authored the initial document and successive updates. By the middle of the 1980s, the OP-06 office codes had taken control of all aspects of naval strategy. Other OPNAV offices, including OP-96, which had had some influence over strategy products, were driven from having any influence over strategy documents. This was an acceptable situation so long as the status quo held for the strategic situation and OPNAV staff organizations remained unchanged. Several key events would ultimately upset these conditions by the end of the decade and force the disassembly of both the Maritime Strategy and the cohort of naval strategists who controlled its evolution.

The people who created and refined the Maritime Strategy were a group of officers whose careers had been informally managed by successive leaders of OP-06. The product of extensive graduate education in political-military affairs, they had been assigned successive, operational assignments within the fleet. The operational analysts in OP-96 were equally well educated and groomed for advanced assignments. The story of these groups and their interactions is important to understanding how the Navy developed " . . . From the Sea," the successor to the Maritime Strategy issued in 1992, as the same officers, in different navy or joint office codes, would be influential in producing it. The programs that groomed them, however, were largely sundered by multiple restructurings in OPNAV and by the Goldwater-Nichols Act of 1986, which mandated a much stronger service commitment to filling joint billets with quality appointees.

The 1970s brought about a renaissance for OP-06, as it worked in tandem with the analytical branches to lay the groundwork for the eventual Maritime Strategy. OP-06 was also in the process of producing a cadre of top-quality officers whose repeated assignments in the branch deepened their understanding of Navy strategy. Admiral Crowe, a future JCS chairman, had multiple assignments in OP-06 before he became its chief in 1978. Vice Adm. James Lyons had three assignments there before taking the helm in 1984. Many of the OP-06 chiefs in the 1970s and 1980s had also been numbered fleet commanders, which further enhanced their authority and influence within OPNAV.

In 1978 OP-06 expanded with OP-603, an even elite strategy shop created by Rear Adm. Bob Hilton in response to threats by the Carter administration to conduct another round of defense reorganization. OP-603 contained an even more exclusive and talented group of officers than the broader OP-06 dedicated to long-range strategic planning. Most had received graduate educations from prestigious schools, such as Columbia, the Fletcher School at Tufts, Harvard, and Johns Hopkins. OP-06 had kept files on officers who had distinguished themselves in their initial OP-06/OP-603 assignments and later requested their reassignment to the office at appropriate career intervals. The roster of OP-603 included a number of officers who rose to flag rank in the 1980s, 1990s, and 2000s, including John Bitoff, Philip Dur, Hank Mauz, Tom Marfiak, Jay Prout, Ann Rondeau, John Ryan, and Joseph Strasser, in addition to European commander Adm. James Stavridis and Pacific commander Adm. Harry Harris. Also among the OP-603 veterans were Maritime Strategy authors Cdr. Stanley Weeks, Capt. Peter Swartz, Capt. Roger Barnett, Capt. Larry Seaquist, and Cdr. Wood Parker. The officers who managed these writers, including Capt. Bill Garrett and Elizabeth Wylie, were themselves former or current OP-603 staff. The large number of flag officers who had served in OP-603 bolstered its influence throughout the operational fleet in a way that other CNO staff offices could not.[157]

OP-96 had similarly influential impact within the service through the flag promotions of office directors like CNOs Zumwalt and Turner and Adm. Harry Train and Adm. M. Staser Holcomb.[158] It also had a stable of officers who were influential beyond the systems analysis office, among them future defense transformation advocate Vice Adm. Art Cebrowski, future CNO Vern Clark, Adm. Dennis Blair, and Adm. Bill Hancock. Except for Cebrowski, who worked in the SSG, these officers were not directly involved in the drafting of the Maritime Strategy. They would see their influence revived when the Navy returned to the business of campaign analysis in the early 1990s.[159] Officers like Capt. Jim Stark, later a rear admiral, and Capt. Roger Barnett, who served in both OP-06 and OP-965 (Extended Planning), the political-military component of the systems analysis office, significantly influenced the development of the Maritime Strategy.[160]

Following the initial, well-received first draft of the Maritime Strategy in 1982, successive political-military strategists from OP-603 continued to update the document as the active fleet put it into action. Cdr. Stanley Weeks returned to sea duty in 1983 and was replaced as the Maritime Strategy's working author by Commander Peter Swartz, a veteran of multiple tours in OP-603 and whom Weeks, along with Barnett, the branch chief, had recommended. Barnett, who had previously served as head of OP-96 and had complained to his superiors when nominated that taking charge of OP-603, a subsidiary branch, was in effect a demotion. His boss, Vice Adm. Art Moreau, offered to "sweeten" the deal to entice him to accept the position. In turn, Barnett requested that Stark and Swartz be assigned to OP-603.[161]

Stark and Swartz became principal writers of the Maritime Strategy in the 1980s. In 1984 they drafted the second classified version, which drew heavily from SSG, operation fleet, and updated intelligence inputs.[162] Seaquist, an OP-603 and SSG veteran who in conjunction with U.S. Marine Corps Col. Phil Harrington wrote the complementary Amphibious Warfare strategy of 1985, drafted the third version, finalized in November 1985. The latter effort drew on operational exercises from the late 1970s and early 1980s involving the prepositioning of U.S. Marine equipment in Norway and the landing of U.S. Marines there to repel Soviet invaders. The addition of Seaquist was especially helpful, as he had reported directly from the SSG in Newport and retained special intelligence access from that assignment that helped in updating the Maritime Strategy with the newest information on the Soviet Union.[163] The CNO's OP-00K (Executive Panel) wrote the fourth and unclassified version of the strategy, released in January 1986, but the drafters of this version came from backgrounds similar to previous authors. OP-60 veteran and NWC graduate Capt. Linton Brooks and Cdr. Robby Harris, with a graduate education in political science from the University of North Carolina, Chapel Hill, drafted it, but Swartz along with Harvey Sicherman, from the Navy secretary's office, provided Secretary Lehman's component and additional support.[164] Naval Institute Press editor Fred Rainbow provided print support for the January 1986 unclassified version published to educate the public on the Navy's strategic mission.

With the release of the unclassified version of the Maritime Strategy, OP-603 veterans launched what would be a number of literary and academic efforts to publicly support the doctrine it presented. Swartz produced annotated bibliographies from 1986 to 1989 to guide supporters and detractors alike through the literature used in arriving at the strategy. Brooks, a writer for the 1986 unclassified version, "crossed verbal and academic swords" with Mearsheimer on the doctrine's merits at a 1985 NWC symposium. Brooks asserted that the Soviet Union controlled its nuclear weapons as tightly as the United States did and that Moscow—"with a military dominated by artilleryman, a strategy focused on land, and a doctrine that suggests that nuclear war cannot be limited"—was "unlikely to cross the nuclear threshold based on at-sea tactical considerations."[165] In 1988 Rear Adm. Bill Pendley, a OP-06 alumnus, tried to connect the U.S. Army's concepts of AirLand Battle and forward defense to the Maritime Strategy.[166] The supporting efforts by OP-603 veterans and others further entrenched the Maritime Strategy within the Navy and deepened the branch's association with it.

As OP-603 continued to update the strategy, its OP-06 parent leadership gained influence with the strategy's implementation by the Navy. OP-06's long history of direct dealings with the Joint Staff as the CNO's liaison with the broader Pentagon allowed it to seek joint input in the Maritime Strategy before the Goldwater-Nichols Act demanded such action. Activist CNOs Hayward and Watkins were eager to implement the strategy within the wider U.S. defense strategy in the 1980s and gave the effort their full support. Naval leaders, notably Adm. Henry "Hank" Mustin—who before taking over OP-06 had commanded operational formations like the Atlantic-based Second Fleet, the force that would bear the brunt of a war with the Soviet Union—took the Maritime Strategy to sea and worked to prove its suppositions. In a 1986 *Naval War College Review* article Mustin argued, "NATO is short of maritime forces to the extent that we cannot perform simultaneously all required maritime tasks to basically implement a defensive strategy in the high north. We must defend forward through offensive operations."[167]

Additional support for the strategist community flowed from Navy Secretary Lehman's background in strategic studies, advocacy for the six-hundred-ship navy to support the Maritime Strategy, personal interaction with individual members of OP-06 and OP-603 on strategic issues, and influence within the Reagan administration. Lehman tended to view strategy as his personal mandate within the Navy, because in his opinion naval officers were no longer well versed in strategy as an art.[168] As Secretary of the Navy, he therefore made efforts to reinvigorate the service's internal culture of strategy, and OP-06, as the center of naval strategy on the OPNAV staff, greatly benefited from his efforts. The U.S. Naval Academy hosted an annual long-range planning conference that although organized by OP-00K was staffed largely by OP-06 veterans. The Washington, D.C., area was also the site of numerous informal strategy discussion groups, including Lehman's Young Turks luncheons in the early 1980s, and of the more formal Strategy Discussion Group, convened by Stark.

The Navy established a two-year master's degree in strategic planning at the Naval Postgraduate School (NPS) in Monterey, California, in 1982, and in 1985 Lehman asked for a mandatory course on the Maritime Strategy to be added. Thus, in August 1986 Cdr. James Tritten arrived at Monterey from the secretary of defense with a mandate from Deputy Under Secretary of the Navy Seth Cropsey and OP-06B Rear Adm. Paul Butcher to "inject *The Maritime Strategy* into the curriculum, so as to reach every student in the school."[169] Tritten, with a doctorate in international relations from the University of Southern California, taught courses in strategy at NPS assisted by fellow Southern Cal alumnus Jan Breemer, also with a PhD in international relations, and Tom Grassey, a former Navy officer with a PhD in philosophy from the University of Chicago.[170] Cdr. Mitchell Brown, an OP-603 alumnus who had written the 1989 Secret-classified update of the Maritime Strategy, relieved Tritten in 1989 while continuing in the role of OP-06 chair of Naval Strategy at NPS.

The influence of OP-06 and its OP-603 component did not stop at official positions, but extended into unofficial settings within the Navy. Successive editions of the Maritime Strategy continued to be widely disseminated and vetted throughout an expanded body of critical thinkers. These included the operations departments of the various forward-deployed commanders, Naval Intelligence and the broader community, NWC Global War Games participants, and SSG members. The after-hours Pentagon office discussion group led by Stark discussed the evolving strategy.[171] The primary writers and articulators of the document, however, remained the small core of officers assigned to OP-603 and its parent, OP-06, and crossover officers from the analysis-based sections of OPNAV who had participated at one time or another in the strategy's development in the early 1980s. Together they constituted a substantial group of officers. By 1983 OP-06 comprised 16 percent of the entire OPNAV staff.[172]

THE ROAD TO GOLDWATER-NICHOLS: A CHANGED WORLD ORDER

OP-06 dominated the production, dissemination, and operational implementation of the Maritime Strategy over the course of the 1980s. The officers assigned to the office, whether junior lieutenant commanders or admirals, were the living embodiment of the strategy. They wrote it. They updated it, gamed it, briefed it, and finally tested it at sea in exercises and presented it to their NATO allies. They directly engaged critics when they attempted to discredit the strategy. OP-06 got a great deal of backup from strategy-minded Secretary Lehman, who had made support for the Maritime Strategy one of the key points of his tenure. The strategists in OP-06, especially OP-603, formed an unofficial strategic enterprise that ensured the continuing success of the Maritime Strategy as the preeminent statement of naval strategy and operational doctrine.

Unfortunately, the close association of the Navy Secretariat and the OPNAV strategy office with a strategy designed largely around one opponent constituted a recipe for problems if the leadership, the opponent, Navy funding, or the staff structure changed, as indeed happened over the course of 1986 to 1988. The changes significantly weakened the Navy's strategic enterprise shaped in the 1980s, leaving it divided and disorganized heading into the most significant geopolitical shift in fifty years.

Navy leadership changes in the late 1980s played a significant role in the fate of strategic planning within OPNAV. Adm. Carlisle Trost, a career submariner and also a former director of OP-96 replaced Adm. James Watkins as CNO in 1986. Trost was supportive of continuing the Maritime Strategy but was more comfortable tasking former OP-96 members now housed in OP-90 and OP-095 (Naval Warfare) with special projects, including long-range planning, rather than assigning them to OP-06, which had performed many of these tasks for Watkins.[173] Soon after assuming CNO duties, Trost also increased the leadership authority for these offices from directors to deputy chiefs of Naval Operations.

In addition to addressing organizational issues, Trost had to confront a restless Congress that was concerned about waste and overspending in the Reagan military buildup and believed that the Maritime Strategy focused too much on the Soviet threat.[174] Trost shifted the argument to one of capabilities rather than pure strategy. He later informed historian John Hattendorf, "I planned to focus my [congressional] testimony on the broader applications of naval power in support of U.S. national interests. . . . Obviously my end goal was to sustain the naval capability which we had and were continuing to build."[175] The six-hundred-ship navy had always been the force structure component that supported the Maritime Strategy's global application. Trost's decision to defend the strategy from a force structure rather than a conceptual point of view, however, represented a departure from the views of his predecessors Hayward and Watkins.

Trost curtailed naval debate on the Maritime Strategy in a July 1987 speech in which he advised the naval strategy community—presumably OP-06 and OP-603—to "take the naval strategy indoors; we have had a full run of public debate."[176] Curtailing the public strategic debate on the Maritime Strategy may have served to improve the chances of retaining naval force structure in the face of Congress' desire to cut the defense budget. A number of defense contractor scandals in the mid-1980s involving procurement issues dismayed Congress. For example, the Air Force purchased coffee machines for C-5 aircraft at a unit cost of $7,622.[177] The bipartisan Military Reform Caucus, which would eventually include more than 140 legislators, formed in response to such scandals and increasing defense costs.

The six-hundred-ship concept was unpopular with Congress due to the rising cost of new construction and maintenance for older ships. Carrier critics, repeating concerns voiced in the late 1970s, argued that the large flattops were increasingly vulnerable to Soviet attack and that their eight to ninety aircraft could be immobilized by a single well-placed hit.[178] In addition, the increasing cost of a carrier and its aircraft became a source of congressional concern. By 1988 a carrier with accompanying aircraft cost an estimated $9 billion to purchase and $500 million a year to operate.[179]

Secretary Lehman, the principal Reagan administration champion of the Maritime Strategy, resigned on 10 April 1987.[180] While some opponents who had personally experienced his wrath thought he should get no credit for the Maritime Strategy's success, others offered grudging respect. John Mearsheimer, a persistent foe, called Lehman "the most effective service secretary in modern times" and one who "never lost a pitched battle involving the 600-ship navy in his tenure."[181] Others who knew Lehman well remarked on the great service he had done in promoting the Maritime Strategy. The naval historian Norman Friedman, who worked for Lehman as a consultant, had stated, "Lehman has given the Navy a rational . . . but I worry that when he goes, it all falls apart."[182] Lehman's geopolitical and bureaucratic skills had been essential in advancing the Maritime Strategy and the supporting force structure as an integral package. While some like Trost might have desired to separate the two concepts, the Maritime Strategy was supported in its direct linkage to the navy's force structure through the CNO's Program Advisory Memorandum (CPAM), which set forth the CNO's warfare area program recommendations for a given year.[183] Lehman had made this specific change during his tenure by shifting control of CPAM input within OPNAV from OP-96 to OP-095 and then to OP-06, where the Maritime Strategy became the starting point for Navy force structure planning.[184] This link was valuable in maintaining the concept that strategy would drive force structure.

Several short-term tenures followed Lehman's six-year stint at the Department of the Navy. His first replacement, former Marine Corps officer and attorney James Webb, served from May 1987 through February 1988.[185] He resigned in protest over Secretary of Defense Carlucci's $12 billion cut in the Navy's 1988 budget, which would have prevented the service from reaching its six-hundred-ship goal.[186] Webb and William Ball lacked Lehman's education in strategy, and further, their short tenures prohibited them from developing the influence and bureaucratic power he had wielded. Webb was followed by William Ball, former director of Legislative Affairs in the Reagan administration, who then stayed on as a placeholder until the Bush administration appointed H. Lawrence Garrett in May 1989. Garrett, unlike his immediate predecessors, would significantly alter naval strategy, from 1989 to 1994.

As CNO, Trost had presided over two of the six iterations of the Maritime Strategy before his retirement in July 1990.[187] Of these, the last two, in 1988 and 1989, attempted to adjust the strategy to account for management of regional instabilities as well as the lingering threat of global war against the Soviet Union. Both also had to account for a personnel change in the Marine Corps, which had been a reliable partner in the development of the Maritime Strategy. The Amphibious Warfare strategy, a well-integrated companion to the 1985 version of the Maritime Strategy, had been produced in close cooperation between OP-06's Capt. Larry Seaquist and Marine Col. Phil Harrington, both with SSG experience.[188]

Marine Corps Commandant Gen. P. X. Kelley had cosigned the 1985 Secret-classified Amphibious Warfare strategy along with CNO Watkins. The document stated that it would "address the uses of naval amphibious forces across the spectrum of conflict while focusing on a global conventional war with the Soviet Union."[189] Marine Corp staff officers Lt. Col. Tom Wilkerson and Maj. Hugh O'Donnell were active participants with OP-603 officers in drafting the early versions of Maritime Strategy. O'Donnell wrote the first unclassified discussion of the strategy in the September 1985 issue of the U.S. Naval Institute *Proceedings*.[190] Navy–Marine Corps cooperation continued into the later 1980s, with Kelley's successor, Gen. Al Gray, and his Plans, Policies, and Operations (PPO) deputy, Lt. Gen. Carl Mundy, contributing inputs and signing the 1989 Maritime Strategy.[191]

General Gray, however, was more astute or more open to acknowledging change in the global strategic situation and adjusting to the mood of Congress than his naval colleagues were. Sensing that the Marine Corps would need to alter its posture toward a post–Cold War world, Gray reconceptualized the Marines as an "expeditionary" force, rather than an "amphibious" force in the late 1980s and "refocused the Marine Corps on warfighting contingencies in the third world to replace the earlier focus on anti-Soviet operations in NATO and northeastern Pacific campaigns."[192] Marine Corps expeditionary units became "special operations capable" but were not grouped under the Special Operations Command, which was created as a separate unified command by Congress in 1987. The Marine Corps' growing independence would turn the creation of strategy on its head in 1990, when the Navy would shift its focus to operations in support of land-based forces. Meanwhile, as the Marines shifted course, some of the Navy's traditional elements based in Cold War strategy began to vanish.

The antisubmarine warfare capability of the Navy had been of significant concern to uniformed and civilian defense leaders since the late 1940s, when the Soviet Navy began to acquire and then reproduce advanced German-designed submarines from World War II. Much of the SSG's work in the early 1980s had been on countering the Soviet submarine threat to U.S. aircraft carriers. The Maritime Strategy postulated an aggressive naval campaign against the Soviets' ballistic missile submarines north of the Greenland-Iceland–United Kingdom gap, but that threat vanished in the early 1990s, causing many to immediately question the Navy's future role and function.[193] The advent of Cold War peace with the Soviets in the late 1980s took a rapid toll on the Navy's antisubmarine forces. By 1990 Navy leaders acknowledged that significant cost savings could be derived from cuts to submarines, maritime patrol aviation, and global antisubmarine warfare sensors.[194] The early retirement of sixteen antisubmarine warfare frigates—one of the causes for Secretary Webb's early resignation and resultant confusion in the Navy's highest civilian office—was just the beginning of major changes to the Navy's force structure at the end of the Cold War.

The Maritime Strategy might have been able to accommodate all of these changes to a degree, but by early 1990 the principal reasons for its existence were rapidly disappearing from the international scene. The December 1989 Malta summit between U.S. president George H. W. Bush and Soviet premier Mikhail Gorbachev had effectively begun the countdown to the end of the Cold War standoff between the two powers.[195] In the absence of an organizing threat, the Navy would be forced to fall back on the maintenance of force structure as a substitute for strategic thought. CNO Trost's successor, Adm. Frank Kelso Jr., would declare in June 1990 at the Senate Armed Services Committee hearing on his nomination that a "military strategy needs a specific enemy" and that "the issues before us today seem ones of naval policy rather than strategy."[196]

While the Navy and especially its strategy community reeled at the loss of their primary opponent, another significant change had been under way since summer 1986 that would profoundly affect the Navy's method of responding to changes in the global strategic situation. The Goldwater-Nichols Act of 1986, passed by overwhelming majorities in the House and Senate and supported by much of the Reagan administration, was in the process of profoundly changing the Navy's operations, administration, authority, and culture. The legislation firmly chained naval forces to joint constructs operating against land targets rather than conducting warfare at sea. It would redraw the boundaries where the Navy operated within, both at sea and administratively within the Department of Defense. It changed naval culture by demanding that the Navy place more of its best and brightest officers in joint, rather than Navy-specific staff billets, and tear down the Navy's informal networks of strategists by scattering them among other commands. These officers still led much of the effort to create a new strategy, but they did so in a very different organizational and operational environment. The analysts who formerly worked in OP-96 eventually returned to preeminent roles in generating Navy programs and the strategic thought that defined their missions. They came to dominate the business of strategy as much as the political military strategists of OPNAV had done in the 1980s. The Maritime Strategy focused the Navy's efforts on a unified campaign against a single opponent, but the collapse of the Soviet Union destroyed that consensus and set the service on a years-long course of strategic drift.

CHAPTER 3

THE GOLDWATER-NICHOLS ACT AND NAVY STRATEGY

In late 1990 veteran U.S. Navy strategist Capt. Peter M. Swartz was preparing to return to the United States after a three-year joint assignment at the U.S. mission to NATO in Brussels. Swartz wanted to return to the Office of the Chief of Naval Operations (OPNAV) and to the business of naval strategy, in which he had been engaged during the previous decade. His mentor in Brussels, Adm. Jim Hogg, the U.S. military representative to NATO's Military Committee, strongly advised him to instead take a position as a special assistant to Gen. Colin Powell, chairman of the Joint Chiefs of Staff (JCS). Swartz reiterated that he was not interested in another joint job, but instead wanted to return to creating and refining naval strategy. As Swartz canvassed various Navy colleagues and friends, he was surprised at how many told him that working for Powell was a "plum assignment." They unanimously urged him to take it. One front-running naval officer went so far as to suggest that if Swartz did not want the job, he should let him know immediately, so he could bid for it. Hogg, growing impatient, gave Swartz an extra day to make up his mind. He accepted the position.

Swartz plunged immediately into his new job, which involved a very close and positive working relationship with Powell just before Iraqi president

Saddam Hussein ordered troops to invade and occupy Kuwait and threatened Saudi Arabia. As Swartz got reacquainted with the Pentagon, he noticed the high quality of Navy talent on the Joint Staff. He had never seen such a high caliber of naval officers assigned there in the 1970s and 1980s. In contrast, when he visited his old haunts and caught up with his previous Navy network in Washington, he was nonplussed by the decline in the experience base and educational backgrounds in some OPNAV shops.

In September 1990 Swartz had an occasion to visit the office of Joint Staff J-8 for input on a project he was working on for Powell. While there, he spoke to Cdr. Joe Sestak, a Harvard graduate he knew by reputation and whose doctoral dissertation on the Seventh Fleet he had read and utilized. Swartz commented to Sestak that he found the disparity in talent between OPNAV and the Joint Staff new and disconcerting. He confided in Sestak that he worried about the intellectual prowess at OPNAV and other key Navy institutions. It was a particular concern for Swartz because he had participated in and fostered intellectual mastery in OPNAV during the 1980s as an author and advocate of the Maritime Strategy, the Navy's Cold War approach to a potential conflict with the Soviet Union. "Captain, you've been away," Sestak responded. "Goldwater-Nichols happened while you were gone, don't you remember? Do you remember how hard you and your colleagues fought against it? Do you remember that you lost?"[1] Sestak's response encapsulated a watershed period for the Navy, from 1989 to early 1994.

OVERVIEW: GOLDWATER-NICHOLS SHUFFLES THE DECK

The Goldwater-Nichols Act of 1986 sought to rectify years of parochial service competition for resources, improve the poor operational planning and execution of joint military operations by the services, and enhance the quality of military advice provided to the president by the JCS. Goldwater-Nichols reduced the powers of the individual service chiefs and increased those of the regionally deployed joint commanders who actively conducted combat operations. The JCS chairman was designated the principal military adviser to the president, whereas previously the whole of the Joint Chiefs advised senior civilian leadership. Navy and Marine Corps officers stridently opposed the legislation, with Secretary of the Navy John Lehman taking on senior members of the Senate and House of Representatives in the process. The Navy was severely criticized for its opposition to a piece of legislation that garnered near unanimous approval from legislators and was universally viewed positively. The legislation would significantly change the way the United States, and particularly the U.S. Navy, approached the business of strategy.

The Navy Responds

While some defense officials, members of Congress, and military leaders welcomed the passage of Goldwater-Nichols, the senior leadership of the military services, especially the JCS at the time, viewed the legislation as congressional meddling in uniformed military matters where none was desired.[2] The U.S. Navy and Marine Corps had opposed it for limiting the independence of their services and forcing their officers into heretofore unpopular joint assignments.[3] Secretary of the Navy John Lehman had vigorously expressed his opposition in congressional testimony and in the media, leaving the impression of the Navy being especially vehement in its position. The leaderships of the Army and Air Force were generally supportive of the reforms it introduced.

The alterations to the military chain of command that Goldwater-Nichols effected completed the separation of Navy leaders from the service's operational forces, an effort that had begun during the Eisenhower administration. Goldwater-Nichols has come to be viewed in a generally positive light, praised by senior civilian leaders, current and retired senior officers, and members of the academic community. Its reforms are often credited, in part, for the quick Gulf War victory in 1991. The Navy's strategy and acquisition experts, however, felt that it damaged their disciplines within the naval service and made them less capable of fulfilling their duties. In effect, strategy had become "someone else's job."[4]

The changes that affected the Navy's strategy community began to be implemented over the course of the late 1980s and into the 1990s. Regional combatant commander–based strategy replaced that of centralized service-based global leadership,[5] and the physical boundaries of the regional commanders increasingly cut across those of the traditional naval geographic command. These changes perhaps had a greater effect on the Navy than on the other services due to the Navy viewing strategy as a global vice regional concept. As the naval strategist Adm. J. C. Wylie noted, for the Navy and the strategic elements of the Air Force, strategy formulation meant "to think in terms of the total world."[6] By contrast, the Army conceived of strategy through theaters of operations, in other words, "a terrain division somehow arbitrary to the sailor or airman, but sound and logical if we move into the soldier's headquarters."[7]

Goldwater-Nichols primarily affected the services at the service chief level by downgrading the authority and capability of service staffs. Of relevance here, the Navy's Maritime Strategy had been created and was maintained at the service staff level. Limiting the authority and duty parameters of the service staffs hampered the Navy's ability to update and create new strategic concepts. The Army's AirLand Battle concept of the late 1970s is often viewed as the offensive strategy equivalent of the Navy's Maritime Strategy. Both were implemented at the operational level of war, but the Army's geographic theater-based concept of strategy allowed for better communication with regional commanders in chief (CINCs). In fact the Army's leadership depended on a close relationship with regional theater commanders to implement strategic concepts.[8] Thus Goldwater-Nichols' strengthening of the authority and responsibility of the regional commanders at the expense of the service chiefs permitted the Army the freedom it needed to conduct its preferred operational level of strategy.[9] In 1989 the Army conducted its Antaeus study on future force postures, and unlike the Navy, acknowledged that with the Soviet threat receding, force size and budgets would decline, and regional contingency operations would be likely in the near future.[10] That same year, as the communist superpower began withdrawing its military forces from Eastern Europe, the Air Force also acknowledged the diminishing power of the Soviet threat.[11] The Air Force chief of staff, Gen. Larry Welch, viewed a smaller force as inevitable and reconciled himself to accepting the Joint Staff strategy concept laid out by Goldwater-Nichols so long as it "did not do violence to people or to the future quality of the force."[12] Thus it would appear that the emphasis of Goldwater-Nichols on regional versus service commanders better suited the Army and Air Force in making the transition to regional strategies more rapidly than it did the Navy and with fewer ill-effects within the force.

The Navy's service staff–based strategists did not fare as well as their Army and Air Force counterparts in the defense reorganization. In addition to removing responsibility for strategy from the Navy's leadership, Goldwater-Nichols effectively dispersed the service's ad hoc, but highly effective cohort of strategic experts who had been responsible for decades of naval strategy, scattering them in assignments on the Joint Staff and the staffs of regional and functional commanders.[13] These personnel requirements forced many strategy experts, like Captain Swartz, into joint jobs instead of their traditional billets on the OPNAV staff. From a different perspective, however, one initial positive effect was that seasoned, knowledgeable, and experienced naval strategists began to populate influential joint staffs, where their capabilities and concepts ensured that the United States continued to sensibly deploy and use its naval power.

OP-06, OPNAV's hub of strategic concepts during the Cold War, had a reasonably good reputation and attracted some of the Navy's brightest officers to the end of the 1980s, after which young officers seeking jobs in Washington increasingly began to recoil from assignment to OPNAV. Instead they began embracing joint strategy duty as the ticket to flag rank as Goldwater-Nichols legislated. In some cases to meet the requirements for joint officer assignment, the Navy was forced to shorten essential assignments at sea, where officers learned core service competencies.[14] Even as late as 2002, a Rand study on how the Navy filled joint billets noted, "There is currently an 'us versus them' perspective on joint duty for naval officers. Joint assignments are considered 'time away' from the officer's warfare specialty and career path, and officers are advised to 'stay Navy' selected and screened for command."[15] Regardless, entering the 1990s many officers had continued to look for joint assignments for their next tour in Washington, which weakened the "bench" at OP-06. Concurrent with this decline of the strategist cohort within the OPNAV staff was the resurgence of operations analysis after being sidelined for seven years following the disestablishment of their OPNAV staff office in 1983.

The end of the Cold War and advent of Goldwater-Nichols resulted in two successive Chiefs of Naval Operations (CNO), Adm. Carlisle Trost (1986–90) and Adm. Frank Kelso II (1990–94), overhauling the OPNAV staff. Support in Congress for Goldwater-Nichols had been nearly unanimous, so the situation demanded that the OPNAV staff be ready to work on joint terms with the Joint

Staff, now under the control of the JCS chairman, who was also designated the principal military adviser to the president. Adm. William Crowe, appointed in 1985, making him the first JCS chairman under the regulations introduced by the act, decided to take a measured approach to the reforms and work in a collaborative fashion with the service chiefs.[16] In contrast, General Powell, who succeeded Crowe in 1989, set out to make the most of his new authority.[17]

Before 1986, the Joint Staff had worked for the service chiefs on a collective basis doing global operations planning, resource allocation, and intelligence among other functions.[18] OP-06 had been the CNO's primary link to the Joint Staff since the 1960s, and attempts were made to cement the strategy office's Joint Staff connection after the passage of Goldwater-Nichols, but they failed due to CNO Trost's view of what constituted his close staff. Unlike his predecessors, Trost was more comfortable working with the analysis branch OP-90 than with OP-96, where he had previously served as director. Trost's changes included designating the directors of OP-095 and OP-090 (Navy Program Planning) as deputy CNOs.[19] Both offices—well populated with analysts, some of whom had previously served in the now-disbanded OP-96—were redesignated OP-07 (Naval Warfare) and OP-08 (Program Planning), respectively, to match joint terms.[20] Thus Trost's decisions on which OPNAV offices he would work closely with served to reduce the influence of the strategy-focused OP-06, which had been the preeminent branch of the Navy staff since the early 1980s.

As Eastern Europeans grew restless under communist rule in the late 1980s, Trost had maintained the focus on the Soviet Navy, which remained formidable despite the general perception of the communist superpower's overall military capability diminishing. The Warsaw Pact and the Soviet Union would both cease to exist in 1991. With the elimination of the communist threat, Kelso, Trost's successor, turned from a focus on global naval strategy against the Soviet Navy to activities designed to preserve force structure for forward presence and the regional threats expected in the emerging post–Cold War world. Such efforts called for the work of budget and force structure analysts rather than the strategy experts who had written successive versions of the Maritime Strategy. JCS chairman Crowe had noted that this would be the case in 1987 in Senate Armed Services Committee testimony on national strategy.[21]

At the end of the Cold War, according to one OP-06 veteran, the Navy needed a "revised story line to match the emerging 'Jointness' of the post–GNA [Goldwater-Nichols Act] reality."[22] For Kelso, this meant a massive reorganization of the OPNAV staff, which included introducing an N code to mirror the Joint Staff offices. Of particular importance, the deputy CNO heading N8 (Resources, Warfare Requirements, and Assessments) was given direct control over the deputy CNOs for acquisition, program planning, and logistics.[23] This change, along with Trost's previous close association with OP-96 and OP-90 further enabled the return of the analysis arm of the Navy staff to power. Although the newly reempowered analysts would not write the strategic concepts that followed the Maritime Strategy, they nevertheless shaped their development and ultimately controlled their dispositions. The Joint Mission Areas (JMA), the process adopted by N8, marked the return of operations analysis to developing naval strategy, albeit from the Army-centric perspective of force structure management over time rather than political-military calculations.

The combination of changes in command structure, the alteration of traditional naval concepts of the battle space, the migration of Navy strategy experts from OPNAV to the Joint Staff, and the return of systems analysts to the fore on the OPNAV staff altered the Navy's concept of strategy. The Navy's most senior officers would no longer control the forces they built, trained, and equipped. The concepts of naval strategy that remained in the wake of Goldwater-Nichols became regional, rather than global in character and would be more influenced by force structure and budget analysis than by strategy, especially toward the mid-1990s. The legislation's joint personnel requirements effectively served to disband the Navy's effective ad hoc strategic experts, dispersing them throughout the joint force. While perhaps useful in the immediate post–Cold War era, these changes would hinder the Navy in the first decade of the twenty-first century as it sought new strategic solutions to a dwindling budget and an aging, contracting force structure.

THE MAKING OF GOLDWATER-NICHOLS

The Goldwater-Nichols Act was the most significant shake-up in the Department of Defense since its birth as the National Military Establishment in 1947 and its restructuring and renaming in 1949.[24] The failure to achieve desired results in the

Vietnam War may have been a catalyst for the defense reform movement of the late 1970s, but the military disasters that followed provided additional impetus for change,[25] including the 1979–81 Iran hostage crisis, problems with interservice planning and communication during the 1983 Lebanon peacekeeping mission and related bombing of the Marine barracks in Beirut, and the October 1983 invasion of Grenada.[26] These perceived operational military failures as well as the performance of the JCS, as the military leadership, came under strong criticism from senior uniformed officers and a growing number of civilian Department of Defense officials. Their voices became more pronounced with the change in presidential administration in 1981 from Jimmy Carter to Ronald Reagan and with it, a promised significant increase in defense spending that former Reagan defense official Lawrence Korb described as a "wartime buildup without a war."[27] The impression of excessive defense spending resulting from soaring military budgets under Reagan caught the eye of some members of Congress and helped stoke legislative branch interest in defense reform.[28]

Uniformed criticism of the JCS and the organization of the Department of Defense came primarily from a small number of senior Air Force and Army officers. Gen. David Jones, USAF, outgoing JCS chairman, said in congressional testimony on defense reorganization in February 1982, "There is very little disciplined long-term planning in defense." He added, "We spend too much time on the scramble for resources and not enough on the oversight of those resources."[29] Jones was critical of the JCS structure and asserted that the advice offered by the Joint Chiefs was neither adequate nor timely in its delivery. He advocated moderate reforms to strengthen the office of the chairman and the Joint Staff to remedy the ills he described.[30] Gen. Edward Meyer, a former Army chief of staff, was even more critical of the JCS system and suggested a more radical solution: eliminating the JCS as an organization and replacing it with a national military advisory council comprised of retired officers, who would not have the same parochial, service concerns as the active duty service chiefs of staff.[31] Meyer's plan would have allowed for direct communication between deployed commanders and the advisory council, with the role of service secretaries and service chiefs significantly reduced.

Civilian staff at the Department of Defense were even more critical of the JCS than senior officers like Jones and Meyer. To them, the two generals represented defense reorganization concepts that had been in existence since the end of World War II and largely based, as the generals noted, on the approach that the services compete for the scarce resources of the early Cold War when Jones and Meyer were young officers and influenced by recent events. The civilian critics of defense organization hailed from a very different background, ranging in rank from former defense secretaries to junior analysts and staffers. Many had served early on in the post-1949 Department of Defense or during the Kennedy and Johnson administrations under Secretary of Defense Robert S. McNamara in analysis positions. Their criticisms focused on the corporate organization of the JCS as a root cause of less-than-useful and untimely operational or administrative advice to civilian leadership. They viewed members of the JCS as parochial servants of their own services' needs and unable to rise above them to meet national defense requirements.[32]

Some senior members among these civilian critics expressed their thoughts in hearings on defense reorganization reform held by the Senate Armed Services Committee in early 1984. James Schlesinger, secretary of defense in the Nixon and Ford administrations, described the structure of the JCS as the "central weakness of the existing system,"[33] and Elliot Richardson, Schlesinger's predecessor, asserted, "Service Chiefs were placed in a position where they are inevitably torn between competing loyalties."[34] Some lower-ranking civilian supporters of reform legislation played key roles in connecting congressional allies of reform with like-minded former senior Department of Defense leaders.[35] Among the civilian supporters were James Locher, a West Point graduate and former Department of Defense analyst at the time serving as a Senate Armed Services Committee staffer, and Arch Barrett, a retired Air Force colonel, systems analyst, and House Armed Services Committee staff member. Both would make significant contributions in the drafting of parts of what would become the Goldwater-Nichols Act.

The Center for Strategic and International Studies (CSIS) and other Washington think tanks provided space where supporters could meet and combine their efforts. From December 1985 through the legislation's completion in November 1986, CSIS hosted the Defense Reorganization Military Reform Project Steering Group, which included a diverse group of academics, former Department of Defense officials, retired military leaders, and members of Congress. Among those taking part were the political scientists Samuel Huntington, Barry Posen, and Edward Luttwak, General Jones and General Meyer, future defense secretary William Perry, and Rep. Newt Gingrich (R-Ga.).[36] The Heritage Foundation and the Brookings Institution also offered defense reform forums through publications and advocacy.

The reform movement had strong bipartisan support within Congress as well as among some well-placed Reagan administration officials and the defense intellectual community. The core of congressional support for reform included bill co-sponsors Sen. Barry Goldwater (R-Ariz.) and Rep. Bill Nichols (D-Ga.) along with Sen. Sam Nunn (D-Ga.), Sen. William Cohen (R-Maine) and Rep. Ike Skelton (D-Mo.), Rep. Richard White (D-Texas), Rep. John Kasich (R-Ohio), and Rep. Les Aspin (D-Wisc.).[37] They felt that greater centralization of power in the office of the JCS chairman would improve the quality of advice available to the nation's civilian leadership. Reagan administration members, including his national security adviser Robert McFarlane, supported the reform efforts, as did David Packard, a former deputy defense secretary whom Reagan appointed chairman of a presidential blue-ribbon commission on defense reform. Secretary of Defense Caspar Weinberger was not initially in favor of the reforms, but later changed his position, for practical reasons, rather than any particular beliefs.[38] Sources vary on the level of Weinberger's acceptance of Goldwater-Nichols, but most suggest grudging acceptance, with conditions, of the final legislative product.

The Navy and Marine Corps leaderships, including CNO Adm. James D.Watkins and Gen. P. X. Kelley, commandant of the Marines, generally opposed the legislation, as it would restrict their traditional freedom of action and give control over shipbuilding and naval and marine operations to other services less well versed in these matters. Numerous naval leaders past and present voiced opposition. Vice Adm. Henry Mustin, head of OP-06 just before Goldwater-Nichols passed, later described the situation as follows:

> Power in Washington is a zero-sum game. The big winners in the Goldwater-Nichols Act were the Secretary of Defense and the Chairman of the Joint Chiefs, and the big losers were the service secretaries and the

> service chiefs. Goldwater-Nichols essentially enabled the creation of a longtime Army dream which had been personified by George Marshall in World War II, which was to have what the Germans called a general staff, with great power and authority. The Navy position on the matter was that that was dangerous over-centralization, that you stifled dissent, and therefore increased the risk of making bad decisions; and that we didn't like it. When I got up there the Secretary of the Navy [John Lehman] made no bones about telling me that, that that's how he felt, and that I was down there to guard the gates against these assaults by the Army and the Air Force.[39]

In a February 1980 American Enterprise Institute article, former CNO Adm. James Holloway (1974–78), an early opponent of the idea of "bad advice," responded to the accusation that the JCS had provided such by calling the allegation a "euphemistic way of saying the JCS did not provide the desired answer."[40] Secretary Lehman quickly become the effective leader of the opposition, issuing the most vocal criticisms of the proposed legislation. Lehman's position was rooted in the Navy's opposition to reform in the late 1940s, at the dawn of the Cold War, and continued in the fight waged by CNO Adm. Arleigh Burke against President Dwight Eisenhower's reform efforts in the 1950s.[41] Lehman argued that the proposed legislation would create inefficient bureaucracy in the Department of Defense and reduce the quality of military advice offered to the president. He also opposed concentrating so much power in the office of the JCS chairman, which would restrict advice flowing to the president to the "opinions and decisions of one man, the chairman himself, and his general staff bureaucracy."[42] Lehman's campaign, well organized but ultimately unsuccessful, served as a rallying point for reform opponents. It even set up a hotline for opponents to offer their support. Goldwater was furious when he discovered the operation and called the number, pretending to be a backer.[43] He later wrote directly to Secretary Weinberger and President Reagan to complain that the effort by Lehman's staff had been illegal.[44]

Few senior naval officers supported the defense reorganization reforms proposed by the Army, Air Force, and defense civilian authorities. Among those who did were the retired admirals Harry Train, Robert Long, and Thor

Hanson, who had joint or Department of Defense analysis experience. Train and Long had been combatant commanders, in the Pacific and Atlantic, respectively, and Train and Hanson had been directors of the Joint Staff.[45] Train, a political-military expert from OP-06, had also directed OP-96, and Hanson had served on the staff of Alain Enthoven, deputy secretary of defense for Systems Analysis.[46] The incumbent JCS chairman, Admiral Crowe, was also in favor of reform, but tended to keep his opinion more closely held.[47] Despite some opposition views being reinforced by findings from Packard's blue-ribbon Committee on Defense Reform, the legislation passed Congress in early October 1986 by a significant bipartisan majority, in the House of Representatives in a 383–27 vote and unanimously in the Senate, 95–0).[48] After the Senate vote, Goldwater called the legislation "the only goddamn thing I have ever done in the Senate that was worth a damn."[49] The Navy had known the outcome as early as November 1985. The JCS, in written testimony to the Senate Armed Services Committee indicated general support for Goldwater's proposals to make the JCS chairman the principal military adviser to the president, to introduce a deputy JCS chairman with the four-star rank, and to develop "some kind of joint personnel management system."[50] Lehman later suggested that the legislation was in effect a retirement gift for Goldwater.[51]

Although hailed as a great triumph for the defense reform movement, the Goldwater-Nichols Act was more of an incomplete armistice than a "victory on the Potomac," as Locher, one of the legislation's authors, called it in his 2002 book. In fact, the defense reformers had favored a considerably more radical plan proposing fundamental changes to the structure of senior military leadership and the armed forces' organization for combat. "Defense Organization: The Need for Change," a Senate Armed Services Committee staff study authored by Locher, contained ninety-one specific recommendations, including replacing the JCS with a joint military advisory council independent of all service functions, as suggested by Meyers; reorganizing the military along mission, rather than service, lines; and removing from the chain of command those service component commanders within the unified commands.[52]

Locher himself dismissed such proposals as diversionary "bullet traps" designed to divert antireform opponents from more moderate goals.[53] Senator

Nunn's staff director, Arnold Punaro, similarly suggested that deception stood at the core of Nunn and Goldwater's efforts to essentially threaten the armed forces with even more radical reforms if their proposals were not accepted.[54] Yet similar recommendations appear in the memoirs of Goldwater as well as those of Sen. John Tower (R-Texas).[55] Analysts influenced by the policies of McNamara for reorganizing the Department of Defense around joint missions, rather than geographic or service constructs, had been making similar arguments since the 1961 Symington Commission, the effort led by Sen. William Stuart Symington (D-Mo.), a former Air Force secretary, that recommended abolishing the separate military departments, replacement of the JCS with a group of senior officers separated from their respective service affiliations, and reductions in the authority of the individual service chiefs to mere administrative and logistics duties.[56] Arch Barrett, Locher's House Armed Services Committee counterpart on defense reform, contradicted the assertion of intentional deception on the part of the members of the House and Senate in regard to the goals of reform. In a 1991 interview, Barrett asserted that the committee reconciliation effort on the House and Senate versions of what became Goldwater-Nichols purposely embraced the reforms that were "politically possible."[57] Barrett's more moderate recommendations formed much of the backbone of the act.[58]

Representative Aspin, the House Armed Services Committee chairman, credits Nichols with being the driving force behind defense reform, more so than Goldwater, who made the later push in the Senate.[59] This was readily apparent to the Navy at the time as well. Deputy Under Secretary of the Navy Seth Cropsey noted in an 11 September 1986 memo to Secretary Lehman, "It is remarkable how much the Senate proposals have faded in favor of those in the House."[60] It appears that pro-reform advocates had a rather long list of objectives that were not met in Goldwater-Nichols. The reform camp's inability to implement the more comprehensive reforms they advocated suggests that Lehman's opposition movement was likely more effective than it seems at first glance. Regardless, the partial reforms of Goldwater-Nichols would create an uncertain climate as the military services grappled with the problem of creating strategy in the post–Cold War era.

PRACTICAL IMPLICATIONS AND EFFECTS

As noted above, Goldwater-Nichols had three significant effects on the creation of military strategy within the services and in the Department of Defense at large. It elevated the JSC chairman to the position of principal military adviser to the president and placed the Joint Staff under the chairman's direct control. It also gave each regional combatant commander greater power over his or her organization and regional strategy at the expense of the service chiefs. These changes further restricted service leaders' ability to influence the development of strategy, the defense budget, and roles and force structures. It also had the effect of diverting talented officers from their traditional roles on service staffs to the heretofore less desirable joint and CINC staffs.

An official Navy spokesperson on the Maritime Strategy stated in 1985 that "no meaningful, single-service strategy was possible in the modern era" and that the Navy considered the Maritime Strategy the "maritime component of the national strategy" in which the Army and Air Force were included.[61] This trend away from service strategy writing affected not only the strategy-producing elements of the OPNAV staff but the acquisition management offices as well. Diverting them to joint assignments, some argued, tended to separate the future leadership of the service from the process that produced the tools of warfare capability they would wield as senior leaders of combat formations.[62]

In short, Goldwater-Nichols fundamentally shifted the balance of power in defense authority from the services to a "joint" construct, but in the words of one critic, Deputy Under Secretary Cropsey, "never offered a positive model of how a more joint military would think or perform."[63] Vice Admiral Mustin described the Navy's position toward the legislation as being "very, very hard over against it" and Secretary of the Navy Lehman as "very hard over against it." He added, "Nonetheless it was the law of the land, and so we had all the transition pains, as the authority for many, many of the issues that affect the armed forces migrated from the services to the Chairman of the Joint Chiefs."[64] Department of Defense Directive 5100.1, issued 3 April 1987, documented the various changes required by Goldwater-Nichols.[65]

As the 1980s came to a close, it became evident that the Navy would need to implement the provisions of the Goldwater-Nichols legislation in an environment in which "senior four-star officers no longer had control of the fleet."[66] While the service chiefs had been removed from the operational military chain of command in 1958 as part of the Eisenhower reform package and no longer commanded deployed forces, they retained significant influence over those forces through their service component commanders. These senior three-star officers had communicated freely with the CNO during the production and evolution of the Maritime Strategy.[67] While anchored in the Navy's traditional responsibility to provide naval force, the Maritime Strategy also served as a "contingent war-fighting doctrine" describing how the Navy proposed to combat the Soviet Union across its multiple regional commands and with a six-hundred-ship navy.[68]

The Maritime Strategy had been the latest in a series of naval strategic documents since the late 1940s that sought to articulate the Navy's place in Cold War–era national strategies. They had generally been produced at the behest and under the guidance of the CNO and the Secretary of the Navy. Some of the regional combatant commanders had resisted the influence of the CNO in this regard, because they, not the CNO, were responsible for the employment of combat units against the enemy. After a presentation of the Maritime Strategy in 1984, Admiral Crowe, while Pacific Commander, had responded, "I'm not sure why the CNO needs a maritime strategy; I need one, but he doesn't."[69] While JCS chairman in January 1987, Crowe told the Senate Armed Services Committee, "There is no such thing as a 'maritime' or 'Navy' strategy for the United States. We have a national strategy and a national military strategy. I do not believe that the scheme known as the 'maritime strategy' is a strategy. It is a conceptual way in which you might use naval forces."[70]

There was a degree of irony in Crowe's statement, for while serving in the mid-1970s as deputy chief, in charge of OP-06, he had been responsible for creating OP-603, the OPNAV staff office charged with strategy creation, and filling it with strategy experts.[71] The effect of Goldwater-Nichols provisions in dividing the fleet into theaters subject to the individual warfighting concepts of individual CINCs, not to mention the CINCs' reluctance to deploy their own ships across CINC boundaries, hamstrung the Navy's attempts to organize, train, and equip its forces to deter or confront the Soviet Union on a coherent global basis.

In regard to strategic primacy, Goldwater-Nichols seemed, at the time, to settle the argument in favor of the JCS chairman and combatant commanders over the service chiefs. The legislation elevated the chairman from a position of first-among-equals to being the principal military adviser to the president and gave the chairman the authority to convene, set the agenda for, and preside over the meetings of the JCS.[72] Title II, specifying that the Joint Staff worked directly for the chairman and not the JCS collective, greatly empowered the chairman's ability to set the broader agenda for the Joint Chiefs.[73] While individual members of the JCS were not prohibited from offering discrete advice to the president on their own initiative the chairman's advice took priority in presidential review.[74] The chairman was also given significant authority over the strategic planning and assessment functions of the JCS, with responsibility for providing strategic direction and preparing strategic, logistics, and mobility plans for the armed forces.[75]

The legislation did not make the chairman a "supreme commander of the military services," as some reformers had proposed, but it did demand that combatant commanders communicate with the secretary of defense and president through the chairman, thus allowing the chairman to act as a "de facto" supreme commander in the eyes of some critics.[76] The service chiefs retained their authority to train, equip, and provide forces to the combatant commanders, but responsibility for strategy appeared, at that time, to reside firmly in joint hands. Some outside observers worried that an empowered chairman might practice "strategic monism," emphasizing one carefully predicted and orchestrated mission or the needs of one service, as opposed to operating as a "strategic pluralist," planning for a diversity of threats.[77] Such provisions and potential threats from an unbalanced chairman could make comprehensive, global service-based strategic concepts much more difficult to create and implement.

The effects of Goldwater-Nichols manifested themselves in early 1987 in the Joint Strategic Capabilities Plan. Intelligence reporting indicated that a Soviet attack would be evident at least two weeks before being launched, thus giving planners time to reinforce Western forces on the Central European front.[78] This appraisal led to planning reassessments on where to focus primary U.S. efforts early in a global conflict. Believing that constrained resources might force decision makers to choose between preparing for a global or a regional war, Joint Staff planners in 1987 had attempted to incorporate greater emphasis on regional planning in the National Military Strategy Document for fiscal years 1990–94.[79] The continued reduction of the Soviet and Russian threat, particularly the decreasing ability to project power into Central Europe and the Persian Gulf, allowed the planners to focus more on regional strategies. Maj. Gen. George Lee Butler, director of J5 (Joint Staff Planning) in 1989, made the projection of increased warning time a justification for greater focus on regional planning.[80]

The Joint Staff might have been planning for the end of the Cold War in the late 1980s, but the Navy was not convinced that the Soviet Union was finished in terms of sea power. CNO Trost had been fighting this assumption since late 1987, when he "realized that there was a perception that the Maritime Strategy was confined to dealing with the existing threat posed by the Soviet navy's increasingly capable naval forces."[81] He was concerned when Congress began to suggest budget cuts as the Soviet threat waned. Trost had been the first Navy chief to visit the Soviet Union, in October 1989, during which he conducted a series of lectures.[82] In addition to his thinking on the Soviet Union remaining a threat, he also sought to convince those in Congress desiring a "peace dividend" to consider the Navy's global missions regardless of the Soviet threat and the force size required to meet them. Trost added elements to operations in the Pacific in the 1988 and 1989 versions of the Maritime Strategy in the hope of shifting the focus away from Europe and the Atlantic, but remained committed to the concept that the Soviet Union was the primary threat to the United States.[83]

The bulk of the Joint Staff, however, was already committed to an impending end to the Cold War and coming to terms with an expected drawdown in defense spending. Thus, in late February 1989, J8 (Force Structure, Resource, and Assessments), stemming from Goldwater-Nichols, presented the "Quiet Study," a review of several force-reduction strategies. The departing JCS chairman, Crowe, did not, however, want to recommend force reductions in the absence of a new presidential strategy,[84] so J8 also produced "Quiet Study 2," which further focused on regional versus global conflicts. The views of Crowe's successor, General Powell—appointed by President George H. W. Bush in 1989—closely aligned with the language of the second study on a shift to a regional strategy, leading him to embrace the document's conclusions. This significantly aided in the transformation from a global to a regional-based strategy.

Powell also embraced "with alacrity" the new authority granted the JCS chairman under Goldwater-Nichols and used it to advance the post–Cold War agenda of change.[85] Powell combined the J5 and J8 projects on post–Cold War forces, which eventually recommended a 25 percent cut in overall military strength and a switch to a regional strategic focus. The briefing "A View to the 90s" encapsulated the thinking of the chairman, with whom the secretary of defense, Richard Cheney, largely agreed. Powell's changes were incorporated into the president's National Security Strategy and the Defense Planning Guidance (DPG), both products of Goldwater-Nichols. Powell considered his new defense strategy "analysis by instinct" rather than reliance on "intelligence, estimates, war games, or computer projections." He later observed, "My thoughts were guided simply by what I had observed at world summits, by my experience at the NSC, and by what I like to think of as informed intuition."[86]

Battle Joined, Battle Lost

General Powell's presentation of planned changes at a 26 February 1990 meeting of the Joint Chiefs and regional commanders was the services' first chance to oppose or propose revisions to the chairman's concept. The Navy, under the leadership of CNO Trost, had disagreed with the naval force structure outlined in "A View to the 90s." Believing the Soviet Union still posed a global naval threat, Trost had two complaints about the proposed force structure directly related to Goldwater-Nichols. First, and most important, wrote Don Snider of one complaint, "The Navy had not been a part of the development of the force before it was 'laid on the table' with the strategy, and thus was not privy to the analysis that validated its size and capabilities."[87] Second, the proposed naval force was too small to be effective in the rotational forward presence mission it was intended to fill.[88] Trost was fighting an uphill battle.

Before planned testimony by Trost on force posture in April 1990, Senate Armed Services Committee members Nunn and John Warner (R-Va.) both said that the chiefs needed to come to the Hill with a different story this year, because it was time to reduce.[89] Trost made one last attempt to make his point two months before his retirement in summer 1990. In a May 1990 article for U.S. Naval Institute *Proceedings*, he wrote that "the Maritime Strategy's origins predate the Cold War" and was "designed to support the entire spectrum of actions needed to represent U.S. global interests as a maritime nation and a world superpower."[90] He reminded readers that despite the changes implemented by Soviet premier Mikhail S. Gorbachev, the Soviet Union "possesses an impressive ocean-going navy and continues to modernize."[91]

Trost's efforts were largely in vain due to the institutional superiority of the Joint Staff and the chairman. Goldwater-Nichols enabled Powell to create naval force structure recommendations without input from the Navy's service chief and made possible congressional favoring of Powell's proposal over the objections of the responsible service chief. As one chief noted, "The planning for the defense build-down was a case of someone determining in advance what was needed, and then seeing that the result was produced."[92] The Navy had believed as early as 1945, as noted during the Richardson Committee hearings on defense reorganization, that if non-naval military authorities were allowed to decide naval force structure size, "there is a real danger that one component will be seriously affected by the decisions of one man to the detriment of the effectiveness of the Armed Forces as a whole."[93]

Powell further strengthened the hand of joint rather than service-based planning in the research, planning, and implementation of the first National Military Strategy associated with the National Security Strategy and DPG. There was broad agreement even among the Navy leadership on a change in focus from global to regional-based strategies, but some global plans against residual Soviet action were retained.[94] These concepts formed the basis of the 1991 Contingency Planning Guidance, which "established a new framework for operational planning based upon both the changes that had taken place in the strategic environment and expected force reductions."[95] In turn, the guidance formed the basis for the Joint Strategic Contingency Planning, the basis for the 1991 National Military Strategy, adopted 27 January 1992.[96] This last document directed regional commanders in chief to "prepare operational plans that focused on regional threats."[97] These plans would be implemented by the regional commanders in the early and mid-1990s, although some of them had been taking regional concerns into account since the 1980s. U.S. Central Command (CENTCOM), which began life as the Carter administration's Rapid Deployment Joint Task Force for the Middle East, focused on regional concerns at its inception.[98] The service chiefs objected in varying small degrees to the new strategy, but when confronted with President George H. W. Bush's demand to reduce the defense budget due to the end of the Cold War, they quickly assented and moved to protect their respective budgets.[99] The results of the Gulf War had appeared to "validate the conceptual underpinnings of the new military strategy," discouraging further argument over its scope and implementation.[100]

The Navy struggled to adjust to the new military strategy, the new force structure determined by outsiders, and the fundamental shift in the service's own maritime strategy concepts. CNO Kelso, who replaced Trost in 1990, had planned to publish a comprehensive naval plan on a logical reduction of naval forces for the post–Cold War world, but could not move fast enough to get ahead of Powell's efforts.[101] His plan eventually appeared in U.S. Naval Institute *Proceedings* in April 1991.[102] Kelso later said, "I never got approval to publish the article in time for it to have the effect I desired. It was finally published after General Powell came up with a 450-ship Navy that he called a base force."[103] He also said about the article, "[It had] absolutely zero effect or impact, because it was not a 'put your step forward.' It was 'Okay, you've been drug down ship by ship now.' In other words, it came after the fact that the reductions had started."[104]

Not only was the senior naval leadership no longer in command of the fleet, its opinions on naval strategy and force structure were rejected in favor of that of an army general supported by a Joint Staff that included naval officers who had been effectively decoupled from naval leadership. While defense cuts became inevitable in the wake of the Cold War, as they had been after World War II and the Korean and Vietnam Wars, in this case the JCS chairman, rather than the CNO or even the Secretary of the Navy, made the recommendation to Congress and the president on which naval forces to retain. The Navy's inability to exert influence on its size, composition, and missions would negatively impact the ability of its leadership to create strategy from 1991 onward.

NEW PERSPECTIVES

The new powers of the JCS chairman also extended to the strategic orientation of the services. Before 1986 naval officers in strategic and operational planning were trained to think of broad areas of ocean as single conceptual units, and the naval organization of the Atlantic and Pacific commands had reinforced that perspective.[105] The chairman's new powers, however, included the right to periodically review and adjust the missions, responsibilities, geographic boundaries, and force structures of each combatant command.[106]

The Navy had historically seen the entirety of the world's oceans as a unitary theater of action uniquely suited to naval control. The service had not fully articulated this concept on paper until the creation of the first version of the Maritime Strategy in October 1982.[107] Naval leaders had been loath to give land-based commanders any control over ocean areas due to their view of the oceans as a unitary battle space.[108] While a global Cold War fit the Navy's view, the end of the conflict allowed for the development of a number of regional strategies encompassing both land and water space, but with a firm terrestrial focus.

General Powell's "View of the 90s" briefing was based on his vision that the disintegration of the Soviet Empire called for new regional strategies that should assume that the United States would remain a superpower due to its military capabilities, forces, and alliance relationships.[109] His approach to developing these strategies involved reshaping not only the force structure but the geographically defined battle space in which that force operated. The naval historian John Hattendorf described the effect of this approach on the Navy as a "structural change in command authority" that "had the intended effect of increasing joint strategic and operational planning in specific geographical locations, but also had the unintended effect of making it more difficult to implement coordinated concepts for oceans—the natural geographical unit of maritime space."[110] This process had begun even before Powell's appointment as chairman.

The 1987 review of combatant command (COCOM) boundaries required by Goldwater-Nichols generated disputes among the services. The Army attempted to revive a previous plan for a subunified Northeast Asia Command centered on the Korean Peninsula, but the Joint Chiefs rejected it.[111] Of more concern to the Navy was a decision on whether CENTCOM, centered on the Persian Gulf region, should assume responsibility for the eastern Mediterranean Sea directly adjacent to the "confrontational" states of Israel, Syria, and Lebanon.[112] CNO Trost counterposed that both the Red Sea and the Persian Gulf be reassigned to U.S. Pacific Command, arguing that "USCINCCENT [CENTCOM commander] could not carry out his mission without command of the seas stretching all the way back to the California coast, which was USCINCPAC's [PACOM commander's] responsibility." The Navy's objections to the proposed changes to COCOM oceanic boundaries illustrate the service's concept of a unified ocean area of responsibility within which the inherent maneuverability, reach, power, and flexibility of naval forces could be optimally deployed and redeployed to meet the nation's challenges. In the end, the JCS only made a moderate alteration, assigning limited areas of the Gulfs of Oman and Aden to CENTCOM. Even so, Secretary of Defense Weinberger had to personally intervene to settle the situation.[113]

The Navy had mixed success in retaining its traditional maritime responsibilities during the 1991 COCOM review. Both the newly established Strategic Command and the North American Command had force structures favorable to naval leadership, but the latter acquired maritime geographic responsibilities over the objections of the Navy and Marine Corps leadership. Powell desired in particular that the Navy gunnery range at Vieques, Puerto Rico, be available for joint exercises.[114]

The early adjustments to COCOM boundaries and areas of responsibility proved to be minor compared to the changes to come in the late 1990s, courtesy of the JCS chairman's greater authority mandated by Goldwater-Nichols and General Powell's efforts to continue the shift from a global to a regional-based strategy. The 1992 DPG stated, "We can shift our defense planning from a focus on the global threat posed by the Warsaw Pact to focus on the less demanding regional threats and challenges we are more likely to face in the future."[115] The regional defense concept was based on four key elements: planning for uncertainty, shaping the future security environment, maintenance of "strategic depth," and continued U.S. leadership to maintain security and prevent the rise of a successor to the Soviet Union.[116]

Although the CINC positions were originally designed as regional commands for a global conflict with the Soviet Union, they took on new prominence after 1991, with those occupying the post becoming active facilitators of a new world order friendly to U.S. interests. Undersecretary of Defense for Policy Paul Wolfowitz presented this new role in a 16 April 1992 memorandum on the contents of the 1992 DPG, writing, "The perceived ability of the U.S. to act independently, if necessary, is thus an important factor, even in the cases where we do not actually do so."[117] Wolfowitz continued,

> Our forward presence helps to shape the evolving security environment. We will continue to rely on forward presence of U.S. forces to show U.S. commitment and lend credibility to our alliances, to deter aggression, enhance regional stability, promote U.S. influence and access, and, when necessary, provide an initial crisis-response capability. Forward presence is vital to the maintenance of the system of collective defense by which the United States has been able to work with our friends and allies to protect our security interests, while minimizing the burden of defense spending and of unnecessary arms competition.

The new post–Cold War national strategy and national military strategy were the products of the civilian presidential administration and defense secretariat, while the principal military inputs came from the Joint Staff working for and with the chairman. The services only provided input related to the defense of their spending programs. The environment in which the Navy produced the Maritime Strategy was a far cry from the new one, in which the service had lost control of the argument about the size and composition of its force and how and where it would fight.

Navy Strategists: In the Crosshairs

The change in the Navy's fortunes was not due to a deficiency in qualified strategic thinkers. Indeed, the service had cultivated a cadre of experts since the days of War Plan Orange, when strategists such as Charles "Savvy" Cooke and Richmond K. Turner accurately anticipated the maritime strategy and course of the 1941–45 Pacific War.[118] This tradition continued throughout the Cold War, with the service mentoring and sustaining experts in naval strategy. While these officers were assigned operational, fleet-related billets during the course of their career paths, they were also rotated through a small number of strategic planning offices on the CNO's staff.[119] They often worked in concert with civilian academics at the Naval War College (NWC), the traditional home of naval strategic thought and culture since the days of Alfred Thayer Mahan, in the late nineteenth century.[120]

These officers were the product of what Hattendorf called a "renaissance in strategic thinking in the U.S. Navy" in response to the tenure of Secretary of Defense McNamara, during which long-range planning had been reduced to a series of five-year planning cycles.[121] CNO Admiral Elmo Zumwalt (1970–74) first sought to create a new cadre of strategists through the NWC. His effort was not entirely successful. The overall curriculum improved, thanks to the efforts of Vice Adm. Stansfield Turner while its president (1972–74), but the school failed to attract enough of the Navy's best to rapidly create a new strategic culture.[122] Zumwalt's other focus, however—strategy concerns in the Pacific and Indian Oceans—did produce the desired strategic culture through the CNO office staffs assigned to work on these issues.[123]

Over the course of the 1970s and early 1980s, OP-06 and OP-00K (Executive Panel), the latter established in 1970, emerged as veritable breeding grounds for naval strategic thinkers. The assigned officers worked in close cooperation with the Office of Naval Intelligence, the fleet staffs, and the Center for Naval Analyses, a federally funded research and development center, and did much of the planning and staff work that led to and included the Maritime Strategy in the 1980s. The Navy had a strategy subspecialty code that officers could acquire through appropriate military or civilian education, but this cadre of strategic experts was informally organized. This was especially true of the strategy experts assigned to the CNO's staff. Capt. William Spencer Johnson, who served multiple assignments in OP-06 in the 1970s and 1980s, recalled that the executive assistant to the flag officer in charge of the office kept a wooden box in his office with file cards detailing those who had served there. This simple filing system recorded the officer's current service billet and when he or she would again be available for service on the OP-06 staff. The admiral in charge of OP-06 essentially had unofficial detailing authority over these officers, and with the support of Naval Personnel Command, could order their return when requested.[124]

A number of former fleet commanders headed OP-06, among them Adm. James "Ace" Lyons and Adm. Charles Larson as well as Mustin and Crowe. Some flag officers and staff officers completed multiple tours in OP-06 offices over the course of their careers, including Crowe, Lyons, Vice Adm. Art Moreau, Rear Adm. Ron Marryott, Rear Adm. Bill Pendley, Rear Adm. T. J. Johnson, Capt. Peter Swartz, Capt. Rodger Barnett, and Capt. William Spencer Johnson.[125] Multiple assignments within OP-06 produced a strong but largely unofficial strategic community of talented men and women within the larger CNO staff.

In the summer of 1981, prompting by Under Secretary of the Navy Bob Murray led CNO Adm. Thomas Hayward to create the Strategic Studies Group (SSG) at the NWC. The group, consisting of upwardly mobile Navy captains and Marine Corps colonels, convened under Murray's leadership and mentorship, assisted by Cdr. Kenneth McGruther, Naval Reserve Cdr. John Hanley, and others. The initial purpose of the SSG, according to McGruther, was to develop ways to "reinforce in the Soviet mind the perception that it could not win a war with the United States, both *before* a war, to enhance deterrence, and at all phases of the war should it occur."[126]

As discussed in chapter two, the first two groups of SSG members became very influential in determining how elements of the new Maritime Strategy would eventually be employed. Murray wanted the group to work on problems of strategy and theater operations broad enough to be useful but narrow enough to be reasonably accomplished. The SSG would not be able to meet these goals in isolation, but instead would need to travel around the world and discuss proposals with senior officers and staffs.[127] Their feedback was important to the builders of naval strategy in OP-60. McGruther, a protégé of Moreau and a former OP-603 staff officer, kept the OP-60 staff appraised of the work of the strategy group,[128] which remained operative throughout the 1980s and supported improvements in the evolving Maritime Strategy.

The naval officers themselves were another important product arising from the OPNAV strategy offices and the SSG. Gaining immense professional expertise from their assignments to these groups,[129] they constituted an expanding cadre of strategic-minded officers trained to both create strategy and anticipate opponents' responses to that strategy. The interactions among the OPNAV strategy offices like OP-603, the SSG, the fleet commanders, and naval intelligence experts generated inspiration to turn a new naval strategy to confront the Soviet Union into plans and a warfighting doctrine useful to operational commanders. This group's combination of operational, academic, and cooperative experience was well suited to the rapid and effective production and updating of strategy-related materials. The changes wrought by Goldwater-Nichols would eventually transform this group from an officially constituted forum to an ad hoc assembly sustained by the members themselves. This transition occurred through the modification of the missions and the composition of these cooperative strategic entities.

One of the most contested aspects of Goldwater-Nichols was the establishment of a rigorous qualification, assignment, and management program for joint duty officers. Due to a perceived predilection by the services to assign less-qualified officers to the Joint Staff, Congress required the Secretary of Defense to submit an annual Joint Officer Management report to the legislative branch detailing the number of joint duty officers, the promotion rates of joint duty officers (including comparisons with non-joint qualified officers), and the billets to which each service assigned the officers.

The requirement of joint duty assignments for promotion to the flag ranks constituted another significant change in officer assignments. The Army and Air Force tended to assign those officers not required for active, operational assignments to staff duty in Washington, D.C., so the services never suffered from a lack of personnel to fill joint assignments. The Navy, however, did not have a similar surplus of officers to assign to joint billets because the force remained operational at sea, as opposed to the Army and Air Force officers, who remained largely in garrison bases. Vice Admiral Mustin, as head of OP-06, later explained the problem as follows:

> What happened in all of this was, it became apparent that the Navy officers' structure was not adequate to man both the Navy and this burgeoning joint arena. There are more officers in Air Force ground than there are in the Navy. At the time the only headquarters that was absolute one-third, one-third, one-third was CinCPac. But none of the others was. We just didn't have enough people to man these, to make

> sure that Navy views were properly represented in the operations of these new commands. So CinCCent, which was created during this time, had a very small Navy representation on the staff.[130]

There was a short timeline for the Navy to conform to the new system. The JCS chairman at the time, Crowe, was insistent and not in the mood to issue waivers to allow flag promotion consideration without a joint assignment even to his own service. Mustin recalled,

> My personal view was that we had to try to integrate the Navy into this new structure, because, like it or not, we were going to have to live with it. It was very difficult. And Bill Crowe had a scoreboard that he was keeping on it. He gave us a year to work that out. The first flag list, [for] which I had been on the selection board, was sent down and asked for a waiver for some really good nuclear guys, [and] we got it. The next time I was not on the flag board. Same thing, asked for a waiver, and Crowe said no, the waiver period's expired; those guys can't be flag officers. Everything sort of came to a boil at that time, which exacerbated the Navy's feuds with the Air Force, with the Army, and with the Chairman himself. It was very difficult.[131]

Mustin and CNO Trost eventually secured some additional waivers, but these proved to only be a temporary reprieve. The focus on joint assignments, especially as a hurdle for promotion to flag rank, caused a significant shift in where the talented officers of each service were assigned.

The Navy staff had suspected this outcome with the passage of the legislation. Capt. Tom Fedyszyn, a former OP-603 strategist with a PhD in political science and then serving in OP-00K, recalled the analysis he did on the promotion rates of O-4 (lieutenant commander) to O-6 (captain) as part of his observations on the progress toward implementation of Goldwater-Nichols at the behest of Deputy Under Secretary of the Navy Seth Cropsey. Assignment to the OPNAV staff before Goldwater-Nichols generally resulted in an 80 percent to 90 percent promotion rate, while the promotion rate for those assigned to the Joint Staff stood at 30 to 50 percent.[132] Fedyszyn knew immediately the implications of the changes for the OPNAV staff in terms of quality personnel. He drafted a memo to CNO Trost explaining the likely outcomes, including his prediction that quality officers would quickly migrate to the Joint Staff in response to the legislation. Trost replied that he was not surprised and laconically agreed that the Navy staff would simply have to adjust to a new reality.[133]

Although the entire OPNAV staff would be affected by the Goldwater-Nichols joint personnel provisions, the strategy branch would in some ways bear the brunt of the changes. OP-06 had risen to prominence during the 1980s in the course of its work with the Maritime Strategy. CNOs Hayward and Watkins as well as Secretary Lehman had valued its inputs and contributions (along with those of OP-00K) to the creation of the strategy and its communication to a wider audience. The emphasis Goldwater-Nichols demanded on joint versus service-centric activities helped bring about a significant reorganization in the OPNAV office structure that weakened the influence of OP-06 on both naval and broader strategic concerns.

During 1992–93 CNO Kelso conducted a major reorganization of the OPNAV staff structure in response to Goldwater-Nichols Act. Vice Adm. Bill Owens, a member of the first SSG, conceptualized and implemented it. OP codes became N-coded offices that mirrored the Joint Staff. The new and powerful N8 (Resources, Warfare Requirements, and Assessments) was introduced to include the warfare "baron" offices of OP-02 (Submarine Warfare), OP-03 (Surface Warfare), and OP-05 (Air Warfare), headed by deputy CNOs. Owens became the first to head the new office.[134] N8 was considerably more powerful than the old OP-06 in the new world in which Goldwater-Nichols determined that services only built, trained, and equipped forces, but did not conduct strategic planning for their use. OP-06 itself became N3/N5 (Plans, Policy, and Operations) and lost influence, as OPNAV had considerably less influence on the Joint Staff now that it worked for the JCS chairman alone and not the collective Joint Chiefs.[135]

Navy Analysts: The Other Strategists

The strategy offices of OP-06 and OP-603 had been among the incubators of future Navy leaders in the 1970s and early to mid-1980, but N8 slowly eclipsed them in this regard. Similar to OP-06, the Navy's analysis shop, OP-96, had produced its own "roll call of heroes" who had risen to high ranks after Secretary of the Navy Paul Nitze established it in 1966, with Capt. Elmo Zumwalt, the future CNO, as its first director.[136] Among the other OP-96 officers who rose to flag rank were Adm. Dennis Blair, Pacific commander and national intelligence director; Adm. Vern Clark, a future CNO; and Vice Adm. Arthur Cebrowski, future director of the Office of Force Transformation. A small number of very talented officers who moved between the strategy and analysis disciplines also achieved flag rank, including Adm. Harry Train and Rear Adm. Jim Stark.

The established academic qualifications and career paths set for analysts served as an enabling factor for their resurgence over the strategists. While not all operations analysts hailed from the Operations Analysis Department of the Naval Postgraduate School (NPS), many had solid science and technology backgrounds from civilian schools. The Navy operations research subspecialty dates from 1951 and was well institutionalized by 1966, when the Navy created OP-96.[137] It was further developed and had its own "feeder" system in the Operations Research program at NPS. The dedicated analysts at NPS, such as Capt. Wayne P. Hughes, a former OP-96 deputy director, continually refined the operations curriculum to turn out top-quality analysts, first to OP-96 and after 1992 to its successor, N81.[138]

In contrast, the Navy's strategy subspecialty suffered from a lack of formal standards and remained an informal enterprise throughout the transition after the passage of Goldwater-Nichols. The Navy developed a chair in naval strategy at NPS in 1988 to develop a more stable career path for Navy strategy experts, but the position was eliminated in a curriculum review in 2000.[139] The position's institutional authority had earlier been diminished after the Maritime Strategy ceased being an official U.S. Navy concept in 1990, and CNO Kelso's OPNAV reorganization in 1992 further reduced the influence of OP-06/OP-603's successor, N3/N5/N513.[140]

The analysts returned to power slowly, gaining in authority and influence over time. Admiral Trost's appointment as CNO in 1986 marked the beginning of the process, with Goldwater-Nichols provisions playing a significant role. In June 1986 the Department of Defense established the Joint Requirements Oversight Council (JROC) as per the act,[141] staffed with relatively low-ranking service vice chiefs of staff and chaired by the Joint Staff director. Goldwater-Nichols required that the four-star JCS vice chairman serve as its chairman. The legislation tasked the JROC with "submitting alternative budget and program recommendations to the Secretary of Defense."[142] The business of long-range forecasting and associated naval planning had lapsed following the reorganization of the systems analysis offices, OP-96 and its OP-965 branch, in 1983. OP-00K and the short-lived OP-00X (Long Range Planning) had undertaken some of the responsibility, but nothing matching those of the analysis branches. The OP-06 strategy branch had no interest in such work, as its staff was fully engaged in updates of the Maritime Strategy.[143] Extended planning was again required in support of the new JCS/JROC mission of long-range program oversight. In the early 1990s this new emphasis on program management over time, the requirements those programs met, and the budgets that supported the programs called for an increased priority in analysis compared to political-military strategy.

The establishment of N81 (Assessments) within N8 exemplified this change, born of the 1992 OPNAV reorganization conducted by CNO Adm. Frank Kelso. The newly formed N8, led by a deputy chief of Naval Operations (three-star admiral), combined the previous functions of the Navy's warfare experts—in undersea, surface, and air warfare—and added a Marine Corps officer–led Expeditionary warfare section. All of these formerly three-star positions, now two stars, were under N8, which was given control of OPNAV-wide program assessment.[144] The reorganization abolished OP-095/OP-07 (Naval Warfare), which had been conceptualized by CNO Hayward as a counterweight to the program assessment divisions and to align programs with naval strategy. The business of assessment required analysts with programmatic experience, rather than political-military strategy experts, to manage the fleet's force structure and planning. The large number of OPNAV personnel assigned to N8 gave it inherent power over smaller, downsized offices, like N3/N5, OP-06's successor. Admiral Owens, the first head of N8, explained the significance of this change: "The reorganization greatly bolstered the institutional power of the Deputy Chief of Staff for Resources, Requirements, and Assessments [N8]. The office that emerged from the staff reorganization had the staff authority to establish requirements for future naval forces, allocate money among those requirements and judge the implications and effectiveness of the allocations."[145]

Owens was also in charge of the analysis-driven process that directly supported N8's powers. The JMA was, in Owens' words, "a new program assessment structure [that] was essentially a matrix that made program advocates justify their programs in terms of their contribution to the new [joint] mission areas."[146] The JMA also served to reduce the power of the three-star flag officer leaders of the surface, undersea, and air warfare disciplines. By reducing the bureaucratic status of the positions, Owens believed that the Navy could focus instead on service-wide innovation and combat effectiveness.[147] Within N8, N81 (Assessments) became the key interlocutor and a worthy successor to OP-96 and OP-965, which once held the bulk of the Navy's uniformed and civilian analysts. The JMAs it serviced and supported were the lineal descendants of McNamara's functional mission organization concepts for the Navy. Civilian analyst Bruce Powers, who joined N81 in 1994, described its mission as follows:

> In N81, we were focused on the first "P" in PPBS [Planning, Programming, and Budgeting System]. That was like the "architect" phase of building a home. The perspective was often that of the whole Navy, and it was always cost-constrained. So proposals for inclusion of additional ships or aircraft types had to be accompanied by trade-offs, or off-sets, of equal cost. Skilled teams of analysts, military and civilian, worked on these trade-off issues. Most of the officers had a master's degree in OR [operations research] from the Naval Postgraduate School in Monterey [where I later taught OR].[148]

Powers further described some of the connections between the 1980s-era OP-96 and N81:

> It [OP-96] was basically the analytical arm of OpNav. It evolved from its earlier days when it did cost effectiveness and other kinds of analyses. It didn't do very well during the Lehman era as Sec Nav, and he cut it back and reduced its size, and reduced its mission. But after Lehman left the Sec Nav job, it was restored to some of its earlier health. And I moved to N81 because of the CNO at the time. Boorda was his name. He said he wanted to re-vitalize N81 and turn it back into what Op 96 had been earlier.[149]

Adm. Mike Boorda's tenure as CNO began two years after the reforms of CNO Kelso created N81. The resurgence of N81 came at the expense of the flag officer discussion process instituted by Admiral Owens.[150]

The SSG also changed in form and content, but perhaps less so than the OPNAV offices. The group went from being a Cold War naval strategy and operations think tank to becoming a broader DIME—diplomatic, information, military, economic—effort.[151] It acquired its first members from outside the Navy and Marine Corps in 1993, and its focus after 1994 became identifying future global trends and their implications for the Navy. The end of the Cold War and the collapse of the Soviet Union precipitated much of this change. The activities of the empowered office of the JCS chairman also played a role, as the chairman, rather than Navy flag officers, assumed responsibility for force-structure recommendations.

Declining Fortunes: Strategy, Budgets, and Cohorts

Admiral Kelso, who replaced Admiral Trost as CNO in June 1990, immediately confronted a host of direct and indirect challenges to the maintenance of a robust naval force structure. The Navy's budget had grown from $57.4 billion in 1981 to $100.3 billion in 1988, but fell back below $100 billion in 1989 and 1990.[152] The service's budget would rise significantly in 1991 to $103.5 billion, primarily due to Gulf War requirements, but then steadily decrease, falling to $79.5 billion in 1997.[153] Kelso had acknowledged in his Senate confirmation hearing that the Maritime Strategy was "on the shelf" and that the six-hundred-ship navy concept should be replaced by a more flexible objective.[154] The end of the Maritime Strategy and change in CNO leadership created a power struggle in OPNAV, as competing offices sought to present new strategic visions to the new CNO. In 1991 this competition produced "The Way Ahead,"[155] which effectively served as Kelso's planning strategy document for the 1990s.[156]

Budget estimates, however, continued to stymie Kelso's efforts to functionally support his vision. He had hoped that the 1991 budget season would kick off with a positive and influential Total Force Assessment briefing to accompany the Navy's budget proposals, but instead he received a sobering and dismal appraisal of the force the Navy might field in the post–Cold War era. Capt. Richard "Dick" Diamond, chief of OP-603 and who delivered the brief, recalled that Kelso responded with a "barrage of scatological invectives and expletives." One particular slide, "The Coming USN Budget Train Wreck," predicted that the Navy "was about to face a major budget crisis that made a new strategic rationale mandatory." This caused the CNO to "go into overdrive" in his negative response.[157] The slide flipper for the brief, Cdr. Paul Giarra, later wrote, "The CNO left the room without providing any guidance to the assembled three-star officers present for the brief," causing great uncertainty for a time.[158]

If the Navy's challenges had been limited to dramatically shrinking budgets, Kelso might have had greater influence on controlling its response to the empowered JCS chairman, but troubling service-specific issues also vied for his attention. He was distracted in particular by ongoing negative publicity from several high-profile accidents and incidents, notably the explosion of the USS *Iowa*'s B-turret in April 1989 during a training exercise almost a year before Kelso became CNO, the Tailhook sexual assault and harassment scandal in 1991, and the 1994 crash and death of F-14 pilot Lt. Kara Hultgreen, one of the first female aviators to fly combat aircraft.[159] In such an environment, Kelso could not concentrate on strategy as well as he would have liked.[160]

Goldwater-Nichols affected not only the Navy offices that created strategy, but also the careers of individual naval officers engaged in the discipline. The new emphasis on joint instead of service offices that the legislation demanded significantly affected officers in the ranks of O-4 (lieutenant commander) to O-6 (captain) who normally would have been recruited to serve in OP-06, which became N3/N5, and other purely service staff positions. Those officers were now drawn to joint positions to meet requirements demanding joint service as a prerequisite to consideration for flag rank. The service solution was to "shorten some assignments and eliminate others" so that joint assignments could be fit into the same nominal twenty-year career plan demanded by the 1980 Defense Officer Personnel Management Act.[161]

Overall manpower reductions at the end of the Cold War further complicated joint assignments. The number of Navy joint billets for officers in the O-4 to O-6 ranks increased by 10 percent from 1989 to 1999 in spite of a nearly 15 percent overall postwar decline in the number of officers in those ranks.[162] A 2001 study concluded that the "deepening" of joint assignment opportunities affected the overall amount of service-based expertise that the average naval officer acquired over the course of his or her career.[163] The experience of the strategy cadre of OP-06 would not initially appear to support this assumption.

The individuals who spearheaded the drive to create the Maritime Strategy in the 1980s found continued employment in the strategy business during the 1990s. As noted at the outset, Capt. Peter Swartz, after some initial misgivings about two consecutive joint assignments, became one of Chairman Powell's special assistants. Diamond took charge of OP-603 in February 1990 and exerted significant influence on the development and coordination of "... From the Sea," the follow-on strategic concept to the Maritime Strategy.[164] Cdr. Joe Sestak contributed what Diamond called the "bumper sticker" for the new strategy: "The Navy/Marine Corps Team Is the Enabling Force for Follow-on Joint Operations."[165] Diamond, along with Capt. Jim Stark and other OP-60, OP-00K, and SSG alumni founded a regular naval strategy discussion group, the Ancient Mariners, that began meeting in 1989.[166] Other groups, such as David Rosenberg's Navy Study Group, which met during 1992 and 1993, would carry on the informal discussion of naval strategy through 2003.[167] A reborn version of this association now called the Strategy Discussion Group began meeting at the end of the 2000s and continues at the time of this writing.

Yet while these officers continued their strategic vocations in Navy and later joint offices involved in producing strategic work, their shoes were not being filled by a new generation of Navy-created and nurtured strategy experts. On the other hand, the analysis arm of the Navy centered on N8 prospered throughout the same thirty-year period thanks to its established career path created by people like Wayne Hughes, the retired captain and NPS professor, and the persistent need for analytical products to support a programmatic and budget versus a strategy-driven Navy. Capt. Robby Harris, a former member of the SSG and OP-00K, called the OPNAV staff in general a "shadow of what it was twenty years ago in both quantity and background" due to the Goldwater-Nichols' joint-officer requirements,[168] which hampered the ability of the Navy to send officers to multiple tours in OPNAV strategy offices. Capt. William Spencer Johnson, the OP-06 veteran, also lamented the decline of multiple assignments, remarking that it prevented officers from acquiring further strategic competence and sustaining corporate memory in naval strategic planning.[169] There was barely time for one assignment in order to meet the joint requirements necessary for eligibility for flag rank.

The lack of repeat experience in OPNAV weakened the Navy's ability to create strategy on its own. According to former secretary Lehman, the joint requirements created excessively large staffs that drew too many officers from experience-generating operational billets.[170] Together, these changes meant a Navy with fewer strategic planners and possibly less operational experience. In addition, being forced to fill a much larger joint staff pool left the Navy bereft of the strategic veterans it had.

It was inevitable that the U.S. armed forces would face significant cuts in the wake of the Cold War and that a new strategy would have to be conceived in response to this sea change in international affairs. Goldwater-Nichols significantly complicated both processes for the Navy. The Navy had been the most significant source of organized opposition to the legislation, and its senior officers at the end of the 1980s and into the early 1990s remained antagonistic to its tenets as the service struggled to adjust to a new international situation and a Department of Defense reorganization. The introduction of an empowered JCS chairman—the decisive voice in determining naval force structure—along with new concepts in combatant commander areas of responsibility and required personnel changes made the process of creating new strategies for the naval service, especially those involving a global responsibility, more challenging in the years after 1992.

Further, Goldwater-Nichols altered the career path of naval officers by mandating joint assignments as a precursor to flag rank. This caused a migration of talented, career-minded officers out of such service offices as OP-60, where they had been carefully trained, mentored, and subsequently assigned important Navy follow-on assignments, and into joint billets in which the Navy could no longer make direct use of their talents. These officers continued to contribute to the process of strategy creation in the 1990s, but there was no longer a strong service staff organization to mentor and aid them in their development. These changes fundamentally altered the process by which the Navy developed strategy and the people involved in that creative process and would play a significant role in the development of the Maritime Strategy's replacement.

CHAPTER 4

THE GULF WAR, REVOLUTION IN MILITARY AFFAIRS, AND STRATEGIC CHANGE

A 1994 dissertation from the Naval Postgraduate School (NPS) epitomizes the Navy's embrace of revolutionary technology through the middle and end of the Cold War and the changing geopolitical and military realities of the 1990s. Written by Lt. John Schulte, a student at the Naval Postgraduate School, "An Analysis of the Historical Effectiveness of Anti-Ship Cruise Missiles in Littoral Warfare" primarily focuses on the development of mathematical equations to predict the effectiveness of anti-ship cruise missiles against U.S. Navy ships, but its historical timeline succinctly illustrates the changes that overtook the Navy's strategy for executing a global maritime war against the Soviet Union. The Schulte Report, as the dissertation became known, details the debut of the modern cruise missile in October 1967, when the Egyptian navy sank the Israeli destroyer *Eilat* in the eastern Mediterranean. The report further details the cruise missile's rise in its capability in the 1980s, from the Falklands War (1982) to the Iran-Iraq War (1980–88), the latter of which included attacks on neutral merchant shipping by both sides and an Iraqi assault on the U.S. guided missile frigate *Stark* in 1987. Schulte's timeline terminates, however, with the 1991 Gulf War, and not with a bang, but with a whimper for the Navy.

Amid the largest U.S. combat mission since the Vietnam War and the single largest deployment of naval vessels to enemy waters since the Korean War, there was no significant clash of arms at sea in the U.S.-led war to drive Iraqi forces from Kuwait. On 25 February 1991, the British destroyer HMS *Gloucester* destroyed one of two Chinese-made Silkworm cruise missiles fired at the U.S. battleship *Missouri,* then engaged in surface gunfire support against Iraqi military targets ashore. An earlier encounter, on 29/30 January, between missile-armed Royal Navy helicopters and Iraqi missile combatants had been a one-sided slaughter, leaving four Iraqi boats underwater without loss of Allied aircraft. Iraq never mounted a determined attack on offshore naval units. Allied naval forces launched land-attack cruise missiles against Iraqi targets and carrier-based aircraft flew sorties in support of the opening takedown of the Iraqi air defense system and later in the short ground war. Warships like *Missouri* shelled targets ashore, but other than the communication networks to coordinate ships' movement and sustain their presence, few if any elements of the Navy's Maritime Strategy were utilized. There was no vast clash of naval arms as envisioned by the U.S. Navy's Cold War strategy adopted in the 1980s.

The Schulte Report has been called one of the most important tactical works of the early post–Cold War era in its emphasis on the need to focus on littoral missile combat. In terms of the Gulf War, it chronicles that the U.S. Navy was largely unable to validate the Maritime Strategy, developed with great effort beginning in 1970. The "action" during the Gulf War was largely in the air and on the ground, with the Navy playing a secondary or tertiary role at best. This turn of events, changes wrought by revolutionary weapons like the cruise missile, and the advent of joint operations largely directed ashore all played a major role in changing Navy strategy in the 1990s.

In 1990 when Iraqi forces crossed the border into Kuwait, the Navy had been working to implement the provisions of the Goldwater-Nichols Act of 1986 and to adjust its strategy and force structure as a result of the end of the Cold War. The Iraqi invasion on 2 August and the subsequent war in early 1991 further complicated the Navy's transition to a new strategy, already made difficult by the reorganization of the military as required by Goldwater-Nichols.[1] The Navy played its part in the Gulf conflict under strategic and operational conditions that did not match those expected when the service planned for war against the Soviet Union. The new joint command and control structures called for by Goldwater-Nichols and introduced in the late 1980s were still unfamiliar and disconcerting to the Navy at the outset of the war.

In addition to the Navy undergoing a difficult transition from its institutional expectations for war based on its Cold War strategy, the reality of combat in the Persian Gulf offered little room for the service to showcase its full set of capabilities in the air and land conflict led by the Army's Gen. Norman Schwarzkopf. The so-called revolution in military affairs (RMA)—under way since the mid- to late-1970s according to experts such as Andrew Marshall, who had led the Office of Net Assessment, and the nuclear strategist Albert Wohlstetter—also complicated the Navy's participation in the conflict.[2] What the Army and Air Force experienced as revolutionary in technological and organizational terms, the Navy observed as evolutionary over time, especially in terms of deep strike and in the command and control of forces. As with the implementation of Goldwater-Nichols provisions, operations analysis played a significant role in advancing RMA, with little room for contributions from the Navy's political-military strategists.

In the Gulf War, the Army and Air Force ultimately validated many of the operational concepts that they had developed for Cold War combat. Some analysts gave the Navy great credit for a logistics victory, but in the end, the service fought a very different war than it had planned for over the previous decade.[3] Many leaders of the Gulf War effort, military and civilian, lauded Goldwater-Nichols provisions as crucial to victory. The Navy leadership had vigorously opposed the legislation, and its trouble adjusting to the changes the law produced as executed in the Gulf War served to put the naval service further on the defensive. In contrast and often at the Navy's expense, the Marine Corps embraced the new environment and did not suffer the same disconnect from broader joint efforts. The effects of the Gulf War and RMA often associated with that conflict clouded the environment in which the Navy sought to create a successor to the 1980s Maritime Strategy.

REVOLUTIONS IN MILITARY AFFAIRS

RMA as a concept was not new when the theory became a major topic in the 1970s. Historians had labeled the introduction of gunpowder and associated modern military organization efforts in the sixteenth and seventeenth centuries as one of the first revolutions. In 1955 the British military historian Michael Roberts first drew attention to a late Renaissance European military revolution.[4] In a lecture at Queen's University of Belfast, Roberts stressed that technology was but one part of the European military revolution, with advances in tactics and strategy enabling larger and more complex military operations with more wide-ranging effects.[5] The technological changes were not confined to gunpowder, but also included the advances in military training needed to employ gunpowder weapons effectively.[6] Roberts' views usefully analyzed changes in ground warfare, but perhaps overlooked how some of the same changes influenced naval warfare and further propelled Western Europe toward overall military superiority vis-à-vis other great powers of the seventeenth century. The military historian Geoffrey Parker observed that Europeans' naval technology along with the strategies and tactics for its employment allowed the West to "turn maritime superiority into global hegemony."[7] Improved sailing warships armed with gunpowder weapons would eventually defeat the naval forces of the Chinese, Ottoman, and Indian Empires. Those European states that did not adapt fast enough to changing naval technology, such as Spain, also faced defeat at the hands of those that did.

Roberts and Parker wrote from the mid-1950s through the mid-1990s. During this period, Soviet military leaders were writing about a more often quoted military revolution—in the development of nuclear weapons—and prophesying the beginning of another—in military technology. The American strategic theorist Bernard Brodie, who called the atomic bomb the absolute weapon, wrote, "Even the most 'revolutionary' developments of the past seem by contrast with the atomic bomb to have been minor steps in a many-sided evolutionary process."[8] Soviet military strategists considered the invention of atomic weapons the key enabler of a "military technical revolution," but as in the case of earlier European RMA, they did not limit their description to ordnance alone. The Soviet admiral Sergey Gorshkov defined the military technical revolution as early as 1976 not only in terms of atomic weapons, but also including "outstanding discoveries in the field of radio electronics and rocket construction."[9] Marshal Nikolai Ogarkov, chief of the Soviet General Staff, lobbied his country's military leadership from 1971 onward to reform its large, unwieldy military force. In 1983 he asserted in the official Soviet defense journal *Krasnaya zvezda* [Red Star] that "bold experiments and solutions are necessary, even if this means discarding obsolete traditions, views and propositions."[10] Ogarkov further stated in a 1983 *Izvestiya* article, "Operational and tactical means of combat are being improved and new ones created on the basis of the latest achievements of electronics and other technical sciences."[11] These developments, Ogarkov further asserted, have led to "highly effective new means of conventional combat" to be developed and introduced, driven by better automated systems of command and control.[12] Soviet defense minister Marshal Dmitry Ustinov was more specific in a 1983 *Pravda* article, in which he identified "reconnaissance-strike complexes with great precision and range" as key emerging U.S. military capabilities.[13] Marshal Viktor Kulikov, Soviet commander of the Warsaw Pact, further elaborated Soviet concerns in 1984 when he described the United States and NATO as "systematically equipping its troops with 'a new generation of conventional weapons, and above all long-range precision weapons, modern means of air defense and radio-electronic combat, and projected command-and-control and communications systems.'"[14] Ogarkov went so far as to suggest in 1983 that the West had already won the Cold War. The journalist Leslie Gelb reported Ogarkov stating the following in a conversation:

> Numbers of troops and weapons mean little, he said. We cannot equal the quality of U.S. arms for a generation or two. Modern military power is based upon technology, and technology is based upon computers.
>
> In the U.S., he continued, small children—even before they begin school—play with computers. Computers are everywhere in America. Here, we don't even have computers in every office of the Defense Ministry. And for reasons you know well, we cannot make computers widely available in our society.
>
> . . . We will never be able to catch up with you in modern arms until we have an economic revolution. And the question is whether we can have an economic revolution without a political revolution.[15]

Nuclear weapons might have been the absolute weapon as Brodie asserted, but Soviet and soon American leaders would recognize that such weapons alone were not enough to guarantee victory in the Cold War.

Offset Strategies and Maneuver Warfare

U.S. leaders did not share Ogarkov's view of the Cold War balance of power in the mid-1970s through much of the 1980s. Andrew Marshall, head of the Office of Net Assessment from 1974 to 2015, reported that his office began following Soviet reporting on U.S. technological advancements in the mid- to late 1970s.[16] Clearly, the Soviet military leadership understood that the U.S. efforts were geared toward developing an offset strategy, whereby the Americans' superior technology could counter the Soviets' numerically larger forces. Harold Brown, secretary of defense under the Carter administration, described this effort in a January 1981 report:

> Technology can be a force multiplier, a resource that can be used to help offset numerical advantages of an adversary. Superior technology is one very effective way to balance military capabilities other than by matching an adversary tank-for-tank or soldier-for-soldier. Other tools that *combine with technology* to this end include doctrine, tactics, and training. Even with the most sophisticated weapon systems, however, we cannot allow the numerical disparities between us and the Soviets to widen further. Thus, we continue to plan our forces on the basis of a "high-low" mix of high performance, high technology systems with less complicated, less expensive systems.[17]

Brown suggested a sense of urgency in the U.S. embrace of advanced technological capabilities. A child prodigy in mathematics and the sciences, Brown had graduated with a bachelor's in physics from Columbia University at eighteen and received a PhD from that same institution in the same subject at twenty-one.[18] He was the first scientist to serve as secretary of defense.[19] From 1961 to 1965 Brown worked as research director of Defense Research and Engineering, under Secretary of Defense Robert McNamara, and from 1965 to 1969 as secretary of the Air Force. He returned to the Pentagon in 1977, after serving seven years as president of the California Institute of Technology. Brown's science and technology background well prepared him to manage the U.S. effort to weaponize advanced technology. In the January 1981 report, he cited significant numerical growth in individual Soviet ground and air units in the 1960s and 1970s, specifically in tanks and other armored vehicles, artillery, and tactical aircraft.[20] According to Brown, the U.S. technological efforts to offset Soviet numerical advantages should first be directed at these Soviet formations.

Brown and his deputy, William Perry, focused their efforts on the development of stealth aircraft, Assault Breaker (a program to defeat a Soviet ground force invasion of Western Europe), and air- and ground-launched cruise missiles as a nuclear-armed counterparts to the Soviet SS-20 medium-range ballistic missiles.[21] Perry later described this effort as one through which "1970s U.S. defense officials saw the opportunity to exploit the new developments in microelectronics and computers to great advantages in military applications."[22] He also contended that the offset strategy "sought to use technology as an equalizer or 'force multiplier' and was pursued by five successive presidential administrations into the 1980s."[23] The potential of precision-guided munitions as an equalizer on the battlefield was another area that interested Perry. In testimony before the Senate Armed Services Committee in 1978, Perry stated, "Precision guided weapons, I believe, have the potential for revolutionizing warfare. More importantly, if we effectively exploit the lead we have in this field, we can greatly enhance our ability to deter war without having to compete, tank for tank, missile for missile with the Soviet Union."[24]

The Defense Advanced Research Projects Agency launched the F-117 stealth aircraft as an experimental effort in 1977; it achieved initial operating capability in 1981.[25] The combination of Assault Breaker, communications technology advances, and stealth aircraft served in the 1980s as the basis of the Reagan administration's buildup of Army and Air Force precision-guided munitions systems and the aircraft and group vehicles to deliver them.[26] Cooperation between the Army and the Air Force aided the development process, with Gen. Donn Starry, from the Army's Training and Doctrine Command (TRADOC), and Gen. William Creech, from the Air Force Tactical Air Command, actively collaborating on Assault Breaker.[27]

The technological advancements under Brown and Perry required new operational theories of war to make the best use of them on the Central European front at the Fulda Gap. Col. John Boyd, an Air Force fighter pilot, laid the foundations for these in 1976 in "Patterns of Conflict." Boyd, an unorthodox combat leader and autodidact in military history and operations research, was especially interested in the relationship between observers and what they think they have observed. Boyd believed many observations to be biased by preconditioned thinking. He sought to "destroy" such thinking and challenged those who listened to him to "construct order and meaning out of this mess."[28]

Boyd applied his ideas on differing observer views to the science of air combat maneuvering, theorizing from historical ground-combat evidence and tactical fighter aircraft combat theory that maneuverability rather than superior force was the key to victory. Boyd wrote, "A fighter that can pick and choose engagement opportunities, yet has fast transient capabilities that can be used to either force an overshoot by an attacker or stay inside a hard-turning defender" is the key component in "creating a faster tempo or [battle] rhythm than the adversaries."[29] This faster battle rhythm would, in Boyd's thinking, allow U.S. commanders to penetrate an adversary's "OODA loop"—his shorthand for the process by which a military organization makes operational and tactical decisions—that is, observe, orient, decide, act.[30] The desired outcome was one in which the tempo of U.S. decision-making and action would be much faster than that of its opponent. The adversary would suffer "confusion and disorder" and be unable to "generate mental pictures of images that agree with the [threat]" or the "faster transient rhythms of patterns they are competing against."[31]

Boyd's message spread informally through a group of influential defense analysts who knew him and respected his ideas. They included William Lind, an aide to Sen. Gary Hart (D-Colo.) and Thomas Christie, a Department of Defense program analyst. Hart as well as Rep. Newt Gingrich (R-Ga.) were also impressed.[32] Upon hearing Boyd's presentation, Rep. Dick Cheney (R-Wyo.) said, "I was intrigued by the concepts he was working on" and thought him to be a "creative and innovative thinker with respect to the military."[33] While largely unpopular among senior defense officials, Boyd's ideas attracted support from reformers seeking to improve the defense establishment's financial stability and operational capability. His theories found acceptance in the Marine Corps in particular. Col. Mike Wyly, a Marine who knew Boyd and followed his work, introduced him to the Marine Corps commandant,

Gen. Al Gray, who like Boyd believed in the doctrine of maneuver warfare.[34] Boyd's theories later found their way, via Wyly, into *FMFM 1: Warfighting*, the Marine's maneuver warfare doctrine authored under Gray's leadership in 1989.[35] The Army, however, would be the first service to produce a new warfighting doctrine, AirLand Battle, embracing maneuver warfare, which would be the key to success in the Gulf War and in post–Cold War struggles with the other services over strategy.

AirLand Battle

The U.S. Army combined Perry's offset technologies and Boyd's OODA loop theories with support from tactical Air Force elements in developing the operational doctrine of AirLand Battle, adopted in 1982. In January 1984 the Air Force presented its own overarching strategy in the *Basic Aerospace Doctrine of the United States Air Force*, AFM 1–1, but its focus on joint operations was limited.[36] According to historian Harold Winton, the document "represented a more coherent explication of airpower principles than its predecessor and recognized some of the potential for the cooperation of air and ground forces at the operational level," but it "stopped short of a fully developed typology of how this synergism could best be achieved."[37]

There were some limited attempts at Navy–Air Force operational-level memorandums of agreement. Among the successful efforts were There agreements on joint refueling of aircraft and equipping B-52 bombers to lay mines and in 1972 on a revolutionary idea from CNO Adm. Elmo Zumwalt to qualify Air Force squadrons in aircraft carrier operations, which was not popular with either service.[38] In another attempt at operational cooperation in Vietnam, the Navy and Air Force held deconflicted (but not joint) air operations, dubbed "route packages," an approach that angered Air Force officers and would return to haunt joint cooperation between the services at the start of the Gulf War in 1990.[39] The Navy made use of the Air Force's Slow Walker Defense Support Program satellites in the 1980s to track closing Soviet aircraft on carriers and both services cooperated on space issues.[40] The Navy steadfastly refused, however, to surrender control of its aircraft to joint command in the 1970s and 1980s, perhaps remembering what had happened in terms of service competition in the 1950s, when the Air Force sought to eliminate the large aircraft carrier in favor of the B-36 bomber. It would be left largely to the Army to integrate all the services' doctrine at the theater operational level of conflict in the 1980s.

AirLand Battle allowed both the Army and the Air Force to exploit Perry and Boyd's contributions, rescued the Army from its post–Vietnam War doldrums, and gave the Air Force a significant role in supporting ground force efforts. The Vietnam War had forced the diversion of significant defense budget resources to operational efforts at the expense of force modernization.[41] The Army compensated with defensive concepts on the Central European front in lieu of modernization, but still suffered from the effects of the long Vietnam conflict, specifically in officer doctrine training. Some of its generals felt the Army so deficient in training and doctrine that they quipped that the Army's principal posture in Europe should be to prepare for its own evacuation in the event of war.[42] Two successive leaders of TRADOC were ultimately able to stem this tide of institutional pessimism.

TRADOC had been created to "centralize the process of reform in training and doctrine" necessary to meet the Soviet and Warsaw Pact force threat in Central Europe.[43] Much of TRADOC's effort involved the development of operational art, described by Naval War College professor Milan Vego as "a level of command intermediate between the tactical and the strategic, one associated with ground command at the level of field army or corps and with the conduct of 'campaigns' that unfold as a series of interconnected battles over time."[44]

German and Soviet World War II operational art were the starting points in developing new U.S. doctrine, as were the lessons learned from the 1973 Arab-Israeli War.[45] The Israeli and Arab armies saw tank losses approach 50 percent of the total vehicles engaged, a figure suggesting the extent to which modern firepower could inflict heavy losses.[46] TRADOC's first commander, Gen. William DePuy, argued that the best way to inflict such losses was to plan operationally and tactically for the worst-case threat of Soviet invasion across the West German border.[47] DePuy's solution arrived in 1976 in the form of a new combat manual *FM 100-5: Operations*.[48] While this field manual continued to promote a defensive Army posture, it prescribed fast-paced action at potential or actual Soviet breakthrough sites on the Central European front. It also recommended the placement of as much firepower as possible in forward areas, but while continuing to emphasize "traditional concepts of attrition and terrain-oriented warfare."[49] DePuy desired "an elastic defense that could cope with Soviet strength and lack of maneuver room in Germany." Wrote military historian Ingo Trauschweizer, "This was to be achieved through the 'superior concentration of combat power in the attack and in the defense through good intelligence, quick decisions and high mobility . . . the only solution for an outnumbered force.'"[50]

DePuy's successor, General Donn Starry, took DePuy's reforms in a very different, offensive direction. Gen. Edward Meyer, Army chief of staff, provided some of the push for this in his criticisms of DePuy's efforts. Meyer wanted a doctrine applicable worldwide, as opposed to DePuy's, which was specific to Europe. Meyer also believed that DePuy's concept was too defensive and not well understood in the Army.[51] Meyer was concerned that DePuy's approach represented a losing effort. "We couldn't fight an attrition war if we wanted to today," he remarked. "We'd be the first attrited."[52]

Starry, although he had been involved in the design of DePuy's Active Defense doctrine, presented in the 1976 field manual, came to view it as a "false start" in the process of rebuilding the Army post-Vietnam and amid the Cold War.[53] His experiences as commander of the 5th Corps in Germany in the mid-1970s also motivated him to seek means of attacking Soviet follow-on forces waiting to be fed into battle.[54] Active Defense had no capability or design to deal with these second-echelon Soviet units. Starry's new concept involved seizing the initiative by being able to "see deep and attack deep at the same time."[55] These two events could happen at the same time—but probably not, in Starry's opinion—but they had to be synchronized at the corps level of command.[56] In this system of "battlefield dynamics," each level of the chain of command from the corps (commanded by a general) to the companies (commanded by Army captains) would maximize U.S. effectiveness and minimize that of the opponent.[57]

To accomplish both seeing and attacking deep into an opponent's reserve forces, Starry placed greater emphasis on maneuverability and coordinated firepower at both the leading edge of a Soviet advance and at the second echelon of Soviet forces waiting to be fed into the battle. Starry also added electronic warfare, electronic countermeasures, intelligence collection, enemy detection, and deception as major elements of his doctrine design.[58] The corps commander was given control of deep surveillance systems, like the Joint Surveillance Attack Radar System, and the physical means of damaging Soviet forces, including the use of Multiple Launch Rocket Systems and the Army Tactical Missile System.[59] Intelligence from the late 1970s through the early 1980s and General Ogarkov's writings indicated that Soviet forces were tactically rigid, had predictable operational deployment patterns (echelonments), and were technologically inferior to NATO troops.[60]

Starry wanted his effort to be joint inasmuch as the U.S. defense system supported this concept before Goldwater-Nichols. He solicited support from both the Air Force and the Navy, but later decided to limit the concept to the Army and Air Force.[61] Starry actively sought advice and content on AirLand Battle from Gen. Bill Creech, tactical air commander of the Air Force. Starry and Creech made use of the Air-Land Forces Agency (ALFA), a joint Army–Air Force coordination body established in 1975 by Gen. Creighton Abrams, Army chief of staff, and Gen. George Brown, the Air Force chief of staff. ALFA was conceived to address the lessons learned from the Vietnam War about service cooperation and as an "independent organization that could cut through bureaucratic 'red tape' to rapidly meet the immediate needs of the warfighter."[62]

The Air Force was already prepared to address the new challenge of supporting the Army on the Central European front. The end of the Vietnam War had led the Air Force, like the Army and Navy, to reassess its role in the broader Cold War against the Soviet Union. The Tactical Air Force (TAF), dedicated to direct support to ground forces, enjoyed a renaissance after the Vietnam conflict. Action in combat played a role in promotion to the general officer ranks in the Air Force, and TAF members had seen a good deal of it in the Korean and Vietnam Wars.[63] More TAF members were also promoted to the general officer ranks in the early 1970s to meet Secretary of Defense Melvin Laird's desire to put younger officers with combat experience into more leadership positions.[64] TAF members learned a great deal from conflicts like the 1973 Arab-Israeli War, in which the "ferocity and nature of the tactical air war . . . seemed more relevant . . . than did Vietnam."[65] They were ready to play significant roles with the Army in planning for combat with Soviet and Warsaw Pact forces on the Central European front.

Cooperation between the Army and the Air Force in creating AirLand Battle stemmed from ALFA. It was not a firm concept at its outset, as Starry did not want it to become what he called "Pentacrete," his term for a Pentagon-approved design that would take massive coordination to change to even the slightest degree.[66] Instead, he wanted a fungible document adaptable to revision in short order. Assisted by his TRADOC deputy, Maj. Gen. Don Morelli, Starry traveled widely in the United States and overseas to deliver his AirLand Battle briefing to U.S. Army and allied armed forces leaderships. AirLand Battle, Starry asserted, was "nothing but a stack of slides" that frequently changed based on input from those to whom it was presented at briefings.[67] In March 1981 it was summarized as a *Military Review* article, "The Extended Battlefield," under Starry's signature. Starry credited Morelli with the catchy term "AirLand Battle."[68] After nearly seven years. years of development, the concept was formally issued as doctrine in the Army's field manual, *FM 100-5*, in 1982 and slightly revised in 1986.[69]

The doctrine, with an emphasis on the operational level of warfare, designated the Army corps the principal action unit. This made sense as the corps was the smallest unit with the requisite organic intelligence, command and control capability, and assigned fire support units to direct the kind of rapid, high-intensity combat the Army assumed would be fought on the Central European front.[70] The corps level of command also supported the airpower coordination vital for attacking Soviet reserve forces waiting to enter battle. Corps-level commands also included control over the nuclear weapons that could come into play if the ground war turned for the worse.

FM 100-5 identified seven key features of AirLand Battle: indirect approaches; speed and violence; flexibility and reliance on the initiative of junior officers; rapid decision-making; clearly defined objectives and operational concepts; a clearly designated effort; and deep strike.[71] These points reflect the influence of Brown and Perry's technical revolution and the operational concepts of Boyd. The concept of deep strike was especially dependent on the products of the military technical revolution of the 1970s. Starry and Creech considered advancing this revolutionary part of the new doctrine as one of their top priorities.[72]

Follow-on efforts included educational support to teach U.S. Army leaders about campaign planning and greater service coordination. The U.S. Army

School of Advanced Military Studies (SAMS) was created in 1981 to advance this effort.[73] More interservice cooperation by Gen. John Wickham, the Army chief of staff, and Gen. Charles Gabriel, the Air Force chief of staff, produced a joint Suppression of Enemy Air Defense agreement governing their services.[74] The agreement supported the deep strike mission by allowing the Army to prioritize the target list while permitting the Air Force to use some Army weapons (missiles) to eliminate selected Soviet targets.[75]

The Army's Gen. Bernard Rogers provided a NATO component to AirLand Battle while serving as the supreme allied commander. He based his concept, Follow-on Forces Attack (FOFA), on his understanding of the precision-guided munition advances from the 1970s Assault Breaker, Air Force concepts for deep interdiction of Soviet airborne assets, and the emerging AirLand Battle doctrine.[76] FOFA was similar to AirLand Battle in that in postulated deep strike attacks on Soviet second- and third-echelon troops. NATO adopted FOFA in November 1984, making it the basis for the alliance's ground and air force operational efforts to repel a Soviet ground invasion of Central and Western Europe.[77]

Army Revolution versus Navy Evolution: Theory and Hardware

While the Army engaged in developing AirLand Battle, the U.S. Navy was just beginning to identify and assemble the components of what became the Maritime Strategy. Both these post-Vietnam responses to mounting Soviet superiority in platform numbers and capability account for military technical advances. They represent two very different approaches toward strategy, operational art, and tactical effort at odds with each other in the 1980s. Interestingly, like AirLand Battle, the Maritime Strategy also began life as a traveling slide stack edited after each presentation.[78] In contrast, however, the Maritime Strategy died with its Soviet opponent, but successive versions of AirLand Battle, codified as an official doctrinal document in *FM 100-5*, survived and remained the Army's blueprint for war into the 1990s in part due to its perceived success in Operation Desert Storm. Of note, General Starry attributed much of Desert Storm's success to regular, realistic Army training, the right equipment, and the right group of military and civilian leaders.[79] By contrast, the Maritime Strategy never had a document number and thus could be ignored or discounted by service leaders rather than survive until the longer, official process of document cancellation.

The political scientist Samuel Huntington and Rear Adm. J. C. Wylie provide some of the best descriptions of the fundamental differences between the Army- and Navy-based strategies. Huntington, exploring the institutional origins of the services' differing views on strategy, argued that the Army was an inherently passive, machine-like organization that waited on civilian leaders to provide it tasking. It was in Huntington's words "the country's general servant, well-disciplined, obedient, performing civil functions."[80] Not all agreed with this passive assessment of the Army's role. In *On Strategy: The Vietnam War in Context*, Col. Harry G. Summers Jr. was quite critical of the passive approach to strategy and national tasking.[81] Summers asserted that without the active commitment of the American people, prolonged commitment to war was impossible.[82]

The Navy, Huntington stated, was a much more independent organization than the Army. It had no civil function—unlike the Army in its active defense of U.S. soil—and believed itself to be the defender of the nation's ultimate frontier. Given this, naval officers were more confident in telling civilian leaders how they intended to defend the nation, rather than waiting for detailed instructions as the Army did.[83] Huntington quoted the innovative Adm. Bradley Fiske in noting that the Navy desired "room to work out its own 'rules of strategy, tactics, and discipline'" free from direct civilian control.[84]

The Navy's concept of strategy was global, rather than regional or theater based, perhaps symbolizing its need for "room to work." Wylie wrote, "The connotation of the word 'strategy' is not the same to the soldier as it is to the sailor or airman," and further explained, "Where the sailor or airman think in terms of an entire world [in terms of strategy], the soldier at work thinks in terms of theaters, in terms of campaigns, or in terms of battles."[85] Although Wylie often grouped the airman with the sailor in terms of how their two services viewed strategy, he recognized the tactical component of the Air Force as being more similar to the Army's in terms of strategic thinking. Wylie asserted, "The 'tactical' air element was in a situation comparable to that of the soldier. He needed his supplies brought to him and he needed his bases to be defended."[86] The Air Force tactical element thought mainly in terms of offensive activity for its part of AirLand Battle, but it was tied to the Army's fortunes in land combat. As Wylie suggested, if the Army proved unable to defend advanced air bases, then TAF would also be susceptible to defeat. This was especially the case in the post-Vietnam era until Desert Storm, when the TAF was largely in control of the service.[87] The Army and TAF concepts that emerged at the end of the 1970s and constituted AirLand Battle in large part confirmed Wylie's view on how the Army and tactical air elements thought.

The Army had rediscovered the theories of Carl von Clausewitz in the late 1970s focusing on his concepts of operational art, which were influential in the development of AirLand Battle.[88] Controlling the ground and air battle with decision-making faster than an opponent's, as per Boyd's thesis, was viewed as a revolutionary concept. AirLand Battle was organized at the operational level of war, its preface clearly stating, "Winning campaigns and battles is the purpose of this manual."[89] The Air Force and Army both promoted the use of the term "strategy" as synonymous with "operational-level warfare." In numerous instances in "Patterns of Conflict," Boyd uses "strategy" to describe what is clearly operational art, as defined by AirLand Battle.[90] Some critics believe the Army misapplied the concept of operational art in its definition of what constitutes a campaign. *FM 100-5* states, "The Operational Level of War involves planning and conducting campaigns. Campaigns are sustained operations designed to defeat an enemy force in a specified place and time with simultaneous and sequential battles. The disposition of forces, selection of objectives, and actions to weaken or outmaneuver the enemy all set the terms for the next battle and exploit tactical gains."[91]

The drafters of AirLand Battle appear to have misunderstood the operational level of war. According to two critics, Mike Kelly and Justin Brennan, *FM 100-5* "removes from strategy its traditional role of planning campaigns and conflates the term 'campaign' with what the Soviets would recognize as an 'operation'—a sequence of simultaneous and sequential battles, connected by a unifying idea and intended to defeat an enemy force."[92] This error was then compounded in the 1986 edition of *FM 100-5*, where the term "operational art" is first introduced in a U.S. military publication. Operational art was described by Kelley and Brennan as "the employment of military forces to attain strategic goals in a theater through the design, organization, and conduct of campaigns and major operations."[93] The U.S. Army's adoption and application of operational art served to promote the concept to the level of de facto strategy. The Army also suggested in its official writings that its definition of strategy corresponded with that of all the other services. A 1982 document, "Doctrinal Perspectives of War," by Gen. Glen Otis, Starry's successor at TRADOC, addressed the differing levels of war, stating, "The doctrinal perspectives of different levels of war applies to all forms of warfare—land, sea, and air—and has impact on all-services—Army, Air Force, Navy and Marine Corps. There is an underlying unity of basic principles and fundamentals that applies to all forms of organized conflict."[94] While the Navy did not share this view, the ultimate dominance of an Army-centric joint force structure at the end of the decade would promote this vision across the services, not just the Army.

In addition to having widely varying concepts of strategy, the Army and Navy also had very different experiences with the idea of a military technical revolution of the 1970s. The Army and to a degree the Air Force readily accepted the 1970s and 1980s RMA as something new and different from past concepts of war. Many of the technological improvements introduced through the efforts of Brown and Perry—such as air- and ground-launched cruise missiles, precision-guided munitions, and long-range aircraft surveillance systems—were originally intended for use by the Army and the Air Force. The Department of Defense's fiscal year 1986 report to Congress listed twenty-eight Army programs designed to produce air-to-ground missile systems and fifteen to create new or improved command, control, communication, and intelligence capabilities.[95] The Air Force had nineteen and twelve such programs, respectively, working to produce similar capabilities.

The Navy had been at the forefront in the development of advanced tactical command and control equipment and precision munitions since the end of World War II. Consequently, it saw the military technical revolution of the 1970s as more evolutionary in character. The strategy it developed from post–Vietnam War assessments was based on countering the Soviet Union, but was entrenched in Navy-specific areas of geography and contained more detailed direction on how to fight the Soviet fleet. The Navy planned to operate in support of the Army's battle on the Central European front, but before doing so would need to defeat its Soviet counterpart and secure NATO's Atlantic and Pacific flanks. President Jimmy Carter and Department of Defense officials were convinced that all of the services should concentrate on the vital Euro-Atlantic theater and the need to repel a potential Soviet ground attack across West Germany and into the heart of Western Europe.[96] As the naval historian Norman Friedman explained, opposition to the Navy's Maritime Strategy focused on the carrier, as carrier strike forces were viewed as a "potential drain of scarce resources better devoted to buying enough Army and strategic air strength to execute the war plan [in Europe]."[97]

In terms of strategy, the Navy rediscovered the basic theories of its primary theorist, Alfred Thayer Mahan, just as the Army returned to Clausewitz. Like the Army, the Navy also wrestled with interpretations, in its case involving the operational application of Mahan's strategic maxims. The Navy also temporarily pursued a defensive sea control strategy, during the tenure of CNO Zumwalt, from 1970 to 1974.[98] Like the Army, however, it returned to a more offensive stance in the 1980s with the Maritime Strategy, the development of which began in the late 1970s, but contrary to Zumwalt's interpretation, invoked Mahan in terms of offensive action.[99] Although the Navy benefited from some aspects of the defense technical revolution in the 1970s, such as those leading to the development of the surface-launched cruise missile, the service had a challenging relationship with the Department of Defense civilians leading that effort.

These differences were especially marked during the Carter administration, with some defense officials, Brown and Robert Komer, under secretary of defense for policy, criticizing the Navy's operational concept of power projection ashore using carrier aircraft. Komer thought carriers excessively vulnerable, and even in the mid-1960s, as a Kennedy and Johnson administration official, declared them "surplus to a nuclear war involving NATO."[100] Komer supported the use of carriers in remote areas like the Indian Ocean as presence units in the 1960s, and later in the 1970s as support forces to the U.S. Rapid Deployment Joint Task Force earmarked for Persian Gulf operations. Komer could not, however, be persuaded to support greater carrier construction at the expense of the modernization of ground and air units designated for NATO support.[101]

Brown believed that smaller flattops with vertical short takeoff and landing represented a better value than the large, nuclear-powered aircraft carrier.[102] The Navy's primary mission in Brown's view was sea control, which meant protecting resupply routes between the United States and Europe.[103] Few offset strategy concepts filtered into the naval service during the Carter presidency. Many of the Navy's own precision-guided weapons programs predated the Carter administration and Brown's effort. The Harpoon cruise missile had begun development in 1969, and the air-launched cruise missile program, the genesis of the Tomahawk, started in the early 1970s before officially merging with the Air Force's effort to do the same in 1973.[104] Brown's annual reports to Congress were filled with references to "offsetting Soviet numerical advantages," but the Navy did not usually figure into this calculus beyond its nuclear-powered ballistic missile submarine force. The Carter defense budgets did allow for an increase in the number of *Oliver Hazard Perry*–class frigates, as a means of "offsetting some of the existing numerical deficiencies in surface combatants required for sea control and defense tasks as well as other operations in ocean areas where there was a less concentrated threat."[105]

While these differences significantly delineated Army and Navy views in the 1970s and 1980s, the services shared some perspectives. Both responded to the unfavorable outcome of the Vietnam War and to the expectation that Soviet numerical strength would continue to grow over the 1980s by, as noted, initially embracing defensive measures, but ultimately rejecting them in favor of offensive means. The new Army and Navy strategic and operational concepts were initially perceived by U.S. NATO allies as threatening to stability.[106] Events at the end of the Cold War and during the Gulf War would remove the strategic rationale for the Navy's preferred strategy, allow the Army and Air Force's operational doctrines to continue, and imprint the Army's operational concept on the Navy with crippling results for the generation of new strategic concepts for the naval service in the post–Cold War era. There is a degree of irony to this in that the Navy's Maritime Strategy was designed for both war with the Soviets and for the maintenance of lower levels of conflict, unlike the Army's, which was geared solely toward high-end confrontations.[107]

The Navy had actively evolved its command and control capabilities after the end of World War II. The Japanese kamikaze offensive had called into question the service's ability to simultaneously project power and defend the fleet from hostile attack. It was estimated that the Japanese flew 2,550 individual kamikaze suicide missions, of which 15 percent ended in a successful impact or near miss sufficient to inflict damage.[108] Continuing development of radar and the proximity-fuzed shell mitigated the effects of kamikaze attacks, but by the conclusion of the conflict, the wartime CNO, Adm. Ernest King, remained dissatisfied with the progress on them. In October 1945 he wrote to the chiefs of the ships, aeronautics, and ordnance bureaus to express his concerns about the future of the fleet.[109] King commented on the slow rate of information display on individual ships under kamikaze attack and the general inability of the fleet to disseminate information fast enough to repel an attack. He recommended a number of improvements, notably, as the Navy digital historian David Boslaugh wrote, "a method of presenting radar information automatically, instantaneously and continuously, and in such a manner that the human mind . . . may receive and act upon the information in the most convenient form, plus instantaneous dissemination of information within the ship and force."[110]

King's call to action stimulated a half century of continuous action by the Navy to improve the rapid transmission of information and targeting data throughout the fleet. Working in conjunction with private industry and academic institutions, the service produced the Naval Tactical Data System, an information exchange system that shared sensor-tracking information from multiple ships. By September 1961 it had been installed on the USS *King* and USS *Mahan,* new frigates later reclassified destroyers, and by the end of that year on the aircraft carrier USS *Oriskany.*[111]

The Navy followed a similar path in the development of precision-guided munitions for war at sea. The kamikaze threat resulted in a family of guided missiles designed to shoot down attacking aircraft before they could attack U.S. naval units, especially the aircraft carrier. The Standard missile family of surface-to-air missile weapons began in January 1945 as a joint project of the Navy's Ordnance Bureau and the Applied Physics Laboratory at Johns Hopkins University.[112] It did not produce a viable weapon until 1953, but it and successor versions gradually became more accurate and lethal.[113] Efforts such as these culminated in the development of a "fully integrated, digitized, ship's combat system," that is, the Aegis system, which first went to sea in 1983.[114]

The Navy's other warfighting elements followed similar evolutionary paths. The submarine and naval aviation arms practiced evolutionary development in pure combat capability. Nuclear power for submarine propulsion was revolutionary in its own right, and the resultant submarines had a radically different primary mission (antisubmarine) than their World War II predecessors (anti-surface warfare). Adm. Hyman G. Rickover, Navy nuclear power chief, made use of the industry and academia partnerships to achieve success. The Navy's aviation component was less successful in that it did not have a powerful shepherd like Rickover to sell its attributes to Congress and protect it from administration officials intent on bending the sea service to their will. Despite this, the aviation Navy introduced new jet aircraft, angled flight decks, air-launched missiles, mirror landing systems, nuclear weapons–armed antisubmarine aircraft, and Rickover's propulsion plant for carrier use in the USS *Enterprise* (CVN 65). These developments took place almost entirely during the 1950s and were service driven rather than originating among civilians in the Department of Defense.[115]

The Navy viewed the realm of tactics as the proper place to discuss these technical improvements , but concepts of naval doctrine began to work their way into Navy thinking in the 1980s as they did in the Army. Unlike the other U.S. armed services, the Navy historically had not viewed operational art or doctrine, exemplified in the Army's *FM 100-5*, as a necessary concept, and this can be seen in how the services viewed the concept of strategy in the 1980s. Navy officers primarily viewed doctrine as an outgrowth of naval tactics. Capt. Wayne P. Hughes, longtime professor of tactical analysis at the Naval Postgraduate School, described doctrine as "the glue of tactics" that "enunciates policies and procedures that govern action."[116] This perspective appears to mirror that of the Army, but Hughes cautioned that while doctrine in naval combat was vital, it should not be dogmatic.[117] Hughes further considered doctrine as greater than tactics in that it encompasses command structure and communication, but is not the equal of tactics; it can only establish the conditions that lead to good tactics.[118] He warned that naval officers should be wary of doctrine in general and "leave room for men of freewheeling genius, for such will be the aces of the next war."[119] This decentralized view of doctrine is remarkably similar to the path pursued by the Army in adopting

AirLand Battle. The ground force incorporated *Auftragstaktik*, a German scheme of mission command, to allow junior leaders freedom of movement to adapt to the "chaos of the next battlefield," where "centralized control of subordinates would be always difficult and sometimes impossible."[120] This commonality in Army and Navy concepts was often forgotten during the 1980s.[121] Misunderstanding between the services over doctrine as a concept persisted throughout the 1990s as well.[122]

The net effect of the military technical revolution was negative for the Navy from the 1970s through the middle 1980s, but ultimately evolved into a positive occurrence due to the development of the Navy's strike capability. The ground- and air-launched cruise missile programs were originally planned as elements of the nation's nuclear weapons capability, but the Navy-produced conventional variant of this effort, the Tomahawk cruise missile, would greatly improve the service's ability to strike targets ashore without risking aircrews to determined enemy air defense systems.

The advent of the Reagan administration allowed the sea service to achieve many of its long-sought goals in force size and preferred global strategy for their employment. The U.S. Army to a degree saw itself a loser in this process and moved to better articulate its own view of strategy through documents like "Who Shall Bell the Cat," an April 1987 study by RAND analyst Carl Builder.[123] The demise of the Soviet menace, however, left the naval service without its preferred opponent, as it retained its forward presence and crisis response functions. As the Navy began to formulate a replacement strategy and attendant force structure, Iraq's invasion of Kuwait precipitated the ideal conflict for proving the utility of AirLand Battle. The Gulf War would strongly validate the Army's concept and Goldwater-Nichols' centralized command structure. The Navy's path to a replacement for the Maritime Strategy was more challenging in that the joint structures the service had so vigorously opposed in the mid-1980s now proved to be the director of one of the nation's swiftest and least costly wars.

A 1991 article, "Going in Harm's Way," by James Roberts, in *Defense* magazine, noted that the Gulf crisis "occurred at a critical time in the development of the U.S. Navy for both strategic and financial reasons."[124] The end of the Cold War had apparently "removed the Navy's prime *raison d'être* at a time when Congress was increasingly balking at the cost of new warships and aircraft."[125] The sea service appeared obstinate about accepting the new joint structures under which the Gulf War would be planned and fought. The Army and Air Force thought of strategy in terms of force structure while the Navy viewed strategy from more of a geographic perspective. The geographically limited scope of the Gulf War favored the Army's interpretation of strategy. The Army and Air Force's tactical and operational concepts of planning also prevailed over the Navy's strategic planning efforts. Accordingly, the new national security and defense strategies that emerged from the Gulf War were more closely connected to Army and Air Force operational concepts than to the Navy's global Cold War strategy. These differing constructs of "strategy" collided at the outset of the Gulf conflict. The naval component commander for the war, Adm. Stan Arthur, said in 1999, "Because Desert Storm was the only major war we have had in a generation, conclusions drawn from it will drive force composition, systems design, and budget decisions for decades."[126] The concept of military strategy appeared to have also been decided by the outcome of the Gulf War, with the Navy clearly on the losing side of the argument.

COMMAND AND CONTROL IN THE GULF WAR: STRUGGLING TO GO JOINT

The effects of the Goldwater-Nichols Act and the end of the Cold War on the Navy would in short order become clear as the military mobilized assets for President George H. W. Bush's response to the Iraqi invasion of Kuwait in the summer of 1990. The Navy had struggled to catch up to the other services in adapting the joint structures required by Goldwater-Nichols, and at the time of the invasion, significant issues remained. These were especially apparent in the upper command relationships for Operation Desert Shield (the military buildup launched on 2 August 1990), Operation Desert Storm (the offensive launched 17 January 1991), and in planning the air war against Iraq. *Desert Shield at Sea*, the Navy's history of the Gulf War, along with *Desert Storm at Sea*, compiled by the Center for Naval Analyses (CNA), identified five early command decisions that affected the Navy's performance during the conflict: control of Navy assets at CENTCOM, the location of Navy command afloat versus ashore, a rotation of Navy leaders, the lack of a strike warfare expert at CENTCOM, and the use of the Marines in the conflict. All of them directly involved joint command relationships and had outcomes perceived as negative by the Navy.[127]

Vice Adm. Hank Mauz, commanding the U.S. Seventh Fleet based in Yokosuka, Japan, was designated commander of U.S. Naval Forces Central Command (COMUSNAVCENT) on 16 August 1990.[128] The Joint Chiefs and civilian leadership felt that a three-star officer (vice admiral) was necessary as the naval component commander under the U.S. Central Command (CENTCOM) commander, Gen. Norman Schwarzkopf. This change from a more independent naval command in the Gulf region to one directly subordinate to the regional CINC would allow an Army general to command the multiple Navy aircraft carriers gathering in the region in support of Operation Desert Shield. Having a three-star officer would also be in line with the ranks of Schwarzkopf's other component commanders, but direct Army command of Navy assets was still a very new experience for the fleet.[129]

Mauz, an experienced surface warfare officer, counted among his many assignments serving in the late 1970s as the premier action officer in the then-new OP-603 in the Office of the Chief of Naval Operations (OPNAV) as the Navy began to shift toward the offensive concepts that would become the Maritime Strategy. In planning the air war against Iraq, he was confronted almost immediately with significant differences in Army (and Air Force) interpretations of command structure and organization than those of the Navy. Mauz decided to make his headquarters aboard a Navy command ship, first the USS *LaSalle* and then his regular Seventh Fleet flagship, USS *Blue Ridge*, after it arrived in the Persian Gulf from Japan, in September 1990.[130] This choice made sense from the traditional Navy perspective because locating COMUSNAVCENT on a specially configured flagship "provided instant communications, a command center, berthing [accommodations], and office space."[131] This choice allowed the naval component commander to remain close to his forces and remain closely apprised of their combat operations, but in the long run it would also result in depriving the Navy of influence in Operation Desert Storm.

Also of note, personnel issues arose in that Mauz and one of his key senior subordinates, Rear Adm. Timothy Wright, had been scheduled to rotate to other commands before the end of 1990. Wright, a one-star flag officer, had been appointed on short notice as COMUSNAVCENT's personal representative at CENTCOM headquarters, in Riyadh, but his presence did not significantly improve the Navy's influence on Schwarzkopf's planning and conduct of the war. A naval aviator with strike warfare experience, Wright was later replaced by Rear Adm. Conrad Lautenbacher in November 1990, before the commencement of active air operations.[132] Lautenbacher, although a quite capable and experienced officer, did not have the same strike warfare experience as Wright.[133]

Mauz was scheduled to rotate back to Washington, D.C., for service on the OPNAV staff in December 1990, and be replaced by Vice Adm. Stan Arthur as commander of the Seventh Fleet and of COMUSNAVCENT. CNO Adm. Frank Kelso wanted Mauz to return to OPNAV to allow Adm. William Smith, whom Mauz was scheduled to relieve, to fill a vacant and presumably important billet on the NATO staff in Brussels.[134] CENTCOM and its air and ground components had non-rotational policies for their commanders in case of crisis or conflict.[135] The Navy now appeared to be violating this rule by rotating out its component commander, Mauz. Wright's rotation and Mauz's move, however, made no sense for two important reasons: communications and proximity. In the new joint command structure, a component commander's physical proximity to the overall leadership of an operation counted for more than it had in the traditional naval command environment. Wright and now Lautenbacher were both capable officers, but as rear admirals they lacked the rank and prestige as their three-star maritime component commander boss in his flagship.

As head of CENTCOM, Schwarzkopf had located his command post in the Saudi capital of Riyadh. While Mauz and then his successor, Arthur, spoke with Schwarzkopf several times each day, their lack of physical presence and face-to-face staff conversations appeared to lessen naval influence on the overall operation. Schwarzkopf was reported by some to have a personal style of command that valued face-to-face discussions over phone conversation.[136] Schwarzkopf asked Mauz if he wanted to stay on as CENTCOM maritime forces commander, but Mauz declined, saying that he did not want to cause trouble for the Navy and in effect screw up the rotation. [137] Schwarzkopf and the Navy staff later claimed that everyone had supported the rotation of Mauz to Arthur and to keep the Navy commander afloat instead of ashore in Riyadh. In retrospect, however, the choice to keep the maritime commander on a ship far from Riyadh and Mauz's early relief appear to have complicated the Navy's efforts in the forthcoming Desert Storm campaign. Officially, the Navy agreed with COMUSNAVCENT remaining at sea, and after the war Mauz asserted that he would not have opted to change command locations.[138] Arthur, however, was less certain. He said in 1999 that COMUSNAVCENT should have been located in Riyadh, but also that if he had needed to be there, the Navy "would have somehow put together an adequate communications package for him."[139]

The naval component commanders' lack of immediate physical proximity to General Schwarzkopf and associated lack of good communications appear to have played a role in other key elements of Operations Desert Shield and Desert Storm. Planning for the air campaign saw the Navy clash bitterly with the Air Force over command and control arrangements and the use of airpower in support of the overall effort. The command arrangements and general differences in strategic ethos between the Army and the Navy led to what the Navy always feared—an Army or Air Force general telling admirals how to conduct naval operations. Finally, a debate over whether to use Marines as active combat participants or as decoys—ultimately the latter was ordered—caused frustration at Marine Corps headquarters in the United States and raised suspicions about the Army capitalizing on Goldwater-Nichols provisions to support its own parochial service interests. The Marine Corps later exploited the reform legislation's provisions to break free of naval domination at the operational level of warfare. As one naval officer later remarked, "After Desert Storm, no longer would the Marines be represented by a Colonel—the Fleet Marine Officer—on a Navy component command staff, supporting an Admiral, but rather they would be their own component, under their own general."[140]

Planning the Air Campaign: What about the Navy?

Conflict over command and control of the air campaign and target designation in support of the ground effort in the Gulf War led to serious disagreement between the Air Force and Navy at the outset of Operation Desert Shield and throughout the duration of Operation Desert Storm. The course of the air campaign was by no means set in General Schwarzkopf's mind as planning commenced in September 1990. The Air Force had begun war planning independently of CENTCOM in early August immediately after Iraq invaded

Kuwait.[141] Led by Air Force airpower theorist Col. John Warden, a service planning group named Checkmate developed Instant Thunder, a plan including dramatic attacks against Iraq's senior civilian and military leadership.[142]

Warden was well known in the Air Force and in the Pentagon as an astute advocate of the war-winning capabilities of airpower. He was sought after for strategic studies assignments even as a relatively junior officer. In 1977, during the Carter administration, Warden had been a member of the Air Force team assigned to evaluate Presidential Review Memorandum 10, a statement on military net assessment and posture review. A junior lieutenant commander, Peter Swartz, found himself confronting Warden as his service opposite member on the review. Swartz felt afterward that Warden had "creamed him" in terms of strategic knowledge and vowed that he would never again be so overmatched on strategy by the Air Force.[143] Meanwhile, Warden went on to become one of the Air Force's premier advocates of offensive action, arguing that the defensive use of airpower imposed too many risks and allowed an enemy to concentrate their own forces in responding.[144] Warden, a military theorist on par with John Boyd, had in 1988 produced a notable book on how to conduct a modern air campaign. Warden believed that the U.S. military had badly neglected operational art and suggested that a single service could conduct operations capable of winning a conflict.[145]

Instant Thunder was in Warden's words designed "to inflict strategic paralysis upon Saddam Hussein's military machine."[146] The plan closely followed Warden's theory on five strategic rings that must be broken to meet conditions for victory in war. Breaking the first three rings required isolating the enemy's leadership from the wider conflict, degrading key production facilities, and disrupting infrastructure with attacks on transportation lines. These actions would then turn the civilian population and troops against their leadership, with the latter destroying an opponent's offensive and defensive military capability.[147]

Schwarzkopf received Warden's brief in Tampa, Florida (the nominal stateside headquarters of CENTCOM) on 17 August. Schwarzkopf's chief of staff, Maj. Gen. Robert Johnson, USMC, asked Warden if the Air Force "had a plan to logistically support a longer air campaign" in case CENTCOM wanted to first destroy Iraqi air defenses before attacking targets in Baghdad.[148] Schwarzkopf liked some aspects of Warden's plan, but wanted his designated air component commander, Lt. Gen. Chuck Horner, USAF, to approve the strategy. Schwarzkopf must have had serious doubts, as he later described Warden as a "member of the Curtis LeMay school of Air Force planners—guys who think strategic bombing can do it all and that armies [and navies] are obsolete."[149] Warden's presentation did not go down well with Horner, who was convinced that a decapitation strike like Warden advocated would be insufficient. The air component commander was also concerned about having someone from "Washington" select targets, as a result of Warden's plan, because he felt that process had been disastrous during the Vietnam War.[150]

Horner appointed Brig. Buster Glosson, USAF, to head the air war planning group, later dubbed the "Black Hole" for the level of secrecy given to its plans and products.[151] Glosson, the outgoing deputy chief of the Joint Task Force Middle East (disestablished in the Desert Storm buildup), adopted a modified version of Warden's plan that identified many of the same command and control and communications and transport targets for early termination, but he spread the campaign over months rather than the original six-day window advocated by Warden. The military historian Steven Metz wrote, "Ultimately, Schwarzkopf and [Gen. Colin] Powell neither rejected nor fully embraced the strategic airpower idea, but allowed it to coexist in parallel with the other parts of the campaign."[152]

The air plan was still in its infancy when it collided with the Navy's alternative plans for air warfare. The key differences between the Navy and Air Force plans were how much focus to give the Iraqi air defense system at the outset of the war, geographic separations of command, and who was in charge. Vice Admiral Mauz liked the aggressive aspect of Warden's plan, but he was unhappy that it sought to suppress rather than destroy Iraq's air defenses.[153] The Navy's representative in the Black Hole, Cdr. Donald McSwain, called the Air Force plan "Distant Blunder," as it was "drafted at the distant Pentagon and a blunder for its emphasis on attacking Baghdad at the outset of the war."[154]

The Navy's experience in Vietnam and its plans for attacking Soviet ground targets required that the enemy's air defense system be silenced before commencing more significant attacks. Mauz had just conducted extensive planning and exercises on this concept while serving as commander of the Seventh Fleet. Whereas standard NATO doctrine discussed the concept of Suppression of Enemy Air Defenses (SEAD), Mauz considered Destruction of Enemy Air Defenses (DEAD) as the more appropriate operational effort and acronym.[155] Mauz and Maj. Gen. Royal N. Moore Jr., air component commander for the Marines, also argued for a "rollback" campaign against Iraq's air defenses before engaging in aggressive attacks against Iraqi command and control and infrastructure targets.[156] Mauz and his staff had developed their overall air warfare concept based on Mauz's experience as commander of the USS *America* carrier battle group, which in 1986 had conducted raids on Libya in Operation El Dorado Canyon, as well as Mauz's more recent Pacific command experience. Mauz backed up his plan with analysis on the Iraqi air defense system provided by Strike Projection Evaluation and Anti-Air Warfare Research (SPEAR), a unit of the Office of Naval Intelligence.[157]

The Air Force had other ideas. Mauz went to see his air component command counterpart, Horner, soon after arriving in theater to discuss their respective allocations for the air war. Mauz wanted to divide Air Force and Navy targets geographically to minimize confusion. This was the way air operations had been conducted during the Vietnam War and had been described as "route packages" for the separate service air components. The Naval Historical Center's account of the Gulf War, *Shield and Sword,* has Horner responding angrily to Mauz's suggestion: "Fuck that! Don't ever talk to me about it again, because we're not going to do it. I'll resign first."[158] Mauz later said that he never used the term "route package," but that Horner had assumed he meant that in their discussion.[159] Mauz also recalled Horner saying that route packages "got people killed in Vietnam."[160] Horner later said the fatalities were perhaps due to some of the challenging assignments the Air Force in particular had received as its share of Vietnam route packages. The Route 6 package shared by the services contained the heavily defended Vietnamese capital of Hanoi and the important port city of Haiphong,[161] so the Navy and Air Force had arguably shared responsibility for the most dangerous packages. Mauz attributed the large number of deaths over Vietnam to "sending aircraft repeatedly to the same stupid targets picked by Washington," not the concept of route packages itself.[162]

While Horner may have opposed anything resembling a route package in coordinating Air Force and Navy strikes from Saudi Arabia and the Persian Gulf, he apparently did not have the same reservations about aircraft based elsewhere, as he approved geographic separation for those assigned to Joint Task Force Proven Force, based in Turkey. According to the *Gulf War Airpower Survey*, a document the U.S. Air Force commissioned in 1993 to create a common reference for Gulf War air operations, Horner had specifically been concerned about the symbolism of geographic separation between Navy and Air Force strike locations.[163] While he did not allow for route packages or a sense of decentralized air operations as advocated by the Navy, he altered the final Desert Storm air plan to include a "major effort to destroy Iraq's air defense system in the first few hours of the war," as the Navy had advocated.[164] The conflict over the plan illustrated another aspect of the gulf between Navy and Air Force concepts of strategy and operational planning that made joint operations challenging.

Leadership of the air campaign revealed additional significant differences between the services. The Navy and Marine Corps as well as the Air Force and Army had followed service traditions in their respective plans for organizing the air war component for Operation Desert Storm. The Navy and Marine Corps preferred a decentralized approach that empowered tactical commanders to take charge of all units (surface, undersea, and air) in different geographic regions. The Navy carrier battle group and the Navy–Marine Corps Air-Ground Task Force were representative constructs of this idea, with one commander in charge of all assets in each formation.[165] The Air Force and Army preferred more centralized control in a unitary chain of command. They only wanted joint coordination at the operational level of warfare and higher. The Joint Forces Air Component Command (JFACC), the organization charged with fighting the air war, exemplified this concept.[166]

The Air Force had published "Joint Doctrine for Theater Counterair Operations," its blueprint for overseas land areas, in April 1986, soon after the Army completed updating its field manual, *FM 100-5*, in 1986 presenting the heart of what became the AirLand Battle concept. The Air Force doctrine constituted the most recent word from the Joint Chiefs on joint air command functions at the operational level of warfare. It held, "The joint force air component commander will be the Service component commander who has the preponderance of air assets to be used and the ability to assume that responsibility."[167] The Navy had participated in crafting the doctrine, and the

CNO and Marine Corps commandant had cosigned it, but many in the Navy never thought they would have to abide by its tenets.[168] The Air Force and its coalition partners would provide the bulk of the airpower for the Gulf War.

The Air Force had 718 aircraft in theater in November 1990 as opposed to the Navy and Marine Corps' combined 581 aircraft.[169] In July 1990, just a month before the Iraqi invasion of Kuwait, Schwarzkopf had war-gamed a potential conflict with Iraq in the exercise Internal Look, during which Horner acted as commander of all air forces, including those based on carriers.[170] The theater counterair document allowed the Marine Air-Ground Task Force commander autonomous control over the aircraft specifically assigned to his or her command, but authorized the joint air commander to overrule decisions as required.[171]

This appointment put the Air Force effectively in control of the air war and subjected naval officers to both JFACC control for the first time and to that organization's battle rhythm in the form of the Air Tasking Order (ATO), a massive document often consisting of hundreds of pages of detailed daily operations specifics and anathema to the Navy's concept of decentralized control of the battlefield. It listed everything, including type of aircraft, mission, call sign, friend or foe codes, takeoff and landing times, time over target, and refueling instructions. SPINS, a supplemental instructions section, provided additional, equally detailed data. The documents, sent to every command every day, caused significant confusion because ATOs had never been transmitted to such a large joint force as that assembled for the Gulf War. In some cases, due to its massive size and the lack of appropriate communications equipment on Navy ships to receive it, the ATO arrived a day late to the aircraft carriers assigned to COMUSNAVCENT, even when sent via satellite with the highest "Flash" message priority routing.[172]

A 1993 CNA study of the Gulf conflict found that many of the naval officers surveyed had had no familiarity with the JFACC and ATO prior to the Gulf War. Before the conflict, they had believed them to be a coordinating but not a command tool and did not expect to receive such detailed instructions on how to carry out their missions.[173] According to the study, Navy aviators were used to receiving more general instructions and tended to "feel they can understand the CinC's objectives well enough to pick out the most lucrative targets to strike."[174] Many naval officers also believed the JFACC had no appreciation of naval issues or the characteristics of naval aircraft, despite the presence of naval personnel at CENTCOM headquarters in Riyadh and their participation in drafting the ATO. *Shield and Sword* notes that the Air Force planners running the air war did not appreciate the potential threat of the Iraqi navy's Exocet-armed aircraft and patrol boats in the Persian Gulf.[175] Naval forces needed to keep watch over the Gulf, the coalition's "right flank," where Iraqi units had the potential to attack allied naval forces.[176]

In fact, the JFACC's staff was often ignorant of the capabilities of naval aircraft and units, which caused confusion in the naval response to missions ordered by the air component commander. For example, Schwarzkopf and Horner were skeptical of Navy claims that its conventional Tomahawk cruise missile would be an effective strike weapon, as they had not yet been fired in a conflict. Schwarzkopf in particular was concerned that the weapons might not even leave their shipboard launch tubes.[177] Also, the Navy weapons that were available had been programmed for missions against Soviet targets and would need to be reprogrammed in order to use them against Iraq.[178] When Glosson prepared his first draft of the air war plan, the missions included one in which six Navy A-6 Intruder aircraft would conduct a bombing raid against a heavily defended target west of downtown Baghdad.[179] The Navy's SPEAR division argued that such an attack was better suited to Tomahawk missiles than manned aircraft. The Air Force resisted this line of argument, perhaps preferring manned aircraft to unmanned weapons. Glosson ordered a series of computer simulations of the attack that also included Air Force F-117 Stealth aircraft,[180] and the results suggested that more than half of the Navy A-6 Intruders and Air Force stealth aircraft would be lost. Such losses would likely have amounted to a significant political and propaganda victory for the Iraqi president.[181] Gulf War chroniclers Michael Gordon and Gen. Bernard Trainor posit that this potential poor outcome was enough to convince Glosson to select the Tomahawk for the mission.[182] In spite of some difficulties, the Navy managed in less than six months to reprogram enough Tomahawks to support the entire Desert Storm air campaign.[183] The costs of the Tomahawk versus those of conventional air-dropped weapons may have been a limiting factor in CENTCOM's decisions on cruise missile participation. Each Tomahawk cost approximately $1.2 million to deliver a thousand-pound warhead, while a two-thousand-pound air-dropped, laser-guided bomb could penetrate more hardened targets for just $73,000 per round.[184] Schwarzkopf later said that Powell had urged him to avoid using cruise missiles due to their high cost.[185]

PLANNING THE GROUND WAR: WHAT TO DO WITH THE MARINES?

In the immediate aftermath of the Iraqi invasion of Kuwait, U.S. and Saudi officials were concerned that Iraqi president Saddam Hussein might order his forces to advance farther south into Saudi Arabia.[186] In support of Desert Shield, the Navy ordered to the Persian Gulf two separate amphibious warfare groups with thousands of embarked U.S. Marines from the East Coast of the United States and from the Subic Bay Naval Base in the Philippines.[187] The employment of Marine Corps units during Operations Desert Shield and Desert Storm further exposed the cleavages between the services under the new joint system.

The two dispatched Marine units were supposed to be prepared for combat in the ground defense of Saudi Arabia but also to affect a forced landing in the rear of Iraqi forces if they advanced into Saudi Arabia.[188] In the haste to get as much combat capability into the region as soon as possible, however, Navy and Marine planners had not loaded the individual ships as was typical for an imminent amphibious assault. Instead, the ships were given a compromise load out, which meant that they were not fully equipped to immediately land on a hostile coast.[189] Due to this lack of amphibious capability, the Marine units were absorbed into the larger ground combat organization rather than integrated with the Navy as usual. Technical communications problems between Vice Admiral Mauz and his amphibious warfare commander, Rear Adm. John LaPlante, complicated the effective relay of this problem to General Schwarzkopf in time to prevent the Marines from being co-opted into the developing ground combat organization.

The Navy and the Marines ultimately worked out their communication and organizational details, but other such snags caught planners by surprise, like decision-making on whether to conduct a major amphibious operation during the war, which also raised issues of service parochialism and knowledge about other service's capabilities. LaPlante and his Marine landing force commander colleague, Maj. Gen. Harry Jenkins, had not yet assembled their entire potential force in November 1990 when first asked about the feasibility of an amphibious attack. With only one Marine Expeditionary Brigade on the chalkboard, "We would get our ass kicked," LaPlante said.[190] Lt. Gen. Walter Boomer, in command of the Marine forces already ashore in defense of Saudi Arabia, did not command the Marine units embarked in the amphibious ships. When pressed by Schwarzkopf on whether an amphibious landing would be necessary to aid the Marines already on the ground in Saudi Arabia, Boomer said it was not.[191] Mauz was concerned about potential mine threats to the amphibious ships, and Schwarzkopf was also loath at potentially sustaining the heavy casualties historically associated with opposed amphibious invasions. After the war, Schwarzkopf said that from the start of the crisis, he and Gen. Colin Powell, chairman of the Joint Chiefs of Staff, had decided to place a high priority on deception. "We worked hard to convince the Iraqis that coalition forces would attack directly into Kuwait supported by amphibious operations," he asserted.[192] The official Army history of the conflict, *Certain Victory: The U.S. Army in the Gulf*, suggests that Schwarzkopf desired to use both the Marines and Army Airborne assault forces "to tie down the Iraqis by making them believe that both options would be exercised."[193] The Army history asserts that this decision distracted seven Iraqi divisions from participating in the main battle to the west.[194]

Despite the generally accepted view among senior leaders that an amphibious attack was unnecessary, some retired Marines, like Gen. Bernard Trainor, accused Schwarzkopf of placing parochial Army concerns ahead of those of the Marine Corps in planning for the ground assault into Kuwait. The CENTCOM commander had been concerned from the outset of the crisis about the ability of his command staff to effectively plan such a complex ground operation. Schwarzkopf, instead of working with his staff in Riyadh or at U.S. CENTCOM headquarters, selected an elite group of Army operations planners from the staff of the School for Advanced Military Studies, at Fort Leavenworth, Kansas. Led by Lt. Col. Joseph Purvis, the group—derisively nicknamed the "Jedi Knights" by Riyadh headquarters—planned the ground war in Kuwait and Iraq under isolated and secretive conditions.[195]

Nicknames aside, Purvis's cell constituted another parochial, largely service-based, planning group, similar to Warden's Checkmate cadre and Black Hole (Air Force) cells, planning the air war in a vacuum in Washington and Riyadh. The Navy and Marine Corps appeared to have been shut out from the campaign planning effort at both its strategic and operational levels; that said, however, the maritime services failed to invite the Army or Air Force to participate in their planning for amphibious operations.[196] These non-joint planning efforts led to further instances of service bickering involving the use of the Marine Corps units afloat. Purvis and his group actively studied the idea of a Marine Corps amphibious assault by the 4th Marine Expeditionary Brigade across a marsh area on the Kuwait-Iraq border near Bubiyan Island.[197] They did not, however, invite Marine representatives to any of their planning meetings for nearly two months. In November 1990, they invited a member of Boomer's staff to participate, but Marines from the shipboard contingent were not consulted.[198]

The Jedi planners had decided to use Boomer's land-based Marines for frontal infantry attacks that in conjunction with a British assault would open a hole in the Iraqi lines through which U.S. Army armored forces would race in a sweeping "left hook" around the Iraqi forces in Kuwait.[199] At a commanders meeting shortly after the unveiling of the Jedi plan of attack, Boomer strongly disagreed with the concept, preferring to keep Marines close to the Kuwaiti coastline, where they could advance to Kuwait City under the protection of Navy ship-based weapons. Schwarzkopf agreed and instructed Purvis and his team to "stop screwing with the Marines."[200]

Accounts vary as to whether the Army planners made the best use of their Marine Corps assets. *Certain Victory* suggests that the Army believed the Marines only capable of playing a supporting role in the campaign. Lt. Gen. Gary Luck, commander of the 18th Airborne Corps, was assigned to protect the Saudi border from a potential Iraqi invasion in November 1990. Gen. Robert Scales, author of *Certain Victory*, noted challenges with Luck's Marine Corps units:

> The Marines prefer to keep ground forces farther back and nearer to the coasts than Army forces and to control the vacated ground using fires from their Harrier ground support aircraft and naval gunfire. The Marines did not have the armored staying power necessary to fight well forward. They had only 123 tanks—all older M60s—that were overmatched by the Iraqi T-72s. With only two other battalions of extremely thin-skinned and vulnerable light-armor vehicles, the Marines were capable of limited maneuvering against the Iraqis outside their narrow coastal enclave.[201]

The Marine Corps history of the conflict, *U.S. Marines in the Persian Gulf*, notes that by December 1990, the Marines ashore under Army command "had a considerable number of M1A1 tanks," courtesy an arrangement between the Army chief of staff, Gen. Carl E. Vuono, and the Marine Corps commandant, Gen. Al Gray.[202] Other parts of the Marines' official Gulf War history point to additional cooperation between Army and Marine Corps planners.[203] While service synchronization in the Gulf War was good, it was "not yet seamless."[204] Perceptions about other service's capabilities could have been due to unfamiliarity. Coordination among the services occurred almost entirely at the strategic level, with limited contacts at the operational and tactical levels. A 1993 assessment by James Winnefeld and Dana Johnson in *Joint Forces Quarterly* stated, "In many ways jointness still stops at the headquarters of the CINCs: they are the lowest level at which joint staffs exist in most theaters."[205]

As Schwarzkopf was trying to clarify the role of his Marine elements afloat and ashore in the region, Commandant Gray became unofficially involved in the CENTCOM planning process. According to Trainor, Gray lacked confidence in Boomer's ability to command ashore and desired greater Marine participation in the form of an amphibious attack in Kuwait or Iraq.[206] Gray visited the Riyadh headquarters in December 1990 and sought to insert himself into the planning process by telling Schwarzkopf that he disagreed with the Marine component of the attack and that Boomer was not up to the task of leading the Marine operation ashore.[207] Schwarzkopf questioned Boomer on Gray's complaints. Boomer saw no reason to change the attack plan and especially saw no need for Gray's suggestion that another three-star Marine general be assigned to the Riyadh headquarters to supervise him. Schwarzkopf rejected all of Gray's suggestions, and the disconsolate commandant returned to Washington bereft of any success in altering the ground war.

Mauz had not been in favor of amphibious operations due to poor beach conditions in the proposed areas for assault,[208] but his successor, Arthur, pressed for an amphibious attack at the outset of the ground war in case the Army advance ashore bogged down. Schwarzkopf rebuffed Arthur, and Boomer reiterated that the Marines ashore could "get by" without one.[209] Arthur recalled after the war, "I knew that neither Schwarzkopf nor Powell wanted to have an amphibious landing. That was the last thing they wanted to have happen. And there was never an occasion where an amphibious landing was going to be necessary to conduct the war the way they wanted to."[210] While there was perhaps agreement at the outset of the Desert Shield deployment on the lack of a need for amphibious operations, there is some evidence to suggest that parochial concerns from the services interfered with further assessment of amphibious requirements. In any case, Schwarzkopf, as the theater commander, had the final say, and the Marines remained aboard their ships.

Despite postwar claims by Vice President Dick Cheney, Chairman Powell, General Schwarzkopf, and other leaders about the marvelous joint effort, primarily as the result of the Goldwater-Nichols Act provisions, the command and control arrangements, the planning for the air war, and the question of how to use the Marines in the conflict indicated that service parochialism remained alive and well. In the Persian Gulf, the Army and Air Force held predominant command positions at the national strategic and operational levels. The focus on land operations against Iraqi forces occupying Kuwait justified those appointments. The Army generals, Powell and Schwarzkopf, and Horner and Glosson—imposed their service doctrines developed in the 1980s for fighting the Soviet Union. Joint integration for the Army and Air Force only applied at the operational level of command and above, and it was unlikely that Schwarzkopf would allow intrusion by the Navy and Marine Corps into planning for the ground and air campaigns, led by the Army and Air Force, respectively.[211] Strategic level integration took place, but was likely hampered by the Navy's refusal to base its commander at Schwarzkopf's command headquarters in Riyadh.

The Navy's assessments in the wake of the Gulf conflict centered on the issues above: command and control, planning and conduct of air war, and use of the Marine Corps. To the first issue, command and control, as noted the two commanders of U.S. naval forces in the war held differing opinions on where to best locate their headquarters. Vice Admiral Mauz thought it best to remain aboard a ship at sea.[212] When the buildup for combat operations commenced, a significant Iraqi maritime threat had existed in the form of mines and small surface combatants armed with Exocet missiles. *Desert Storm at Sea* suggested that a ship facility had better means with which to communicate with other fleet units than one located on shore. It further stated that there had been a real concern that the Iraqis might invade Saudi Arabia and that the Navy wanted no part in a land-based headquarters that could possibly be overrun by hostile ground forces.[213] Vice Admiral Arthur thought his headquarters should have been located with the rest of the joint force leadership in Riyadh.

Schwarzkopf lacked experience handling naval units, and further, his stint as the Army component commander during the 1983 Grenada invasion under naval leadership, when he had to commandeer Marine Corps helicopters on USS *Guam* to transport Army Rangers to rescue U.S. hostages, did nothing to raise his opinion of the naval service's professionalism.[214] Given this, the physical presence of a senior naval officer would have served to assert the Navy's role in the mission far earlier and with better results. In an ironic twist of fate, it should have been an admiral's turn to lead CENTCOM at the time of the Gulf War. The service had nominated Vice Adm. Hank Mustin for the position, but according to Mustin and others, Powell, then national security adviser for President Reagan, wanted an Army general for the position.[215] Mustin later described Secretary of Defense Frank Carlucci, who acquiesced to Powell's demand, as a "tower of Jello" for not standing up to such blatant Army parochialism.[216] Adm. Bill Owens, Carlucci's military assistant, also advised that Mustin was not the right man for the CENTCOM position.[217] The Navy's denuded presence at CENTCOM headquarters did not contribute to its situational awareness. The one-star naval liaison officer in Riyadh, Rear Admiral Wright, was not apprised of or invited to any of the key briefings, such as on Colonel Warden's Instant Thunder strike plan. Wright later observed,

"Decisions were made in Riyadh on the spot by 'people with faces,' and by implication not by electronic communications."[218]

The Navy's account of the Gulf War suggests that the Navy's indifference to past joint efforts in the Persian Gulf region, such as Schwarzkopf's Internal Look exercise in July 1990, and a reluctance to engage with CENTCOM's U.S.-based headquarters staff in Tampa contributed to the Navy's attitude toward establishing its headquarters in Riyadh.[219] It also suggests that while the Navy had good reason to focus on maritime threats from both Iraq and Iran during the Gulf conflict, it had a historically fragmented command structure for Persian Gulf operations that hampered effective deployment against either threat. *Desert Storm at Sea* notes this problem, stating that the prewar Navy commander of the Middle East Force should have perhaps been absorbed into the larger COMUSNAVCENT organization early in the crisis.[220] In general, senior Navy leaders assumed that elements from the larger fleets would support the small naval forces generally assigned to the Gulf region for patrol work during the Cold War.[221] The authority given the regional combatant commanders by Goldwater-Nichols proscribed such direct service leadership of campaign elements. In fact, no service leader could visit the Gulf region without Schwarzkopf's permission.[222]

Concerning planning and execution of the air war, although it might be easy to look back and suggest that the Navy should have had a stronger presence at the JFACC in Riyadh from the outset of war planning, the joint doctrine supporting the concept of the JFACC was less than five years old in 1990.[223] Exercises late in the Cold War using a JFACC and an ATO had been regional and held in Europe where only the Army and Air Force could participate. In addition, much of those exercises had been simulated. As a result, many naval officers had no idea what to expect when the operational JFACC was introduced for the Gulf crisis.[224] The Air Force's computer system for the Gulf War JFACC and ATO had been developed by the 9th Air Force and was not a universal system with which the Navy was familiar.[225] The ATO remained slow and cumbersome to prepare and transmit throughout the conflict and skewed more toward offensive rather than defensive operations. It would have been useless, for example, in countering surprise Iraqi naval activity in the Gulf. When remnants of the Iraqi surface navy attempted a breakout from Iraqi bases to internment in Iranian ports on 30 January 1991, ship-based aircraft and helicopters outside JFACC control and not subject to the ATO responded.[226]

Desert Storm at Sea suggests that naval staff members quickly became discouraged in trying to influence the JFACC, believing it had "no appreciation of the necessity for and benefits of striking naval targets."[227] The JFACC's operations director, Maj. Gen. John Corder, USAF, perhaps put it best when he said, "He who controls the target list controls the war."[228] Additional problems included such basic issues as refueling for carrier-based versus land-based aircraft. For example, Navy carriers used a fuel suitable for shipboard use, JP-5, a less-explosive and more-stable fuel than the more flammable A-1 fuel used by Air Force jets.[229] Arthur regularly complained that naval aircraft, which generally had shorter ranges than their Air Force counterparts, could not get adequate tanking support from the Air Force–operated campaign air-tanking effort.[230]

As for the role of the Marines, the option of conducting an amphibious landing during Operation Desert Storm appears to have been rejected from the outset by Powell and Schwarzkopf based on the possibility of high casualties and because of the limited geography of suitable beaches where such an operation could be mounted.[231] They preferred instead to have the amphibious force serve as a distraction and deterrence force to keep the Iraqis planning for an amphibious attack that would never come. Postwar intelligence assessments presented to Lieutenant General Boomer suggested that the Iraqi army had well-fortified the coast of Kuwait, but personal inspection by Marines afterward suggested the fortifications were poorly constructed.[232] The work done, however, indicated that the Iraqis indeed believed the allied forces would launch an amphibious attack.[233]

The amount of pressure placed on the CENTCOM leadership by the Marine Corps commandant to conduct an amphibious attack is debatable. General Gray was on the record in *Desert Shield at Sea* as saying that an amphibious-capable force was in effect the "strategic reserve" of the Desert Shield and Storm campaigns.[234] The friendly account of Gray's career by Col. Gerald H.

Turley, a former staff officer of the commandant, suggests that Gray was determined to find a role in the Desert Storm campaign for an amphibious attack.[235] The Navy's history also asserts that Gray had wanted to conduct such an attack, but if not done, the afloat Marines could be used as an accessible reserve if needed for continued ground operations.[236] Gray had pushed hard through Maj. Gen. John Sheehan, the Marine Corps representative on the COMUSNAVCENT staff, for an amphibious landing in Kuwait.[237] Such an attack was initially approved, but the amount of damage to property in Kuwait, as well as problems clearing mines on the invasion beaches led to the plan being shelved.[238] Gordon and Trainor believe that Gray felt that there was not enough emphasis in the CENTCOM theater on amphibious operations. Gray had the Marine Corps warfighting center at Quantico, Virginia, prepare to present his service's version of Colonel Warden's Instant Thunder brief and the Army Jedi's ground warfare–planning effort for amphibious warfare.[239] The plan was war-gamed, and 10,000 friendly casualties were expected in one week of fighting.[240] The Marines transmitted the plan to Vice Admiral Arthur in theater, but it found no allies and was never pursued.

While Gray did not get the amphibious action he desired, Boomer's Marines on the ground in Iraq and Kuwait executed many of the maneuver warfare concepts Gray had attempted to inculcate in the Marine Corps since becoming commandant in 1987. The Marines 1989 *FMFM 1: Warfighting* was Gray's attempt, in the view of Capt. Terry Pierce, an expert in naval technology innovation, to "return the Corps to its roots in warfighting learned in the Banana wars, but shelved during the set piece battles of the Pacific and Korea."[241] As the significant troubles facing the Soviet Union became apparent in the late 1980s, Gray preferred to focus on Third World contingency operations rather than the Navy's global Maritime Strategy.[242] Gray retired soon after the Gulf War and was replaced by Gen. Carl E. Mundy Jr., who also wanted to move the Marine Corps beyond mere amphibious warfare and toward a more holistic concept of operations in coastal areas on the littoral, that is, both land and sea.

When the Gulf War ended in March 1991, it was readily apparent that the Navy would need to adjust to a new reality in the post–Cold War world. It would have no peer opponent fleet to fight, and the Army and Air Force concepts of strategy and operational planning would prevail. In a 2005 email,

Capt. Joseph Bouchard, a former planner in OP-06, encapsulated the Navy's dilemma:

> The Navy was very slow to react to the doctrinal implications of the collapse of the Soviet Union and was unprepared doctrinally for Desert Shield and Desert Storm. Desert Storm was fought using joint doctrine based on AirLand battle. That made sense. Iraq was in effect a continental theater, but it means that the full capabilities of naval force were not exploited in Desert Storm. This was manifested in many ways as well as documented in the studies of Desert Storm.[243]

While the naval service could do little to change the geographic and political conditions under which the Gulf War was fought, it could have been more directly engaged in shaping the lessons and emerging views on the nature of the post–Cold War world. The military historian Steven Metz suggests that the Gulf War created a new strategic paradigm due to its timing and its overwhelming success. With the Soviet threat dissipating, the United States needed a new paradigm, and Desert Storm "provided an instant perception of clarity" for U.S. leaders, who knew how to deal with the consequent challenges.[244]

AFTER THE GULF WAR: TOWARD A POST–COLD WAR STRATEGY

The Gulf War would have a significant impact on U.S. strategy, defense organization, and operations for the next two decades. The Navy had been slow to react to the crumbling Soviet threat in terms of tactics and organization for battle. Adm. William Owens, a former vice chairman of the Joint Chiefs, wrote in 1995 that the Navy had been successful in carrying out its Desert Storm missions of strike warfare and maritime interdiction because "it was able to modify its operational doctrine that—along with the weapons, systems, and training it generated—proved ill-suited to the Gulf War."[245] He further asserted that the war did not present any of the expectations of the Maritime Strategy, which assumed that opposing aircraft, submarines, and other forces would contest U.S. control of the seas in one or more oceans.[246] Owens declared that all of the tactics associated with war at sea, such as fire-and-forget cruise missile combat and especially decentralized command and control, had been replaced by the "deadly skirmishing of littoral warfare."[247] He summarized the results of the Gulf War as follows:

> Both the Army and the Air Force had come home from the first of the new-era conflicts—Desert Storm—with their entering doctrines intact. The Air Land Battle concept that the Army developed after Vietnam held up well in Desert Storm's one hundred–hour ground campaign, and the concept of strategic bombardment, long an Air Force doctrinal belief, seemed vindicated by the victory. . . . But while the Army and the Air Force came out of the conflict believing that the operational concepts they had developed during the latter decades of the Cold War were still valid for the new era, this was more difficult for the Navy to do.[248]

Naval strategy needed more time to change. Adjustments had been under way since the late 1980s. One naval analyst, Ron O'Rourke, noted that the Navy had actually begun to move away from a purely Soviet focused strategy as early as mid-1988, when congressional and Reagan administration financial support for the six-hundred-ship navy began to wane. Noting one of the first public indications of this change, he cited a January 1988 speech to the National Press Club by Secretary of the Navy James Webb, who stated that the U.S. should reduce emphasis on Western Europe and the static defense of land areas in favor of more maneuverable forces that can "deploy and fight wherever they are needed without access to overseas land bases."[249] Adm. Carlisle Trost, however, remained firmly in support of the Maritime Strategy throughout his tenure as Chief of Naval Operations, from 1986 to 1990.[250]

In 1988 the Marine Corps began to study Third World contingency operations quite unlike the amphibious landings proposed for the Gulf War. The shift from an amphibious toward an expeditionary capability helped to move the Marine Corps away from the Navy's Maritime Strategy, and in terms of command and control arrangement, tended to put the Marines directly under the COCOM, not the Navy component commanders' authority. The Navy itself showed signs of adjusting in 1989 when William Ball, as outgoing Secretary of the Navy, emphasized the ability of the Navy to conduct operations independent of base access and overflight rights in his posture statement to Congress.[251] Secretary of the Navy H. Lawrence Garrett continued along this path in his fiscal year 1991 statement to Congress, emphasizing the capability of aircraft carrier battle groups, in particular, as an example of "flexible, mobile, maritime forces" that could be "on station [to] preserve our nation's position of strength around the globe."[252]

The Navy still faced a number of significant obstacles despite this emerging strategic transition between the Maritime Strategy and a new regional power-projection concept. This was an ironic situation given that just two decades earlier, CNO Zumwalt had emphasized the Navy's ability to provide forward presence.[253] CNO Adm. Arleigh Burke had argued in the wake of the Korean War that the Navy had the best force for waging limited war.[254] That notwithstanding, the Maritime Strategy was primarily oriented to the global threat presented by the Soviet Union and its Warsaw Pact allies. The disappearance of the Soviet threat took with it the justification for the six-hundred-ship navy as the numerical measure of necessary naval strength. In ground campaigns, like Desert Storm, submarines, carrier battle groups, and ships carrying Tomahawk missiles could obviously play a role, but the Navy needed to convince Congress how many could be supported in the post–Cold War environment.

While there was some confusion within the senior naval ranks on how to move forward as Admiral Owens suggested, the Navy's political-military strategists led the way to creating a post–Cold War strategic framework. They would do so in an environment organized by joint, rather than service, structures and controlled by a growing emphasis on force structure analysis as opposed to geopolitical strategy. Playing significant roles in this process were the absence of a unifying enemy in the form of the Soviet Union, the reorganizations in the Navy staff and the broader Department of Defense required under the Goldwater-Nichols Act, and the effects of RMA and its supposed archetype product, the Gulf War.

CHAPTER 5

MAKING THE CHANGE IN NAVY STRATEGY

By early 1990 it had become evident to many in the Navy's strategy community that a replacement was needed for the Maritime Strategy. The collapse of the Eastern European communist governments of the Warsaw Pact over the course of 1989 strongly suggested that even if the Soviet Union survived, the global threat it posed to Western interests would be diminished. The end of the Cold War as proclaimed by President George H. W. Bush and Soviet premier Mikhail Gorbachev in December 1989 at the conclusion of their summit in Malta accelerated the process.[1] The Maritime Strategy, developed over the course of the 1980s, focused mostly on meeting the global Soviet naval threat. Some kind of strategic reorganization along regional lines had appeared likely as early as 1987, when Joint Staff planners reviewing the national military strategy suggested a more regional and less global approach. This fell in line with the greater powers being given to regional commanders following implementation of the Goldwater-Nichols Act of 1986 introducing a joint structure for the military. The legislation serves as a useful reference point in the origins of post–Cold War strategic reorganization.[2]

Many of the same people who had been involved in the development of the Maritime Strategy in the 1980s led the way toward crafting a replacement. As in the 1980s the process relied on staff from the Office of the Chief of Naval

Operations (OPNAV), think tank experts and scholars, and senior officers. The changes brought about by the end of the Cold War, the Goldwater-Nichols Act, and the 1991 Gulf War, however, dictated a different product with much-reduced influence on both the Navy and national strategy compared with its predecessor. Geopolitical assumptions about the emerging post–Cold War world demanded a very different product. Littoral and land-based operations, rather than blue water naval strategy, would play the lead roles. Littoral warfare was a new concept for naval planners, some of whom held that the area of engagement extended from coastal regions to six hundred miles inland, which would include 80 percent of the world's capital cities and 95 percent of the global population.[3] The Marine Corps, previously just a component part of naval planning, was to be integral to developing the new strategy.

The inevitable post–Cold War drawdown in military strength complicated the development of a new strategy by demanding greater OPNAV focus on budget and programmatic functions. Thus, N8 (Resources, Warfare Requirements, and Assessments), the programmatic arm of the OPNAV staff, significantly increased its power and influence between 1991 and 1994 at the expense of the strategy and policy divisions. By 1994, a de facto strategy based on management of the force structure rather than meeting a threat applied as the Navy approved and disseminated successors to the Maritime Strategy to the fleet.[4]

The apparent success of joint approaches in fighting the Gulf War, in particular in regard to Army and Air Force operations, demanded that the Navy's follow-on strategy parallel that of the other services. This required a fundamental shift in the Navy's traditional geographic and threat-based strategy-planning process. Under the joint system, planners drew "lines in the water" that linked naval forces with land-based commanders more closely than at any time in the previous century. The end of the Cold War, the Goldwater-Nichols Act and resulting reorganization of the OPNAV staff, and the Gulf War had brought about significant changes by 1994. They fundamentally altered the Navy's strategy from a global focus in support of general U.S. interests to one delimited by maintenance of the newly imposed joint force structure within designated regional boundaries. These changes would dictate how the Navy viewed and conducted strategic planning for the next two decades.

THE MARINE CORPS: BEYOND THE MARITIME STRATEGY

The Marine Corps had begun moving past the Maritime Strategy even before the collapse of Soviet power. As commandant, Gen. P. X. Kelley had been a strong supporter of the strategy and its design of using Marine units on the flanks of a Central European conflict between the NATO alliance and the Warsaw Pact. This cooperative effort culminated in the Marine's 1985 Amphibious Warfare Strategy, a document that closely complemented the Navy's own Maritime Strategy. Amphibious Warfare was regularly practiced in Exercise Teamwork, in which U.S. Marines landed in Norway, collected prepositioned equipment, and deployed to counter a northern Soviet offensive.[5] Vice Adm. Henry Mustin, the NATO strike fleet commander in 1986, had assessed that the potential loss of Norway to the Soviets would "be a determining factor in the Battle of the Atlantic" and would represent as severe a loss as that of Iceland or Greenland.[6] In the event of war, operations were planned in the Mediterranean, in Greek Thrace, and in the Turkish Dardanelle Straits to prevent the Soviets from opening a second southern front against NATO forces.[7] There were also plans for landings on the Soviet Pacific coast to distract enemy forces from the main Warsaw Pact offensive on the Central European front.[8]

Kelley's successors had different ideas on working with the Navy. The naval historian John Hattendorf noted, "The U.S. Marine Corps momentarily moved away from concentration on such closely integrated, strategic, high-end warfighting cooperation with the Navy to develop more independent or Marine Corps–led operational concepts focused on lower-intensity regional contingencies."[9] Gen. Al Gray, who succeeded Kelley as commandant in 1987, brought with him a new ethos of maneuver warfare. Gray had seen one of the briefs by Col. John Boyd, USAF, on the "OODA loop"—observe, orient, decide, act—while serving as commander of the 2nd Marine Division at Camp Lejeune, North Carolina, in 1981,[10] after which he became a strong supporter of Boyd's maneuver warfare concepts. Boyd told the Marines to think "beyond the beachhead," on which they of course focused for amphibious operations, and instead to think about how best to engage the enemy regardless of the terrain.[11] He advanced the operational warfare ideas and practices of Gen. George

Patton and General Erwin Rommel, comparing their maneuvers across wide areas of territory to the set-piece amphibious warfare operations the Marines had conducted in the Pacific and during their counterinsurgency efforts in the Vietnam War.[12]

Gray established a maneuver warfare innovation group within the 2nd Marine Division, whose members included future CENTCOM leader Gen. Anthony Zinni; Col. Ray Smith, who would lead Marines in the Grenada invasion; and Col. James Myatt, who would lead a Marine division in the Gulf War.[13] One of Gray's instructors in this effort was Col. K. D. Schreiber, a German emigre whose father had served in the Wehrmacht in World War II and died fighting the Soviets on the eastern front. Schreiber had attended the German General Staff College, formerly the Kriegsakademie, and had been instructed in maneuver warfare techniques by German generals who had fought in World War II.[14] When Gray became Marine Corps commandant in 1987, his own maneuver warfare theories spread beyond the 2nd Marine Division and throughout the Corps. It attracted new disciples in one future commandant, Gen. Charles Krulak, and the influential Gen. Paul Van Riper.

The final product of Gray's efforts was the *FMFM 1: Warfighting*, the 1989 Marines Corp operational manual encapsulating his thoughts on the nature of war and in particular how the service should prepare for and execute combat operations. It represented a firm step away from the Marine Corps' amphibious roots and intended use during the Cold War. According to the manual, "The Fleet Marine Forces must be organized to provide forward-deployed or rapidly-deployable forces capable of mounting expeditionary operations in any environment. This means that, in addition to maintaining their unique amphibious capability, the Fleet Marine Forces must maintain a capability to deploy by whatever means is appropriate to the situation."[15] During the Gulf War, the Marine Corps 1st and 2nd Divisions were employed similarly to Army formations instead of for the amphibious warfare operations they had prepared to conduct as elements of the Maritime Strategy on the flanks of the Central European front. This change in operational employment distanced the Marines from the Navy in terms of strategy as well as operational art. It would have significant consequences for the Navy when it began the process of developing a replacement for the Maritime Strategy in late 1990.

"THE WAY AHEAD"

In 1990 Adm. Frank Kelso II brought to his job as Chief of Naval Operations (CNO) a perspective on naval organization that was perhaps as radical as that of Adm. Elmo Zumwalt (1970–74) two decades earlier. Kelso had read a book by the American management expert Edward Deming, attended one of the business guru's three-day seminars, and even invited him to dinner.[16] Kelso would later assert, "What most impressed me was his dedication to what he was doing. He was 90. He really did not have to work anymore, but he was dedicated to changing the work ethic in this country."[17] Deming's fourteen points to good management included elements that the CNO thought could be applied to the Navy, including eliminating slogans, work quotas, and annual evaluations that might not reflect an associate's true performance. In applying Deming's system to the Navy, Kelso restyled the idea of Total Quality Management into Total Quality Leadership (TQL), based on concerns that operational naval officers at sea self-identified as leaders and saw managers as people sitting behind a desk.[18] The Navy TQL program never got the support Kelso desired from most of the service's leadership: no one admiral was in charge of its implementation; Kelso never described in detail what the program was meant to achieve; and civilians dominated the department's TQL office, rather than the experienced military professionals necessary to translate TQL tenets to the operating forces. The program did not survive beyond Kelso's CNO tour (1990–94), but because it was implemented at the outset of his term, it left its mark on Kelso's reorganization of OPNAV and affected the creation and influence of " . . . From the Sea," the replacement for the Maritime Strategy.

One of Kelso's first projects was to establish a "strategic rationale for a continued robust USN force structure in the face of the impending CJCS [chairman of the Joint Chiefs of Staff] Base Force, which at the time [late 1990] was still speculative, though all but inevitable."[19] Remarks made 2 August 1990 by President George H. W. Bush at the Aspen Institute had clearly indicated that military budget cuts were coming. Before that, the JCS chairman, Gen. Colin Powell, had already taken steps to support a major downsizing, and Bush had approved the "draft blueprint for America's future defense configuration" during a 26 June 1990 Oval office meeting.[20] At that point, Kelso was still in the confirmation process to become CNO. Powell's determinations strongly disadvantaged Kelso's efforts at a counterproposal from the outset.

The U.S. Air Force had released "Global Reach–Global Power," its future concept study, in June 1990. It emphasized the combination of strategic nuclear deterrence, tactical fighter and bomber squadrons, and space and special operations forces. The document pegged the joint and especially allied applications of these forces as crucial to the uncertain security environment of the 1990s.[21] The document also succinctly identified the air service's primary missions in strategic deterrence, theater operation and power projection, mobility through airlift and tankers, controlling the "high ground" of space and securing partnerships with U.S. friends and allies.[22] The document firmly couched itself in the joint language ushered in by Goldwater-Nichols and gave the Air Force a solid foundation in the operational level of war in the post–Cold War era.[23] Kelso knew that the U.S. Navy needed a similar vision.[24]

In a 2002 interview with the naval historian Paul Stillwell, Kelso remarked, "Look, we understand that this is a different time, a different era, and we will try to accommodate to the change."[25] There were, in fact, a number of reasons for Kelso to be positive about a future that no longer included the Soviet Union as the Navy's singular opponent. The National Military Strategy of 1989 and Defense Planning Guidance for 1990 still suggested that substantial forward presence was required against a possible Soviet (or Russian) resurgence of power.[26] Morale within the service was high, and modernization efforts introduced in the latter part of the Carter administration and accelerated during the first Reagan administration had begun to reduce the average age of ships and aircraft.[27] It was in this setting that planning began for Kelso's attempt to alter the Navy's strategic course to suit the post–Cold War world.

"The Way Ahead," which appeared in the April 1991 issue of U.S. Naval Institute *Proceedings*, emerged as the first product in this effort.[28] A joint memo from Secretary of the Navy H. Lawrence Garrett III and Kelso on 23 August 1990 had provided general guidance to the project that culminated in the document. It laid out three challenges: the necessity of maintaining an adequate industrial base, identification of how many ships and aircraft the Navy could afford to operate in the future, and an examination of the size and shape of the twenty-first-century Navy with the replacement of current ships and aircraft.[29]

The two major decisions transmitted in Garrett and Kelso's memo would significantly differentiate the process of strategy development from the approach in the 1980s and the weight afforded to the Marines Corps in terms of strategic planning. OPNAV's OP-603 had begun an unofficial effort to replace the Maritime Strategy in early March 1990, some three months before Kelso's confirmation, but due to reluctance by the deputy CNO for OP-06 to assume control over the project, it was taken over and exploited by other OPNAV offices.[30] Capt. Richard Diamond, who led OP-603 from 1988 to 1991, would recall, "'The Way Ahead' had everything to do with the personalities/motives of the key players involved."[31]

The OP-06 incumbent in 1990 and 1991, Vice Adm. Robert "Barney" Kelly, was not as assertive in pushing for a defined role for his office as his predecessors had been.[32] In the absence of such pressure, Kelso appeared to turn to those officers with whom he had worked in the past decade, including OP-07 (Naval Warfare) leader Vice Adm. Paul David Miller, who had served with Kelso in John Lehman's Navy Secretariat.[33] In the end, although OP-603 continued to provide many of the concepts for the Navy's further strategy products in the early and mid-1990s, it was apparent that the strategy division had lost some of its influence. The deputy chief of Naval Operations in charge of OP-06 and the OP-603 staff did much of the work developing "The Way Ahead," but the deputy CNOs for OP-07 and OP-08 (Program Planning) claimed much of the credit. Personalities also made for different outcomes in terms of which OPNAV staff office could claim the new strategy products as their own.

In addition to other elements of OPNAV writing strategy, the Marine Corps was given a coequal place in crafting "The Way Ahead" at the instruction of Garrett and Kelso in their memo. This stood in contrast to the development of Maritime Strategy, to which the corps directly and considerably contributed, but only when and where invited by the Navy to do so and with a focus more purely on the Navy's ends. Commandant Gray and Lt. Gen. Carl Mundy, deputy commandant for Plans Policy and Operations, had been sending officers to work with OP-603 strategists and the CNO's personal office, OP-00K (Executive Panel), since CNO Adm. Carlisle Trost's tour (1986–90). The Marines began to exploit the contacts it had developed with OP-603 in recent years to put its stamp on the new document.

OP-603 had been the center of post–Maritime Strategy thinking since March 1990, when Diamond, at the time leading the office, hosted an unofficial Saturday meeting to discuss elements of a future strategy with interested OPNAV staff members.[34] The group agreed that the future of the U.S. Navy was about supporting combat ashore, being an emergency crisis response force in the world's littoral areas, and downgrading the previous focus on warfare disciplines like antisubmarine and antiair warfare.[35] The consensus of the Saturday study group was that a small team of officers from OPNAV and the Marine Corps commandant's office were best suited to produce a strategy that incorporated these concepts.[36] OP-603 also held a monthly, catered luncheon to which notable guest speakers on naval strategy were invited to generate discussion on strategy development.

Kelso struggled to catch up intellectually with General Powell's Joint Staff-driven post–Cold War force structure and strategy production effort that resulted in the Base Force concept, Powell's design for the post–Cold War military, in 1991. Powell assumed a nominal 20 to 25 percent cut in the strength of each of the armed forces,[37] including reducing the Navy to between 400 and 450 ships. The bulk of the planning for the Base Force had taken place before Bush's Aspen Conference appearance, leaving Kelso little time to produce a response. Trost, Kelso's predecessor, convinced that he had little chance of saving the Maritime Strategy's six-hundred-ship navy, had been working on a notional 450-ship force. Secretary of Defense Dick Cheney and much of Congress approved of the Base Force, and Kelso accepted it when he became CNO, convinced that the plan might be an "anchor against pressures for further reductions" in fleet size.[38] To acknowledge the need for reductions in force size, Kelso assured Congress that he would not seek new ship designs during his tenure as CNO.[39] Thus he had to explore avenues other than fleet size to articulate his vision for the post–Cold War Navy.

Prefacing Diamond's efforts at OP-603 and with the broader Washington, D.C., naval strategy community, beginning in 1989 monthly "strategy lunches" hosted by Capt. Jim Stark, an OP-603 alumnus and at the time director of OP-00K, had begun bringing together people in the Washington, D.C., naval community with political-military affairs backgrounds, dubbed the Ancient Mariners, to fuel discussion on post–Cold War naval operations.[40] Diamond would later credit Stark as the "founding genius of this important and much unheralded back-room shaper of Navy strategic thinking and cross-pollination."[41]

Diamond assigned Cdr. Michael Dunaway to be the lead author for OP-603's early unofficial effort to draft a theme document for the new strategic era. In a major difference from the 1980s process that produced the Maritime Strategy, Diamond directed Dunaway to work directly with Maj. Al Heim, USMC, from the commandant's Plans, Policies and Operations (PP&O), to combine Navy and Marine Corps thinking.[42] Heim's inclusion in the process was the natural product of the ongoing cooperative efforts among OPNAV's OP-603, OP-00K, and the Marine's PP&O.[43]

Diamond presented the results of this unofficial effort to his OP-06 boss, Kelly, on a plane ride back from the 1990 Global War Game.[44] It had been a challenge from Diamond to get Kelly's attention for his new strategic concept. According to Diamond, Kelly was a reluctant leader of OP-06, holding the "pol/mil weenies" under his authority in disdain.[45] Kelly saw himself as an "operator," not a staff officer; many in OP-06 and OP-603 thought him to be "more concerned with protecting the carrier/naval aviation community" than making radical revisions to the Maritime Strategy. He preferred to take direction from the CNO on every issue rather than offer new ideas himself. His staff viewed him as a "speed bump" to new ideas who often responded "Who asked for this?" when presented with new ideas.[46]

At one point Diamond had confronted Kelly on how his posture and remarks had lowered morale in the offices under his authority, and although Kelly admitted that Diamond was probably correct, he did not change his behavior. Diamond later said that OP-603's end-of-the-week, Friday afternoon celebrations were called "pol/mil weenie roasts," a term that Kelly did not find amusing.[47] Kelly's disinterest in OP-603's ideas perhaps relegated them to the duration of a boring plane ride back to Washington, D.C., but what made the flight significant was that Kelly had invited a fellow passenger, Vice Adm. Paul David Miller, deputy CNO for OP-07, to also view Diamond's brief. Miller, like Kelso, had previously been a member of Secretary Lehman's close staff. After commanding the Seventh Fleet in Japan, he returned to Washington, along with Kelso and a number of other former Lehman-era staff officers, including Cdr. Rick Wright, now Miller's flag writer and "idea man." Capt. Daniel Murphy, who drafted Trost's 450-ship navy plan, became Kelso's executive assistant, and Capt. William "Wild Bill" Center, another OP-603 alumnus, joined Miller's staff as its unofficial "briefing builder." Center's very "advanced" Apple Macintosh PC churned out "colorful and engaging" briefing slides for which the OPNAV graphics shop at that time could produce no equal.[48]

Miller decided that the OP-603 brief had merit but needed "catchy graphics and a snappy title."[49] He wanted to move it forward in his office rather than wait for Kelly to promote it within OPNAV. He asked Kelly for a copy of Diamond's briefing and proceeded to develop it using his own staff. Diamond later suggested that Kelly might have been more interested in his upcoming appointment to the four-star Pacific Fleet Command rather than, as Diamond recalled, having OP-603 "bore him with the history of Western Christendom and never give him quantitative information."[50] Miller proved to be successful in his advocacy, with the 23 August memo from Garrett and Kelso tasking his OP-07 with the development of what would became "The Way Ahead."[51]

OP-603 staff, including Diamond and Cdr. Paul Giarra, remained the primary briefing presenters despite OP-07 having been given overall authority. They delivered a presentation to Commandant Gray on 7 September 1990 at Marine headquarters. Gray was, in Diamond's words, "very enthusiastic" about the brief and made five specific recommendations:[52]

- inclusion of an amphibious strategy, or he would not recommend the document's use to the CNO;
- inclusion of a message to "John Q. Public" that the team of the Navy and Marine Corps could do the job in question, that is, forward deployed operations in littoral spaces;
- for the brief to become "an enduring comprehensive strategy document" that would be "widely distributed and not programmatic";
- mention not only joint operations, but combined operations with allies as well; and
- a focus "on the larger strategic thrust of maritime issues" to make the document viable and to earn his and the CNO's approval.[53]

The general also included some observations on the operational aspects of the document, including sealift, deployment patterns, and force components. Of note, no Navy flag officer attended the brief with Gray and the drafters, but perhaps the outcome was preordained given the senior officers personally involved in its creation.[54] Diamond recalled that CNO Kelso, Vice Admiral Miller, and General Gray worked out the details after the briefings on "The Way Ahead" around the kitchen table in Kelso's Washington Navy Yard quarters during several weekend work sessions. Secretary Garrett lent his name to the document after agreement on the basic elements.[55]

Unlike the Maritime Strategy, which had begun life as a classified product, "The Way Ahead" was unclassified and published in an open forum, in the U.S. Naval Institute *Proceedings*. The various authors of the Maritime Strategy, as well as the naval historian John Hattendorf, have suggested that the older strategy's distribution in classified format had helped to strengthen its influence within the uniformed Navy, as classified documents contained more pertinent, operations details.[56] Broader dissemination enabled by an unclassified document was useful for influencing outsiders, such as academics and experts at think tanks focused on strategic issues, but uniformed audiences must be won first through a classified version that in the words of two Navy strategists "shows the insiders that we are serious."[57] The Maritime Strategy gained much of its initial credibility with Navy officers when it was presented as a classified document. That there was no classified version of "The Way Ahead" might be a factor in it not being as successful in terms of influencing serving officers.

"The Way Ahead" attempted to identify and deal with uncertain conditions. It was in direct response to Bush's Aspen statement that future U.S. defense policy would be based on "deterrence, forward presence, and crisis response and force reconstitution."[58] It emphasized traditional elements of naval strategy—such as power-projection capability and the need for a surge capacity to "get adequate combat power rapidly to the scene of action"[59]—and addressed them in the "joint and combined environment" that Gray had demanded, but also acknowledged the need for flexibility in active employment due to the 25 percent force structure reduction imposed by Powell's Base Force concept. The strategy laid out shifted the Navy from geographic or threat-specific force requirements to support of the president's national security strategy, which was subject to rapid change.[60]

Despite the document's origins within the OPNAV staff, it turned out to be more of a success for the Marine Corps. The Navy withstanding, the other services had accepted the concept of expeditionary warfare for more than two decades. According to Dunaway, who drafted "The Way Ahead," "The USMC more or less won the idea that all naval operations were inherently expeditionary." It represented "an important concession for the Navy to come around to the USMC way of viewing the world."[61] Perhaps this resulted from the Marine Corps' confident understanding of its place in the world at the beginning of the post–Cold War era. Gray had spent the 1980s developing Boyd's maneuver warfare concepts. Dunaway called Gray's *FMFM 1* "the best and probably the only true neo-Clausewitzian warfighting strategy written by any of the services in the last 40 years, Maritime Strategy notwithstanding."[62]

"The Way Ahead" represents Kelso's first attempt to recapture the initiative in defining the Navy's size and roles and missions largely lost through Powell's Base Force concept. According to Hattendorf, the strategy was prescient in its expectations for the future, even if its influence was short-lived.[63] The naval historian Peter Haynes suggests that the release of "The Way Ahead" just a month after the end of Operation Desert Storm minimized its overall impact on the Navy's process of rethinking its purpose after the Cold War.[64] While opinion on the Navy's performance was divided, enough OPNAV staff members were convinced that the full capabilities of naval forces were not exploited during the Gulf War. This alone was enough to cast some doubt on the influence of the new strategy.[65] It also did not set firm priorities against which to budget for the near or immediate future.[66] This lack of direct connection between budget and force structure would plague "The Way Ahead" and future Navy strategy products for the next two decades.[67]

Kelso was dissatisfied with "The Way Ahead": "The article itself badly disappointed me, because by the time it came out it looked like, 'Well, hell, all you're doing is writing an article to say what the status quo is at the time you've written the article.' So that disappointed me a lot, because I really wanted to lead the curve, not be hanging behind it all the time."[68] The doctrine had limited direct influence in the short term—quickly waning after its creators resigned, retired, or transferred to duties outside OPNAV.[69] Official Navy posture statements to Congress did not mention it after 1993.[70] The naval strategist Capt. Peter Swartz has suggested that "The Way Ahead" was better suited to the 2000s than the 1990s.[71] Having defined general naval requirements and responsibilities, it gained in importance in the next quarter century.

"THE NAVY POLICY BOOK"

The next step in the post–Cold War Navy strategy development process was another unclassified document released in May 1992 that focused more on internal process than strategy and was in part driven by the Navy's need to respond to the allegations of sexual abuse and harassment brought to light by the Tailhook scandal. "The Navy Policy Book"—also influenced by CNO Kelso's interest in Deming's Total Quality Management theories but taking as its model a United Parcel Service policy document—generated a broad base of input from the fleet.[72] Less than forty pages long and billed as "a single reference of the most important guiding principles of our Navy,"[73] it included chapters on vision, guiding principles, and strategic guidance, but did not qualify as a strategy document. Captain Diamond, who penned the document's strategy and policy chapters, referred to it as "the Company owner's manual," providing a "concise summary of what the Navy was about to the rank and file sailor or officer."[74] Capt. Judy Myers, USN (Ret.), who helped draft elements of the document as a commander in N00K (Executive Panel), described the document as Kelso's effort to "institutionalize what the Navy was as an organization and that people, accountability, responsibility, and good stewardship were critically important to us and in fact part of our culture."[75]

"The Navy Policy Book," generally well received, represented Kelso's second attempt to recapture the initiative in developing the Navy's strategy and operational concepts in the post–Cold War world. Although not a strategic work, its organization around core values and concepts served to make it a common point of reference for future concepts.[76] The Naval Institute *Proceedings* book review praised it for its focus on people but also called it a series of "homilies."[77]

The document's publication coincided with the unveiling of the report by the Navy's inspector general and the Naval Investigative Service detailing events at the Thirty-Fifth Annual Tailhook Association Symposium on naval and Marine Corps aviation, held in September 1991 in Las Vegas, where, investigators alleged, a "reported 83 women and 7 men had been the victims of assault and sexual harassment."[78] As noted, "The Navy Policy Book" was in part written in response to the Tailhook scandal, but also in light of other events from the late 1980s and early 1990s that "called actual Navy values into question."[79] The release of several Navy and Department of Defense reports on the Tailhook scandal along with reporting on previous Navy mishaps and corruption probes, including ongoing investigations into the USS *Iowa*'s turret explosion and the FBI's "Ill Wind" investigation of Navy contracting procedures, distracted Kelso from his internal process and strategy improvement efforts.[80]

BUILDING ". . . FROM THE SEA"

Kelso's third and most successful attempt to shape the post–Cold War strategic environment was the 1992 white paper ". . . From the Sea." He ordered the document for a variety of reasons, but most specifically in response to the failure of "The Way Ahead" and "The Navy Policy Book" to convince Navy and Marine Corps leaders, as well as the Joint Staff and the Office of the Secretary of Defense, that the Navy was indeed adapting in accordance with the altered strategic environment.[81]

". . . From the Sea" built on several efforts, including those of OP-603 (Strategic Concepts), analysis of the Navy's performance during Operation Desert Storm, projected force requirements needed for the post–Cold War environment, and the findings of outside groups and think tanks on future U.S. Navy strategy and operations. The concept put forward in it continued to emphasize traditional U.S. Navy roles, including the need to "command the seas" and ensure freedom of commercial maritime passage.[82] The main thrust of the document, however, was its focus on joint operations in littoral areas where expeditionary forces would do most of the fighting, including land-based operations by Marines or other ground forces. Its concept of "maneuver from the sea" was described as being much like the Army and Marine Corps concept of maneuver warfare on land. A new naval doctrine would be developed to support the concept of sea-based maneuver warfare.[83] ". . . From the Sea" expanded on concepts developed for "The Way Ahead" and used the teamwork methodology of "The Navy Policy Book" to implement the new strategy across the Navy and Marine Corps.

". . . From the Sea" served its purpose in providing the Navy a vision for the post–Cold War era. Hattendorf calls it a successful effort in that ". . . From the Sea" became an influential document among senior naval leaders and defense civilian experts.[84] It constituted a consensus about what the Navy did to replace the unraveling 1980s Navy identity forged around the Maritime Strategy.[85] The paper also legitimized and focused the Navy on the mission of land attack warfare.[86] Unlike Kelso's previous attempts at strategy and policy, ". . . From the Sea" survived his retirement and that of the Navy secretaries associated with its creation. In fact, its influence endured in Navy planning documents for the next two decades.

Although perhaps successful in creating a strategic vision for the post–Cold War Navy, ". . . From the Sea" could also be considered a long-term failure as far as sustaining strategic thought within the Navy. Many felt it unwise to suggest that the United States held "preeminent control of the seas," as it claimed.[87] Others also argued that it gave the Marine Corps too much influence and control over naval forces. ". . . From the Sea" referenced joint operations but said little about how the Navy and Marine Corps might integrate their efforts. Fans of the revolution in military affairs faulted it for insufficient transformative thinking and for reflecting Cold War biases.[88] Like "The Way Ahead" and "The Navy Policy Book," ". . . From the Sea" was also presented as an unclassified document and as such lacked the institutional influence among serving officers that a classified version might have generated.[89] Most significant, ". . . From the Sea" had no direct connection or influence over the Navy's budget and programming process.[90] The service's budget requests are its primary connection to Congress. Since the 1980s Maritime Strategy, the Navy had used its strategies primarily to market specific programs rather than to bolster strategic planning. This lack of connection between Navy strategy and program funding would prove to be a fatal flaw for not only ". . . From the Sea," but also for successive Navy strategic documents to this day.[91]

The end of the Cold War removed the unifying, common threat of the Soviet Union and replaced it with uncertain regional threats. The Goldwater-Nichols Act of 1986 gave greater authority to regional commanders and reduced the need for a service-based strategy; the 1991 Gulf War soon showcased the power that a regional commander could wield. Service chiefs like Kelso, having lost their strategic authority, ultimately turned to the business of preserving force structure and devising operational art for its employment under regional commander control.

"... From the Sea" grew from the same desire to create a successor to the Maritime Strategy that produced "The Way Ahead." Additional impetus stemmed from the OP-603 brief that Capt. Dick Diamond delivered to Kelso in July 1991 that led to the CNO becoming distraught and then enraged by future force projections that the Navy's force structure would plummet over the next twenty years.[92] Despite OP-07, through Vice Admiral Miller, co-opting Diamond's brief for the core of "The Way Ahead," the success of the document meant, as Diamond saw it, "We in OP-603 were not completely out of the picture yet." Given this, Diamond further stated, "We continued to work the OP-603, Headquarters Marine Corps, and OP-00K alliance and continued to refine our brief."[93] In the wake of "The Way Ahead," Diamond's team regained strategic momentum with the introduction of new leadership and a new task—a broad OPNAV effort to specify the naval force structure required for the world described in "The Way Ahead." As for leadership, Vice Adm. Leighton "Snuffy" Smith, an OP-095 (Naval Warfare) and Strategic Studies Group (SSG) alumnus, replaced Kelly as director of OP-06, and Rear Adm. Ted Baker became Smith's deputy, leading OP-60.

The Naval Force Capabilities Planning Effort (NFCPE), the project for determining the requisite force structure, was envisioned as an easy exercise to first confirm whether the Navy's existing force structure was up to the challenges of "The Way Ahead" world. It ended up becoming a months-long process, stretching from November 1991 through March 1992. Kelso assigned Smith, in his new capacity, to take charge of developing a coordinated response to the issues posed by the NFCPE.[94] Smith initially questioned whether a coordinated document was even possible. He told Diamond at his checkout meeting before leaving to assume command of the cruiser USS *Bunker Hill* in Yokosuka, Japan, "Based on my thirty-five years of experience I can assure you that this here Littoral Warfare Shit ain't never gonna fly in this man's Navy."[95]

Despite whatever initial objections Smith may have had, he assumed his task with enthusiasm. He enlisted his deputy OP-06, Rear Adm. Jim Cossey, and OP-60's Baker, in the effort, and eventually expanded the flag oversight leadership of the project to five officers, including two Marines.[96] Navy and Marine Corps officers at the O-4 to O-6 rank did the bulk of the work, however, along with analysts from the Center for Naval Analyses (CNA). Secretary of the Navy Garrett instructed the group to "create a new, zero-based plan for naval forces spanning the next fifteen to twenty years and provide, in effect, an entirely new strategic concept for the naval forces of the United States."[97]

According to Swartz, the purpose of ". . . From the Sea" was to leave the 1980s Maritime Strategy behind, provide a basis for the 450-ship fleet needed for the post–Cold War era, and to provide the Navy with something akin to the Air Force's "Global Reach–Global Power" doctrine. The Navy also sought to prove that it did not need input from the Joint Staff and Chairman Powell to determine its force structure and employment.[98] ". . . From the Sea: Preparing the Naval Service for the 21st Century" would be released in September 1992 and published subsequently in U.S. Naval Institute *Proceedings*.[99]

A Bumpy Start

The NFCPE process that developed the new strategy involved a fairly large and talented group of field grade Navy and Marine Corps officers and CNA analysts who were led by Vice Admiral Smith and Lt. Gen. Hank Stackpoole, Marine Corps PP&O chief, as cochairs. Rear Admiral Baker and Maj. Gen. Matthew Caulfield, USMC, provided direct oversight of the team.[100] The project had three phases, with the first running from October through December 1991. According to Capt. Edward A. Smith, who took part in the effort, the first phase attempted to determine "what had and had not changed in the national security environment and what the implications of the changes were for the roles and missions of naval forces." This phase included war games, flag officer conferences, and multiple working groups organized to evaluate the new strategic order from a zero-based analysis that essentially looked at what the "naval forces did for the national good that justified the money taxpayers spent to build and to maintain them."[101]

Bill Manthorpe, deputy director of Naval Intelligence, gave one of the most significant briefings in the first phase.[102] He contended that notwithstanding the collapse of the Soviet Union, "High seas threats presented themselves at regular intervals of about every 25 years."[103] This put Manthorpe and others at odds with the conventional wisdom that a fundamental, history-changing event had occurred with the Soviet Union's demise. One person who disagreed with Manthorpe, CNA analyst Thomas Barnett, wrote that the brief led to the division of NFCPE participants into three camps: the "transitioneers," who believed the United States should deal with small threats in order to ensure a transition to a safer post–Cold War world; the "big stick" contingent, who wanted to prepare for the next Operation Desert Storm against a regional hegemon; and the "Cold Worriers," who thought the United States should follow Manthorpe's advice and prepare for the rise of the next great superpower that might "sneak up" on it in the coming decades.[104] Manthorpe later wrote, "Would the Pentagon help to build a 'new world order' in this fractured security environment crammed full of lesser includeds, or would it retreat from this fractious world to focus on 'the Big One'? The answer is, the Pentagon tried to do both."[105]

In the short term, the Navy made use of Barnett's assessment if for no other reason than to assume the mantle of change that perhaps fit the zeitgeist of the immediate post–Cold War era. The first document from the NFCPE, "The Strategic Concept of the Naval Service," incorporated strands from all three of the camps identified by Barnett. Smith was not impressed with the product, describing Baker's effort on the document as "a rehash of the old one [i.e., The Maritime Strategy], and it wasn't very good."[106] The working groups returned to CNA, their base of operations, to continue their deliberations, but Smith remained dissatisfied. "I went out and got updates, and I just wasn't happy. I mean, it just wasn't clicking," he later said.[107] Smith ultimately decided to condense the NFCPE working group:

> Finally one day I was just totally frustrated. They'd had working groups, and I called them together and I said, "Okay, goddam it, here's the deal guys. Let's condense this thing. We don't have to solve world hunger right here. What we need to do is find out what the Navy's going to do, how it's going to operate. If it's not going to be threats, then do we build a capabilities-based force? And I don't want to go threat-shopping. That's not what we are here for, so we're not looking to find a problem

> with the Chinese or the Pakistani's or whomever, but think about the kinds of missions that we're going to have to do and break those things down, and let's see if we can attack it that way."[108]

Smith's comments are perhaps unsurprising given the initial guidance he received from CNO Kelso, who later recalled, "The Navy need[ed] a planning document that's credible in the political and military arena."[109] The Maritime Strategy had done the job in the 1980s, but Kelso noted, "Well, here we are going into a new world with no planning document. I wanted a piece of paper that we could use and sell to Congress and to the Joint Staff of the OSD [Office of the Secretary of Defense]— that this is what the Navy's job was in the years ahead of us."[110] Thus it should be expected that Smith would rebuff any repetition of past great power strategies.

Smith's rejection of "The Strategic Concept of the Naval Service" constituted the end of phase one of the NFCPE. Phase two involved a smaller team and featured new leadership in the form of Col. Thomas Wilkerson, USMC, who had recently been selected for but not yet promoted to brigadier general. Wilkerson was no stranger to the business of maritime strategy writing, having worked on the second edition of the Maritime Strategy in 1983. Smith and Stackpoole remained in their supervisory positions and a "gang of four" Navy and Marine Corps flag officers—Rear Adm. Dave Oliver, Rear Adm. Phil Coady, Gen. Charlie Wilhelm, and Rear Admiral Baker—nominally supervised the effort. Wilkerson became the driving force behind the second phase of the NFCPE, and the supervisory flag officers gave him significant autonomy in the process. Wilkerson, assisted by Capt. Rusty Petrea, USN, and Lt. Col. Chip Gregson, USMC, did most of the work.[111] They totally rewrote "The Strategic Concept of the Naval Service," with Marine Corps requirements figuring equally, and later predominantly, in the thinking of some of the naval officers involved.[112] The product from Wilkerson's work was forwarded to Smith, who along with Maj. Gen. Charles Krulak, USMC Combat Development Command, continued to refine it.

Smith, much happier with the new product, later recalled, "Rusty [CAPT Petrea] and his crowd had come up with a new approach—much like I had been thinking. We were going to listen to this presentation about 'From the

Sea.' After it was done, I had basically heard in a very concise outlined form pretty much what I had told them earlier."[113] Unfortunately, the new concept did not have a good name. The Air Force had in Smith's opinion, "One hell of a bumper sticker with 'Global Reach, Global Power.'"[114] Smith wanted something similar and even offered a week of free leave to his staff for a winning name. While Smith did not claim responsibility for much of the content of the final product, he did claim credit for the name:

> I had this document in my briefcase and I was sitting at my breakfast table at home in Fairfax, Virginia, one morning about 5:00 o'clock [*sic*] eating my Cheerios or whatever the hell I was eating. The briefcase was open, and right on top of it was this piece of paper, and it had "Engagement from the Sea." It had several different titles, "Engagement from the Sea," "Power from the Sea," "Diplomacy from the Sea," and I looked at that thing and suddenly I said, "You know, it could be anything from the sea. So why don't I just put three dots down here: '. . . From the Sea.' You can fill in what you want. And I did it, and that's how we came up with the name."[115]

The review process did not, however, end with Smith's triumphal naming of the document. Phase three involved more rewriting of the document, with Smith, Petrea, Krulak, Owens, and Sean O'Keefe, the new Secretary of the Navy, all making contributions. Cdr. Jim Stavridis gave the document a final polishing with support from Scott Truver, a contractor.[116] Smith submitted the final product to CNO Kelso and Commandant Mundy, who approved it and sent it on to the acting Secretary of the Navy, Dan Howard, who had replaced Garrett following his resignation in mid-1992 in the wake of the Tailhook scandal. Smith and Howard did not get on well. Smith recalled, "So I took this thing down [to the Secretary of the Navy's office] and this is where I got into a shouting match with Dan Howard. He didn't like it "' . . . From the Sea,' and unfortunately it was going to be a Secretary of the Navy kind of thing and not the CNO."[117]

After Congress confirmed O'Keefe to replace Garrett in July 1992, Smith continued his battle to get the document approved. Despite ongoing disagreements, there was also progress. Cdr. Jim Stavridis, then on O'Keefe's staff, served as an additional editor and go-between for the increasingly frustrated

Smith and the new secretary. Smith recollected, "Well, finally it got to be an editing contest between O'Keefe's office and my office, and the guy doing the editing up there was Jim Stavridis; I think he was a Commander at the time. Smart guy. I recall a couple of times we'd get on the phone and I'd just get so damned frustrated. I mean literally I was having chest pains, and my blood pressure was probably off the top of the scale, and I'd just slam the phone down and stomp around."[118]

After some additional changes, Smith resubmitted the document, Kelso and Mundy again approved it, and it went to O'Keefe for approval. While attending a war game in Newport, Smith received the message from O'Keefe's office telling him that it would be approved if Smith removed a seven-page section on the importance of "forward presence/engagement" of naval forces.[119] Smith reluctantly agreed, and the final, signed version was saved on Commander Stavridis' computer.[120] The effort pleased Smith, who later said the best compliment he received while on active naval service was for his work on ". . . From the Sea":

> Kelso had a flag conference in D.C. It wasn't all the flag officers. I think it was just three stars. I briefed the first time there in the barrel, and the idea was once we got this thing written we were going to brief it and get flag officer buy-in. I briefed "From the Sea" to these three stars, and there were some two stars in there and four stars as well—probably about 25 guys in that room. I remember when I was in the briefing and I was looking around the room, and I realized I had their attention. I continued on and finished the briefing. And there was this pause and I said, "Now, I'll be happy to take any questions." And they applauded. I went home that night and I told my wife. I said, I think I've gotten the highest compliment that you can get. These guys applauded after I finished my presentation. I'd never heard of it, never seen it before in my life, and so that was the story.

Fans, Critics, and Peacetime Presence

". . . From the Sea" represented a major turning point in U.S. naval policy. Its opening paragraph boldly stated, "The world has changed dramatically in the last two years [1990–92] , and America's national security policy has also changed. As a result, the priorities of the Navy and Marine Corps have shifted, leading to this broad assessment of the future direction of our maritime forces."[121] The slogan for the new concept was "Naval Expeditionary Forces—Shaped for Joint Operations Operating 'Forward . . . from the Sea'—Tailored for National Needs."[122] It stood as a fundamental step away from open ocean warfighting as envisioned in the Maritime Strategy and movement toward joint operations in a littoral zone that some planners conceived as extending six hundred-plus nautical miles inland from the coast.[123]

" . . . From the Sea" also called for the unprecedented establishment of a Naval Doctrine Command. The Navy had in the past avoided specific doctrines for naval forces. According to Wayne Hughes, operations analysis professor at the Naval Postgraduate School, "In part it had come at the urging of the Marine Corps, which saw the advantage of applying 'operational art,' standing between strategy and tactics."[124] The command, established in 1993, published its first work, "Naval Warfare," Naval Doctrine Publication-1, in spring 1994. Modeled on previous joint publications, it would be the Navy's attempt at something approaching the successful doctrinal publications of the Army (*FM 100-1*), Air Force (*AFM 1-1*), and the Marine Corps (*FMFM 1*).[125]

This new strategic situation and environment played directly to the strength of naval forces. ". . . From the Sea" stated that naval forces would operate forward at advanced conditions of readiness that did not require the additional staging and advanced basing needed by the other services to operate in similar environments. Naval forces were swift, self-sustaining, armed with a considerable strike capability, and possessed of the necessary command and control sophistication to host either a naval or joint force commander.[126] The Naval Expeditionary Force represented the joint force's connection to its supply base in the continental United States, a connection ". . . From the Sea" emphasized: "Forward logistics, prepositioning, and strategic sealift, coupled with strategic airlift, are the keys to force sustainment."[127]

Although acknowledging joint operations, ". . . From the Sea" focused much more on the Navy and Marine joint partnership than relations with the Army and the Air Force. In addition, its references to joint operations with the other services did not necessarily mean full integration.[128] Vice Admiral Smith later said that Army and Air Force input had not been sought for ". . . From the Sea."

Instead, the Navy leadership considered congressional and Joint Staff support as more relevant in gaining acceptance of the document.[129]

Professor Jan Breemer of NPS viewed ". . . From the Sea" as part of the rehabilitation of the surface warfare branch of the Navy after years of being secondary to the service's naval aviation and submarine components.[130] The surface navy's Aegis system SPY-1 phased array radar and accompanying combat system had originated in the defense of carrier battle groups but grew to become a complete battle force integration system. Mated with the new Tomahawk cruise missiles, a weapon on which development began in the 1970s for the surface force on the order of CNO Zumwalt, it offered a potent, unmanned strike alternative to conventional aircraft. During the NFCPE process, key members of the group, including naval aviators, offered support for the idea of surface force land attack as a ". . . From the Sea" component.[131] A consensus emerged on the dispersed capability of Tomahawk land attack cruise missiles fired from surface force and submarine platforms as a primary enabling capability for the " . . . From the Sea" concept.[132]

The Navy and especially the Marine Corps leadership were happy with " . . . From the Sea." Kelso later stated, "At the headquarters level we needed to establish a strategy and program base on which to build for the future. And in my judgement the short white paper '. . . From the Sea' was a pretty good start."[133] Kelso spread the credit noting, "Snuffy [Vice Admiral Smith] had a significant role in it. But the basic document, the basic idea of the document was written by a bunch of Marine O-6s and Navy O-6s, and commanders and lieutenant commanders. I mean, it's the kind of document that had a lot of fingers in it, and a lot of people now would like to claim credit for it. I don't think any one person deserves credit for the document."[134] Kelso also praised Secretary O'Keefe for his efforts in making ". . . From the Sea" a useful product. He acknowledged, "Mr. O'Keefe deserves a lot of credit for pushing to get it published. I think he recognized from sitting down in OSD that the Navy needed something like this in order to be able to get OSD focused on what the Navy was going to do, and so he pushed hard to get the document out early in his tour as Secretary of the Navy."[135]

Marine leaders were perhaps even more pleased. In a January 1994 article in U.S. Naval Institute *Proceedings*, Commandant Mundy lauded the document's ideas on command and control, battlespace dominance, power projection ashore, and sustainment of forces. In particular, he cited the willingness to allow the "blurring of the line between the land and the sea" and that "the commander may need to be a Marine instead of a sailor, depending on the circumstances."[136] In regard to Marine command, he added, "A good case in point would be peace enforcement operations like those in Somalia, where there was no serious threat to the naval task force and where the focus of all efforts was clearly on events ashore."[137]

There was of course plenty to disagree with in regard to the content of ". . . From the Sea." Kelso remarked, "You could find somebody who did not like something in it as well as somebody who liked something in it."[138] He acknowledged, "A lot of naval officers felt it had too much Marine in it," but at the same time, "The Marines wanted more Marine ideas."[139] Kelso later asserted that the document did not have enough "blue water warfare" concepts, stating, "Yes, it was absolutely focused on littorals, and it did not have enough about carriers and submarines and whatever."[140]

Vice Admiral Smith regarded ". . . From the Sea" as the high point of his nearly four-year assignment as deputy CNO for OP-06. He later said, "There were a lot of other things that happened in my tour as N3/N5 [OP-06's successor], but that was clearly one of the biggest. I think if I made a mark, it was there."[141] Frank Hoffman, a Reserve officer and national security analyst, was one among the Marines who believed that they did not receive sufficient attention. "Most Marines were fairly excited by the hope that the Navy would finally recognize the changes in the international security environment and finally break loose from its strategic stupor and internal parochialism," he wrote, noting disappointment with the lack of focus on peacetime presence operations. Similar to concerns voiced by Smith, Hoffman observed that the document stresses the "potential application of Navy and Marine forces as the nation's primary crisis response tool and studiously ignores presence and peacetime tasks in support of political and economic objectives."[142] Many critics within the Navy considered it a major shortcoming to remove, as ordered removed by O'Keefe, the section on the peacetime presence mission.

Capt. Edward Smith, an original member of the NFCPE, described this negative view of ". . . From the Sea" as perhaps influenced by those outside the sea services who assume that "navies fought navies" as their primary function.[143] The collapse of the Soviet Union should have logically curtailed the need for a larger naval force, but the NFCPE effort found quite the opposite to be the case. The NFCPE examined the period of 1946 to 1991 and discovered that in the 325 instances in which U.S. armed forces had responded to a crisis of some kind, only 12 percent involved encounters with Soviet armed forces.[144] The NFCPE group also found that 83 percent of all crisis response efforts from 1945 to 1991 involved naval forces, 95 percent of responses from 1986 to 1991 included naval forces, and 70 percent of all of them from 1977 to 1991 required aircraft carrier support.[145] The forward presence of naval forces as being crucial to the support of U.S. overseas interests would, therefore, appear to be clear, so why did O'Keefe order the presence mission excluded?

History played one role in the decision. In a 1993 CNA paper, Capt. Linton Brooks, one of the Maritime Strategy authors, reminded readers that although Navy officers recognized the importance of peacetime presence it was of secondary importance in the documents at hand but "allowed the Navy to prepare for war."[146] Brooks also noted that in periods of budget shortfalls, presence forces tended to be cut more readily than those purely dedicated to warfighting.[147] The influence of Congress and defense policy experts also played a role. Combat requirements, not presence efforts, drove the defense-spending process, and in the absence of a Department of Defense document identifying "presence" as a mission, the Navy had to focus on warfighting requirements to secure its budget requests. In a Program Objective Memorandum (POM), the document listing all of the Navy's program requirements, O'Keefe specifically cited the need to make the Navy's strategic concepts match its budget requests.[148]

Criticism over the lack of forward presence in ". . . From the Sea" proved to be relatively short-lived. The incoming administration of President Bill Clinton ordered the Bottom-Up Review to assess defense requirements in March 1993. The final report on this effort, published in October 1993, included language similar to both "The Way Ahead" and ". . . From the Sea" in terms of the importance of forward naval presence: "To address the new regional dangers and seize new opportunities, we have developed a multifaceted strategy based on defeating aggressors in major regional conflicts, maintaining overseas presence to deter conflicts and provide regional stability, and conducting smaller-scale intervention operations, such as peace enforcement, peacekeeping, humanitarian assistance, and disaster relief to further U.S. interests and objectives."[149]

The Bottom-Up Review also noted that at the operational level, forward presence required enough naval force to meet two nearly simultaneous major regional conflicts and also to support other, smaller regional operations. Overseas presence was recognized as a major mission, especially in terms of aircraft carriers. The big flattops were seen as flexible assets, and their ability to operate independently from shore bases made them well suited to overseas presence operations, especially in areas like the Persian Gulf, where land-based military infrastructure was relatively scarce and underdeveloped. The naval force size specified by the Bottom-Up Review reflected the requirements of overseas presence as well as warfighting in two major conflicts. Such specific support for presence as a distinct military mission gave the Navy the justification it needed to further articulate this mission area and use it as the basis for budgetary decisions.[150] Kelso clarified the impact of this decision:

> They (the Clinton administration) accepted the fact that if the Navy was going to be forward deployed on a continuous basis, that was a basis for force levels. In other words, in the past the only thing that had been acceptable was, "How much do you need for when you're going to fight?" And that had been large enough to take care of the forward deployment base. But as you get smaller and smaller, that is no longer large enough. So we were allowed to use the idea that if it takes *X* destroyers to keep one forward deployed, you need *X* for one on a continuous basis or how many carriers and all that sort of thing. I was a significant recognition of the need for forward-deployed forces within the Navy.[151]

The service would further expand on the need for presence as a funded mission in the follow-on to "... From the Sea," the aptly titled "Forward ... From the Sea" in November 1994.[152]

" ... From the Sea" also faced analysis and criticism from national and international security scholars and experts. NPS professor Breemer called it the "end of naval strategy," but also conceded that the Navy's new strategy was well within historical norms. He believed that the remnants of the Soviet

Navy could at best "survive" and that the United States was prudent in devising a new strategy in "an ocean without challengers."[153] " . . . From the Sea" represented a top-down change similar to what the Navy experienced in the wake of World War II, as described by the political scientist Samuel Huntington in 1954, when the service shifted from a war at sea organization to one where naval strikes supported land campaigns, such as in the Korean War. Breemer's greatest concern was that the Navy could not change its culture fast enough to shift from a footing rooted in war at sea to a modern version of "cross ravaging," whereby the forces primarily concerned themselves with attacking land targets.[154] Regardless, Breemer complimented ". . . From the Sea" as "short and straightforward" in message.[155]

The British naval historian Geoffrey Till had a less critical opinion, writing, "With the publication of *From the Sea* (1992) . . . the navy's preoccupation shifted from sea control to land control. 'Naval Strategy,' declared Jan Breemer dramatically, 'is dead.' This did not mean that sea control ceased to matter; it meant only that the U.S. Navy and its allies would now be able to switch their attention to its reward: the capacity to project power ashore, especially in the world's troubled littorals."[156] Till cited Huntington and Sir Julian Corbett as having ideas that prefigured those in ". . . From the Sea."[157] It seemed clear to these scholars that although the change from open ocean blue water to littoral operations might be difficult for the Navy to accept and execute, there were well-known precedents for how to accomplish it.

Some critics viewed " . . . From the Sea" as the means to sustain muscular naval force structure. Cato Institute analyst Christopher Preble argued that " . . . From the Sea" did not fully take into account U.S. security roles in a post–Cold War world and that maintaining a large fleet in the face of inevitable budget cuts would result in "strategic over-extension, and a 'hollow fleet' incapable of performing its missions effectively." He suggested that a 275-ship fleet, rather than the 450-ship outfit that Kelso was trying to maintain, would be better suited for U.S. needs and that regional powers should assume more of the burden of protecting the free flow of global trade.[158]

Despite these criticisms, " . . . From the Sea" largely succeeded in establishing a new vision for the Navy and for the Navy–Marine Corps team in the joint post–Cold War world. Hattendorf noted, "'From the Sea' had wide influence within and outside the Navy. It was extensively used as a basis for flag officer speeches and in testimony before Congress, and it was favorably noted by civilian defense analysts. At the same time, it clearly reflected how the fleet was currently operating and resonated with contemporary thinking about the Navy."[159] The Marine Corps got equitable footing with the Navy, and in some cases, as Rutgers University international relations scholar Edward Rhodes noted, "The Navy was acknowledging the Corps as at least an equal partner, and possibly as the critical partner, in naval operations."[160]

New Strategy, New Structure

" . . . From the Sea" sowed the seeds for its own obsolescence and the isolation of the greater Navy strategic community responsible for its production. The conditions that made the break with the 1980s Maritime Strategy and the development of " . . . From the Sea" possible also enabled the wholesale reorganization of the CNO staff in ways that left its strategy branch isolated and without sufficient influence to refine its product. The continuing effects of Goldwater-Nichols and analysis of the Gulf War accelerated this trend. The Navy's strategy branch continued to produce further guidance on post–Cold War operations, but each had less impact compared to " . . . From the Sea."

CNO Kelso, a champion of the strategy community who strongly supported the effort that resulted in " . . . From the Sea," had to be equally acknowledging of the Department of Defense's budgetary process controlling the size and capability of the service he led. With " . . . From the Sea" in place, he sought to remake the Navy staff in order to preserve as much as possible the newest fleet force structure to support the new littoral warfighting mission with the Marine Corps and the broader mission of forward naval presence. In adopting some of Deming's management theories in reorganizing OPNAV, Kelso empowered the staff's budgetary deputy chief of Naval Operations to fundamentally remake the process by which the Navy determined what forces to buy and in what quantities to purchase them. Goldwater-Nichols necessitated this in part, but it was also in response to the more limited defense budgets of the post–Cold War era.

Kelso later revealed Secretary O'Keefe to have initiated this effort, stating, "After publication [of '. . . From the Sea'], he [Secretary O'Keefe] took that document and did some very smart things. He got the Navy and the Marine Corps leadership together . . . and said, 'We're going to have a war game, a paper war game, a talking war game about what this is going to mean to the Navy and to the Marine Corps, and not only that, we're going to align our programs to fit this. We're going to put our money where our mouth is to fit this program.'"[161]

Kelso's OPNAV reorganization began in October 1992 and ended in February 1993.[162] It consisted of three key elements: the redesignation of the OPNAV office codes from the traditional Navy preface of "OP" to the Joint Staff "N" code system; the abolition of OP-07 (Warfare Integration), the addition of deputies for Doctrine and Liaison (with forward commanders), and the downgrading of several three-star deputy CNO codes to two-star positions; and the subordination of the Navy's warfare deputy CNOs to a greatly empowered three-star deputy CNO for N8 (Resources, Warfare Requirements, and Assessments).[163]

Changing the OPNAV office codes had been contemplated since the passage of Goldwater-Nichols to align the Navy with the Joint Staff and other services.[164] The reductions in rank were also in response to the legislation—which cut the number of three-star deputy CNO's on the OPNAV staff from six to five—with additional reductions in OPNAV staff numbers stemming from Chairman Powell's Base Force concept.[165] Kelso preferred that the OPNAV staff, rather than the operational fleet, absorb the losses, and as a result, relinquished one hundred fifty officer and enlisted positions.[166]

Kelso had not been happy with OP-07, instituted by his predecessor, Hayward, to serve as an "honest broker" among the surface, submarine, and air warfare platform sponsors.[167] Kelso later remarked, "Many officers did a lot of hard work, a lot of assessing ideas, but in the end the money was given to the warfare sponsors and they fought hard to keep their money, and they always needed more than they had. OP-07 had, I think, a significant influence on whether we would support ballistic missile defense from our ships. Admiral J. D. Williams, when he was OP-07, believed strongly that we should, but he could have done that from anywhere. He did not need an entire organization to do that."[168]

The platform sponsors—N86 (Surface Warfare), N87 (Submarine Warfare), and N88 (Air Warfare)—lost their direct reporting access to the CNO and were grouped under the new and powerful N8 (Resources, Warfare Requirements, and Assessments). They were also downgraded in rank from three- to two-star positions in accordance with congressional requirements.[169] An additional two-star officer billet for N85 (Expeditionary Warfare) was added as required by " . . . From the Sea" and would alternately be headed by a Navy and Marine Corps officer.[170] The surface warfare chief (N86) had previously held many of the Expeditionary Warfare officer's responsibilities, and this addition constituted a net loss for the surface warfare community.[171] An additional two-star billet, N83 (CINC Liaison) , for communication with forward-deployed commanders, was added in recognition of the greater influence wielded by those commanders in the wake of Goldwater-Nichols.

The most important and lasting piece of Kelso's reorganization was the creation of N8 and the selection of its leader, Vice Adm. William Owens. According to Peter Swartz, Kelso "saw changing the process [of OPNAV management and decision-making] as more important than changing the organization."[172] Kelso later stated, "I believed that the 'give and take' [of decision-making] needs to be at the flag officer level in OPNAV, and I wanted them to have to focus all the time on what we really needed to do as a Navy and how we needed to spend our money as a total Navy."[173] Kelso also wanted additional input for the OPNAV flag officer decision-making process. "I wanted them [OPNAV] to bring in people from the outside to talk to us if they had things that we could use that we weren't traditionally using."[174] Kelso knew exactly whom he wanted to lead the new office:

> I brought Admiral Bill Owens back from Sixth Fleet, because I thought Bill was the right guy for N8. He's a very hard worker, and he's a smart guy, and he's innovative, and that's a great combination to have in an officer in the Navy. A lot of people do not always agree with Bill, but I don't think that anybody can argue that he is not smart, that he is not a very hard worker, or that he is not innovative, and he's honest. He does what he thinks is right. So Bill in my judgement did not need the old OP-07 and the old OP-095 organization trying to tell him how to do his job all the time.[175]

Owens was a veteran submariner just then completing an assignment as Sixth Fleet commander in the Mediterranean. He had been a member of the original

SSG and had created innovative operational concepts for antisubmarine warfare in the North Atlantic and the Norwegian, Barents, and Mediterranean Seas. Owens later said that while with the SSG he became aware of the world of possibilities when all of the naval warfare "unions"—surface, subsurface, and aviation forces—worked together and joined the other services to achieve an objective.[176] Owens' Sixth Fleet assignment had given him the opportunity to explore a number of post–Cold War operating concepts, including the creation of Maritime Action Groups, composed of submarines, surface ships, and patrol aircraft, and the use of the amphibious warfare ship USS *Wasp* as a light carrier/sea-control ship, using its Marine Corps AV8B Harrier jets for antisurface and antiair warfare missions rather than only to support Marine units ashore.[177]

Owens fully agreed with Kelso's thinking and plunged into his new assignment with enthusiasm and aiding in Kelso's OPNAV reorganization. He later stated, "The first task I undertook upon becoming Kelso's resource director in late summer 1992 was to destroy the enemy within—an archaic and antiquated structure within Navy headquarters [OPNAV] that had artificially divided the service into fiefdoms centered on surface ships, submarines and naval aviation, institutionalizing an internal rivalry among the traditional 'warfare communities' at the expense of innovation and combat effectiveness in the overall force."[178] Owens also knew how he intended to carry out Kelso's vision of an assessment process involving the whole of the OPNAV staff flag officer leadership. He later explained, "Our first task was to come up with a new scheme to identify the Navy's priorities in making budget decisions as well as to assess combat capabilities. We had to come up with a way to encourage and hasten a new way of thinking about how the Navy would go to war in the twenty-first century."[179]

Owens' scheme to promote Kelso's vision was the "Joint Mission Areas [JMA] Assessment Process." Announced to the fleet in February 1993 as a follow-on policy paper to ". . . From the Sea," it identified six Joint Mission Areas and two Support Areas around which to construct OPNAV planning and decision-making. The JMAs consisted of Joint Strike, Joint Littoral Warfare, Joint Surveillance, Joint Space and Electronic Warfare/Intelligence, Strategic Deterrence, and Strategic Sealift/Protection and the support areas of Readiness/Infrastructure and Manpower/Personnel and Shore Training.[180] The missions and support areas were assigned to teams led by flag officers and senior members of the OPNAV staff. Their mission was to assemble inputs from the fleet and from the Joint Staff and other services on which systems and programs the Navy should base its budgetary requirements and to create an integrated investment strategy within each discipline and to propose programs and systems for inclusion in the Defense Department's Planning, Programming, and Budgeting System (PPBS). The CNO Executive Steering Committee and the OPNAV Resource and Requirements Review Board (R3B) had the responsibility of accepting or rejecting the recommendations of the JMA and Joint Support teams. The R3B would then advise the CNO, Marine Corps commandant, and Secretary of the Navy on which programs and systems to approve for entry into that defense budget cycle's POM. The JMA follow-on paper stated that the purpose of introducing the JMA was to achieve consensus throughout OPNAV. The word "consensus" was underlined in the original text to stress its importance.[181]

This end state starkly contrasted with that of the previous system, in which the individual deputy CNOs for the warfare disciplines battled each other to win the approval of the CNO for their warfare area requirements and subsequently funding support. Owens later described the process as follows: "For roughly two decades, decisions within the Navy about the allocation of resources had been worked out within a staff structure dominated by five spokesmen. Three of these were Vice Admirals who advocated the perspectives and resource claims of the Navy's three warfare communities. There were the so-called 'staff barons,' a term meant to imply their relative independence and equal power status. Their 'fiefdoms' were naval aviation, surface warfare and submarines, and included the research, development and acquisition bureaucracies that worked for and within these platform categories."[182]

The 1992 OPNAV reorganization effort had been aimed specifically at reducing the power of the barons. It created a larger and more substantial fiefdom for Owens as head of N8. The demoted warfare barons, along with N83 (CINC Liaison) and the new N85 (Expeditionary Warfare) fell under Owens' control, as did N80 (Programming) and N82 (Fiscal Management).[183] Of particular note, Owens was given control of N81 (Assessments), the descendant of OP-96, in operation from 1960s through early 1980s. N81 was the key to the JMA process. According to the JMA memorandum, "The Assessments Division N81 oversees the assessment process for N8 and provides analytical resources to support the efforts of the JMA and SA assessment teams. The Assessment Division is also charged with integrating the results of the separate assessments into a (single investment strategy the Investment Balance Review (IBR)) [*sic*]."[184] While originally designed as an integrator of cross-OPNAV flag officer products, N81 "increasingly became the heart of the JMA process and overshadowed the collective role of the participant flag officers."[185] The 1992 reorganization marked the return of analysis to a position of power in OPNAV equal and in some ways superior to that of the old OP-96 analysis division, which had been disbanded in 1983.

As 1993 drew to a close, it appeared that Kelso had accomplished many of the goals he had set out to achieve upon becoming CNO. His plan to implement consensus-building and cooperative flag officer input to the Navy's programming and budgeting process, derived from Deming's TQL method, was being implemented through the reorganization of OPNAV and creation of N8.[186] Moreover, ". . . From the Sea" appeared a useful foundation on which to base the overall effort. Kelso later said, "Well, that ['. . . From the Sea'] provided N8's planning a tremendous tool. With this document, he [Admiral Owens] had something against which to assess his program. It was the cleanest way to do business that I had ever seen the Navy staff engage in. I do not want to take any credit for much of this, except that I was there, and I backed Bill Owens when a lot of people did not want to travel in that direction."[187]

There were also key demotions in the power and influence of OPNAV positions not under the direct control of N8. The deputy CNO for OP-06, who had developed ". . . From the Sea" from concept to the signature of the Secretary of the Navy, was weakened in rank and influence by the OPNAV reorganization. The office, recoded as N3/N5, saw a number of rank reductions in its subordinate flag officer positions. Its OP-65 (Nuclear Weapons Policy) division was downgraded to a branch. OP-64 (Fleet Operations and Readiness) and OP-61 (Political/Military and Current Plans Divisions) had to share the same flag officer director as N31/N52 (Plans, Policy, and Operations) branch.[188] It's OP-60 directorate, redesignated N51, and its OP-603

(Strategic Concepts) branch, now N513, survived, but neither had a role within N8's JMA process. Of note, OP-603 lost its position as the first OPNAV office to review POMs. In this capacity, OP-603 had conducted a strategy appraisal as part of the CNO Executive Board (CEB) review prior to the other POM appraisals. The CEB was eliminated as part of the reorganization. Subsequent lists of POM development assessments make no mention of a strategy assessment.

The reduction in authority and responsibility of the OPNAV offices concerned with strategy was perhaps not surprising given the magnitude of change that had taken place from the end of the Cold War through the Gulf War. Whether by deliberate design or benign neglect, senior Navy leaders viewed ". . . From the Sea" as a definitive document that would not require significant revision for some time. Kelso later asserted, "In my judgement, the short white paper ' . . . From the Sea' was a pretty good start and I notice it has not changed much [as of 2009]. They've fiddled around with it, but it's still pretty much the same thing if you look at it very hard, so nobody's come up with a lot better since then."[189] Owens had a similar opinion. "From the Sea," he wrote, "recognized that for the foreseeable future, the Navy's control of the seas would not be challenged and argued that the primary role of U.S. naval forces would be the application of joint military force in littoral areas."[190] There appeared to be little need for an OPNAV strategy branch in an environment where the strategic situation appeared so settled.

Owens later described how the "shock" of Operation Desert Storm contributed to the changes he worked to implement from N8. "Desert Storm," he noted, "the first post–Cold War conflict, was a magnificent battle—and a doctrinal disaster for the U.S. Navy. Our naval forces performed well. There was no failure of nerve on the part of the men and women who fought there. The Navy was successful, however, because it was able to modify its operational doctrine, a doctrine that—along with the weapons, systems, and training it had generated—proved ill-suited to the Gulf War."[191] There were those who disagreed with Owens' assessment. The military analyst Col. Harry Summers suggested that the Navy had been successful in that its "initiative in preparing to build a sea bridge to Europe enabled it to build just such a bridge to the Middle East. The amphibious threat from the marines kept Iraqi divisions pinned down in static defenses."[192] Summers concluded that this effort was made possible only through the Navy's investments in the 1980s, both in ships and in the offensive Maritime Strategy.[193] The CNA Corporation's analysis of the conflict commissioned by the Navy identified both positive and less-effective elements of the Navy's role in Operations Desert Shield and Desert Storm. Overall, it found that the Navy and Marine Corps performed well, but suggested improvements in command and control and the management of precision-guided weapons. It found no major strategic or operational errors in the Navy's conduct of its part of the conflict.[194]

Navy leadership in the early 1990s was more concerned about warfighting than its logistics doctrine. According to Owens, "Little in Desert Storm supported the Maritime Strategy's assumptions and implications. No opposing naval forces challenged us. No waves of enemy aircraft ever attacked the carriers. No submarine threatened the flow of men and materials across the oceans. The fleet was never forced to fight the open-ocean battles the Navy had been preparing for in the preceding twenty years. Instead, the deadly skirmishing of littoral warfare dominated."[195] Thus, Owens concluded, "For the navy, more than any other service, Desert Storm was the midwife of change."[196] The distinct focus on operational warfare, at the expense of a broader, specific service strategy and policy in the joint era would continue to dominate the thinking of senior Navy leaders and make pure strategic considerations gradually less important.

The 1990s saw further attempts by the N3/N5 (Plans, Policy, and Operations) to refine the arguments made in ". . . From the Sea," but with gradually less impact over the decade. The Clinton administration's acceptance of the need for forward-deployed naval forces came as a welcome development, but continued budget cuts threatened the Navy's already weakened force structure.[197] Secretary of the Navy John Dalton, who wanted to put a Clinton administration imprint on ". . . From the Sea,"[198] produced "Forward . . . From the Sea," which reiterated many of its predecessor's concepts, but specifically focused on forward naval presence and the centrality of Combat-Credible Presence, for some representing further justification for the existing force structure. President Clinton's 1994 National Security Strategy supported forward presence as a concept that "demonstrates our commitment to allies and friends, underwrites regional stability, gains U.S. familiarity with overseas operating environments, promotes combined training among the forces of friendly countries, and provides timely initial response capabilities."[199] Despite this support, Clinton's Bottom-Up Review set the goal of a 346-ship Navy by 1999.[200]

Credible Combat Force came about as an effort to counter the shrinking fleet recommendation. Rear Admiral Phillip Dur, director of N51 (Strategy and Policy) and an OP-603 alumnus, and Capt. Joe Sestak, his N513 (Strategic Concepts) deputy, proposed the concept to defend existing Navy and Marine Corps forward presence and Navy force structure requirements to the administration and to the 1994–95 Congressional Roles and Missions of the Armed Forces Commission.[201] The new "buzzword," as some called it, was also an attempt to avoid reducing the number of aircraft carriers below twelve ships. Dur and Sestak did not actually give the brief. Instead, the CNO, Marine Corps commandant, and Secretary of the Navy spoke.[202] Other notable appearances before the commission included those of Maj. Gen. Tom Wilkerson, USMC, who had played a lead role in writing ". . . From the Sea"; Capt. R. Robinson Harris, who had written the unclassified version of the Maritime Strategy but at the time was serving in the Navy's Office of Legislative Affairs; and Scott Truver, who helped draft the ". . . From the Sea."[203] "Forward . . . From the Sea" emphasized the same concepts of Navy and Marine Corps cooperation as ". . . From the Sea," but also discussed "enduring contributions in strategic deterrence, sea control and maritime supremacy, and strategic sealift."[204]

MOVING "FORWARD . . . FROM THE SEA" INTO THE TWENTY-FIRST CENTURY

"Forward . . . From the Sea" did not achieve the same level of influence as its predecessor, despite the massing of familiar offices and experienced staff leaders and authors in support of it. The strategy offices essential to the 600-ship navy of the Cold War and the 451-ship force of 1992 no longer wielded the same influence as they had in previous decades. The real determinant of fleet size was embodied in the Navy POM as managed by Admiral Owens in N8 (Resources, Warfare Requirements, and Assessments) and through documents issued from that office, such as "Force 2001: A Program Guide to the United States Navy," issued in July 1993, and the annual POMs in support of Navy budget objectives. These documents influenced the Bottom-Up Review that preserved the Navy's desired number of carriers but reduced the number of escorts based on the absence of significant threat and the simultaneous need to cut forces to stay within budget.[205]

While "Forward . . . From the Sea" had some initial success, it had little impact on POM development because it was focused on blue water programs and failed to "script a convincing story about how a littoral strategy works."[206] It was further criticized as a rehashing of the Navy's Cold War presence operations and provoked backlash from the Army and Air Force due to its "parochial focus on uniqueness of naval forward presence."[207] Only "boots on the ground," combined with robust land-based (as opposed to carrier-based) aviation could actually influence others.[208] The emphasis on force structure analysis in support of limited defense budgets was clearly the province of the analysts as opposed to the strategists.

N81 (Assessments) continued to increase its power within OPNAV over the next decade, into the early 2000s. The demand for analytical assessment instead of strategy in support of fleet size and operations carried on in the wake of the 1992 reorganization and the 1993 Bottom-Up Review. When recruited in 1994 by CNO Adm. Mike Boorda (1994–96) to work in N81, Bruce Powers, a veteran Navy operations analyst, said Boorda told him that he desired "to revitalize N81 and turn it back into what OP-96 had been earlier."[209] Boorda fundamentally shifted the composition of officers selected for the SSG in favoring analytical over strategic objectives. Since the SSG's establishment in 1981, it had been devoted to developing operational solutions to questions posed by the Navy's strategic documents. According to John Hanley, SSG adviser at NWC, "The SSG's approach was to identify strengths that U.S. and allied forces could apply against Soviet weaknesses in the maritime theaters to attack the Soviet Union's strategic sensitivities in a global war."[210] Boorda altered this fundamental mission in 1995 when he "redirected SSG from 'strategy' to generation of 'innovative future naval warfare concepts.'"[211] This move served to disconnect both NWC and one of the Navy's most upwardly mobile groups of officers (in terms of flag-level promotions) from direct work on Navy strategic concepts. Boorda was more interested in this, developing

"Navy Joint Operational Concept," a joint Navy–Marine Corps document generated between March 1995 and February 1997 by Capt. Joseph Bouchard, chief of N513 (Strategic Concepts).[212] The document proposed expanding on the Navy and Marine Corps cooperation introduced by " . . . From the Sea" and create a new "operational maneuver from the sea," a concept to further link the efforts of the two naval services. The idea ran up against N8, however, which saw it as an attempt by the Marine Corps to steal Navy budget funding.[213] It attracted other opponents, including the new Naval Doctrine Command and the naval aviation community, both of which felt threatened by closer Navy–Marine Corps cooperation. Secretary of the Navy Dalton also objected and decreed that "Forward . . . From the Sea" remain the Navy's strategic concept during his tenure.[214]

Boorda's tenure was tragically cut short by suicide in May 1996. His successor as CNO, Adm. Jay Johnson, had no interest in a new Navy strategy or operational concept and instead designated "The Navy Operational Concept" as an internal Navy document. It was published in the May 1997 issue of *Seapower* but had little influence.[215] The Navy's shrinking budget was of more concern than strategic concepts. The Navy would be reduced to 354 battle force ships by 1997, and the Quadrennial Defense Review that year recommended a mere 305 ships.[216] Additional elements of the Navy strategic community were further diminished over the course of the 1990s, leading them to pursue more private than official service-organized efforts. The Admiral Charles M. Cooke Conference for Naval Strategists and Planners, an influential event in the 1980s during the height of the Maritime Strategy's influence, held its last gathering in 1995.[217] Continued examination of Navy strategic concepts became more of a cooperative and private affair as well in the absence of influence within the OPNAV staff. In 1992 the distinguished naval historian and Navy Reserve intelligence officer David Rosenberg inaugurated a Navy strategy study group in the Washington, D.C., area that continued until 2005.[218]

In 2000 Adm. Vern Clark, a 1970s-era alumnus of OP-96 succeeded CNO Johnson.[219] A former director of J3 (Operations) and the first business school graduate to be appointed CNO, Clark would deftly manage organization, training, and equipment provision to the service. Clark desired a "readiness-based"

Navy, especially after the 11 September 2001 al-Qaida attacks.[220] In 2002 Clark told Vice Adm. Kevin Green, the incoming deputy CNO for N3/N5 (Plans, Policy, and Operations), that the Navy did not need a new strategy, as it already had one—the POM.[221] Similar attempts by N3/N5 to reintroduce strategy input to the POM over the course of the first decade of the twenty-first century failed. The fleet that emerged in those years was based almost exclusively on analysis. In 2000 Clark assigned control of the Navy's thirty-year shipbuilding plan to N81,[222] which would be instrumental in developing Clark's Sea Power 21 concepts from 2003 to 2010.[223] Some officers viewed "Sea Power 21" as a legitimate strategic document, albeit with caveats, but others had a less salutary view of what they considered yet another white paper in a stream of many over the decade. In an address to the NWC's graduating class of 2016 in Newport, Vice Adm. Frank Pandolfe, a member of Clark's staff said, "If the heart of the Maritime Strategy was an operational war plan, *Sea Power 21* fundamentally was a vision document."[224]

Vice Adm. John Morgan, leader of N3/N5 from 2004 to 2008, had more success than Green in pushing strategy documents to a wider audience, but N81 still outpaced him in terms of POM influence. "The Navy Operating Concept for Joint Operations," written by N513, had been little cited in POM documents or within the press. Succeeding strategy documents were also ineffectual. The Navy Strategic Plan in support of POM 08 (2006) was signed off on six months too late to be of significant influence on its intended POM cycle.[225] The Navy Strategic Plan for POM 10 (2007), deliberately targeted at Navy Department programmers supporting POM development, had some influence in the development of "A Cooperative Strategy for 21st Century Seapower," released in 2007.[226] It had extensive support to ensure a "fit with the OPNAV POM process,"[227] but classified as Secret, it did not get wide distribution as a result. The POM 10 strategic planning effort was lost to a degree in the turmoil of the end of the George W. Bush administration, during which operations in Iraq and Afghanistan and Pakistan dominated Department of Defense thinking.[228] It reflected current and near-term Navy programming already in place rather than attempting to influence future efforts. It did not include Marine Corps input and had no mechanism to secure OPNAV support, as did the N8/N81 POM development process.[229]

Morgan's greatest triumph was perhaps "A Cooperative Strategy for 21st Century Seapower." Championed by CNO Admiral Mullen (July 2005–September 2007), it was drafted by N3/N5 (N51) author Cdr. Bryan McGrath as a triservice effort in support of POM 12.[230] It had widespread influence in the broader U.S. and international naval community and within U.S. government circles, but again failed to impact its intended POM target, as it had no direct connection to POM development, as did the pre-1992 CNO Program Analysis Memorandums, formerly drafted by OP-96 and later N81, inputs to the POM process.[231] The distinct lack of a formal relationship between strategy and the programming process allowed Navy programmers to ignore strategic input from 1992 through the beginning of the second decade of the twenty-first century.

By contrast, N81's formal connection to the programming process provided it broad influence. The thirty-year shipbuilding plan has in effect served as the Navy's de facto strategy document from 2002 to date. Its main supporting element is the Naval Force Structure Assessment (FSA), described in OPNAV Instruction 3050.27 (12 February 2015) as a tool that "determines long-term Navy force structure objectives to support a global posture of distributed mission-tailored ships, aircraft, and units capable of regionally concentrated combat operations and peacetime theater security cooperation efforts."[232] The 2012 FSA was used to "determine a post-2020 requirement for 306 ships in the battle force and emphasized forward presence while re-examining resourcing requirements for operational plans and defense planning scenarios."[233] More recent FSA's have called for 355 ships, but unlike the six-hundred-ship navy of the 1980s, there is as yet no John Lehman counterpart to serve as the chief navigator for the course to that fleet strength.

The rise of China to great power status and the return of a revanchist Russia to global mischief has provoked an official return to a period of "Great Power competition" for the U.S. military and awakened a renewed interest in grand strategy. To its credit and despite decades of strategic slumber the U.S. Navy, unlike the other services, has again begun to produce strategy documents detailing the service's global role in securing U.S. interests and combating would-be opponents. These include the 2015 "Cooperative Maritime Strategy," a 2018 classified Naval Strategy, and "Advantage at Sea," an unclassified product of the Navy, Marine Corps, and Coast Guard promulgated in December 2020.[234] There has also been a slight lessening of N8's iron grip on the POM process with CNO Adm. John Richardson's establishment in 2016 of an OPNAV N50 division assigned to, like that the OP-603, create Navy strategic documents, but also develop an initial strategy input to the POM, the first such direct input from the strategy branch since 1992.[235] This division became part of a reborn N7 (Warfighting Integration) division in 2020, but its future was uncertain toward the end of that year. There has also been renewed interest in the operational level of war in the Navy's development of a distributed maritime operations doctrine for naval forces as a tool for executing new strategies. The drafting of these documents suggest that the Navy retains a strategic outlook despite decades of being in a joint harness with the other services. The overall defense environment, however, remains less amenable to such concepts.

Congress discussed the need to reduce the number and size of joint staffs in 2016 in order to give military personnel more active training in warfare disciplines, but the idea that one service alone might manage the efforts of others in a given area of operations still registers as "parochialism." One needs to look no further than the 2010 Navy–Air Force AirSea Battle concept, which was rapidly altered to include first a Marine and later an Army component in 2015, so as not to appear too much in favor of one service over the other. Goldwater-Nichols had long lasting effects in that it altered what had at times been a chaotic, but competitive strategy environment among the services to one of "enforced parochialism," where each service tended to get its share of the defense budget whether needed or not for current and future defense needs. A 2016 review of Goldwater-Nichols at thirty by the Congressional Research Service (CRS) asked how the Department of Defense could spend $600 billion every year and still not achieve all U.S. goals, for instance even after the expenditure of nearly $1.6 trillion and more than fifteen years of conflict in Iraq and Afghanistan.[236]

One of the proposed solutions in the report might have an answer: "More decentralization, through retaining or bolstering semi-autonomous military services, properly guided by OSD decision-making and resource allocation processes, thereby promoting creativity and innovation through competition."[237] The idea of a defense marketplace of ideas seems to fly in the face of

Goldwater-Nichols' concept of efficiency through centralization, but thirty-four years of what has been in effect "defense socialism" does not seem to have solved the budgetary or strategy issues as desired.

Congress also retains a laser-like focus on the budgetary aspects of defense while giving little consideration to the products of that spending, other than for their "value" through long-life expectancies of ships and other naval hardware. Following CNO Clark introducing the thirty-year shipbuilding program in 2000, Congress decided to make it an annual Navy requirement, to be submitted along with the budget, starting with the FY2003 defense budget.[238] The strategy and even the operational employment of that document's product registered little with the legislature other than for investigations into major accidents, such as those from the summer of 2017 when two Navy destroyer collisions in a short span of time resulted in more than twenty dead sailors and two ships out of commission for months. The lack of connection between strategy and defense expenditures will remain a problem for the near future.

The people part of Navy strategy development remains equally stagnant. A new strategy subspecialist category was created in January 2015.[239] Anecdotal evidence from the NWC, Naval Post Graduate School, and OPNAV staff, suggests that few, if any of these graduates, are employed in actual naval strategy duties. The creation of N7 (Warfare Integration) may help alleviate that problem by taking control of not only the strategist cohort but also their education and detailing. At the time of writing, the role of this CNO deputy office continued to develop.[240]

There is however hope for new maritime strategic content. The Navy, Marine Corps, and Coast Guard have embarked on a new triservice maritime strategy as a replacement for both the 2015 Cooperative Naval Strategy and Richardson's successive Designs for Maritime Superiority. Advertised as the hereditary successor to the 1980s Maritime Strategy, this joint effort shows great promise. It also faces a number of potential minefields as it navigates its way to approval from three service chiefs and a Department of Defense whose senior leadership is currently populated with a large number of West Point graduates. Renamed Advantage at Sea, the triservice maritime strategy awaited final CNO approval before publication. It will be an unclassified document, calling into question again the validity of such documents as opposed to classified ones presented to a smaller, more senior, and more exclusive audience of naval leaders.

The 1980s was a decade where the naval services had largely come to terms with their force structures, strategies, and operational concepts. The 2020s look a lot more like the 1970s, when the future *Oliver Hazard Perry*–class frigate was labeled "unsurvivable," the AEGIS program ten years late and a billion dollars over budget, and the aircraft carrier an unneeded platform vulnerable to cruise missiles. It will be hard to develop a functioning triservice strategy in the current, contentious environment.

Within OPNAV itself, the business of "strategy" has seen another reorganization under the aegis of N7 (Warfighting), created in 2020 and composed of pieces of OPNAV N3/N5, N8, and the Navy's education field. N7 has the potential to become an OPNAV power center as N8 has been since 1992, but its dynamic founder, Vice Adm. Stuart Munsch, departed for the Joint Staff J7 position in the summer of 2020. As Peter Swartz has reminded his readers, OPNAV offices come and go and often are a function of personalities and enduring missions. N8 has always had a hold on the POM cycle so vital to the Navy's planning. It remains to be seen whether N7 can find as secure a future in the OPNAV organization.

CONCLUSION

The Navy's concept of strategy, the products its concepts engendered, and the staff organization that created them in the Office of the Chief of Naval Operations (OPNAV) were fundamentally altered as a result of the end of the Cold War, passage of the Goldwater-Nichols Act of 1986, and the results of the 1991 Gulf War. The end of the Cold War eliminated the primary opponent around which the Navy had organized its strategic concepts since the late 1940s. This event alone would have caused a major alternation in Navy strategy and spawned products very different from the 1980s Maritime Strategy. In that "end of history," some also saw the possibility for systemic organizational change. The reorganization of the OPNAV staff in 1992 by CNO Adm. Frank Kelso was one such a change. Kelso later said to Paul Stillwell, his oral history interviewer, "I would tell you that I do not think the organization could have been changed without the changes taking place at the end of the Cold War. I believe there are opportunities for change. You cannot make such changes without the right conditions for change."[1]

The provisions and changes stemming from the Goldwater-Nichols Act were influential in the replacement of the Maritime Strategy with ". . . From the Sea" and later documents. The legislation aimed, according to the naval historian John Hattendorf, to eliminate the unproductive service parochialism that had stymied past attempts by the Department of Defense to create a joint service doctrine and a new joint military command organization that responded to civilian leadership instead of prioritizing service concerns.[2] Goldwater-Nichols strengthened the chairman of the Joint Chiefs of Staff, placed the Joint Staff under the chairman's control, and further empowered deployed regional joint commanders, who would presumably oversee the global contest against the Soviet Union should one occur. These changes served to strengthen the combined arms joint doctrine that the Department of Defense and many members of Congress desired.[3]

The reorganization resulting from Goldwater-Nichols affected the Navy more significantly than the other services and was in some ways more crippling for it in the post–Cold War era. In strengthening regional commanders' authority, joint leaders altered long-held concepts of maritime strategy and redrew the Navy's theater map of the world. As Hattendorf observed, "The majority of these dividing lines were placed in the middle of oceans, dividing them up in ways that were quite foreign to maritime thought. At the same time, the new divisions placed land areas, not maritime theatres, as the central focus for each region, in some cases even dividing coastal areas from their related open ocean regions."[4] Naval strategy planners had to develop new doctrines and strategies to function in this new environment, not only different in terms of potential opponents, but also in terms of strategic geography. Capt. Bill Manthorpe's prediction of a rising peer competitor every quarter century was dismissed in favor of a world order perceived through regional geography. While acceptance of a regional model was not detrimental to planning, the supposition of a new or returning peer competitor with a global reach should have remained in the strategic literature past the early 1990s but succumbed to end-of-history predictions that ultimately never came to be.

The Goldwater-Nichols' legislation had a negative effect on the quality of personnel assigned to OPNAV, particularly the strategy branch staffs. While trained strategy experts such as those who developed ". . . From the Sea" remained well after the Cold War, they were not replaced by the same quality of personnel who sought service on the Joint Staff and in joint commands, which under the new rules was the best path to flag rank. The entire strategy cohort dispersed, and force structure management replaced geographic and threat-based considerations in long-term planning.

The outcome of the Gulf War and the military technical revolution that preceded it also played a significant role in how the Navy replaced the Maritime Strategy with " . . . From the Sea" and subsequent strategies. Navy resistance to the passage of the Goldwater-Nichols Act, while perhaps necessary in trying to maintain traditional operational freedom, was counterproductive in terms of fighting the Cold War and the Gulf War. The war in the Persian Gulf highlighted the organizational competence and capabilities of the Army and Marine Corps ground forces and the Air Force, but not the Navy's. As Adm. Bill Owens noted, "Desert Storm confirmed the operational doctrines that the Army and Air Force had developed over the last two decades, but also demonstrated that the Maritime Strategy—the basic operational concept governing Navy planning since the early 1970s—was not fit for the post–Cold War era."[5]

The Navy's lack of strategic and operational validation, combined with not quickly adapting to the joint provisions of Goldwater-Nichols, and its inability to influence Gen. Colin Powell's Base Force concept produced a climate of uncertainty within the ranks of naval leadership. Kelso identified this "tumbled state" as a major factor in his desire to seek significant change. The changes he introduced, however, tended to be process driven rather than focused on a detailed new strategy. The lack of a classified version of ". . . From the Sea" (thus depressing buy-in among naval officers), the document's focus on the operational level rather than the strategic level of war, and its failure to connect strategy to the service's budgetary lifeline to Congress collectively condemned it to the ranks of background material, or a "vision," rather than the leading element in the development of a new maritime strategy. These events marked the demise of the Navy's Cold War strategy system. The end of the standoff with the Soviet Union, passage of Goldwater-Nichols, and conduct of the Gulf War not only fundamentally affected the change in naval strategy from 1989 to 1994, but continues to determine how the Navy produces strategic products to this day.

NOTES

INTRODUCTION

1. O'Rourke, "Future of the U.S. Navy," 289.
2. Howarth, *To Shining Sea*, 547.
3. Keller, "Last Soviet Soldiers Leave Afghanistan."
4. Bush and Scowcroft, *A World Transformed*, 148.
5. Pendley, "New Maritime Strategy," 66.
6. O'Keefe, Kelso, and Mundy, ". . . From the Sea," 93.
7. Jaffe, "Development of the Base Force," 22.
8. Echevarria, "American Operational Art," 137.

CHAPTER 1. NAVAL STRATEGY, 1945–1980

1. Gaddis, *Strategies of Containment*, 4.
2. Bradford, *America*, 261, 262.
3. Jablonsky, *War by Land, Sea, and Air*, 144.
4. Jablonsky, 174–75.
5. Raines and Campbell, *Evolution of Army Ideas*, 6.
6. Barlow, *From Hot War to Cold*, 64.
7. Dorwart, *Eberstadt and Forrestal*, 72.
8. Hewes, *From Root to McNamara*, 129.
9. Hewes, 135.
10. Dorwart, *Eberstadt and Forrestal*, 83.
11. Raines and Campbell, *Evolution of Army Ideas*, 36.
12. Barlow, *From Hot War to Cold*, 66.
13. Isenberg, *Shield of the Republic*, 111.
14. Isenberg, 104.
15. Builder, *Army in the Strategic Planning Process*, 25.
16. Palmer, *Origins of the Maritime Strategy*, 10.
17. Palmer, 12.
18. Dorwart, *Eberstadt and Forrestal*, 90.
19. Dorwart, 104.
20. Dorwart, 105.
21. Dorwart, 105.

22. Barlow, *From Hot War to Cold,* 86.
23. Barlow, 94.
24. Dorwart, *Eberstadt and Forrestal,* 147, 148.
25. Palmer, *Origins of the Maritime Strategy,* 42.
26. Barlow, *From Hot War to Cold,* 111.
27. Barlow, 111.
28. Palmer, *Origins of the Maritime Strategy,* 37.
29. Palmer, 30.
30. Barlow, *From Hot War to Cold,* 176.
31. Jablonsky, *War by Land, Sea, and Air,* 178.
32. Jablonsky, 176, 180.
33. Barlow, *From Hot War to Cold,* 179.
34. Barlow, 180.
35. Barlow, 180.
36. Barlow, 177, 180.
37. Forrestal, Memorandum, 9.
38. Forrestal, 11.
39. Rearden, *History of the Office of the Secretary of Defense,* 409.
40. Barlow, *From Hot War to Cold,* 188.
41. Lederman, *Reorganizing the Joint Chiefs of Staff,* 18, 19.
42. Lederman, 19.
43. Isenberg, *Shield of the Republic,* 150.
44. Barlow, *From Hot War to Cold,* 201.
45. Rearden, *History of the Office of the Secretary of Defense,* 144.
46. Barlow, *From Hot War to Cold,* 202.
47. Barlow, 212.
48. Barlow, 212.
49. Rearden, *History of the Office of the Secretary of Defense,* 49.
50. Barlow, *From Hot War to Cold,* 220, 221.
51. Palmer, *Origins of the Maritime Strategy,* 67.
52. Barlow, *From Hot War to Cold,* 236.
53. Barlow, 227.
54. McFarland, "1949 Revolt of the Admirals," 61.
55. McFarland, 61.
56. Palmer, *Origins of the Maritime Strategy,* 80.
57. Rearden, *History of the Office of the Secretary of Defense,* 75, 548.
58. Palmer, *Origins of the Maritime Strategy,* 77.
59. Palmer, 77.
60. Palmer, 82.
61. Wheeler, "Naval Aviation in the Korean War."
62. Wheeler.
63. Marolda, *United States Navy and the Korean War,* 33.

64. Marolda, 33.
65. Baer, *One Hundred Years of Sea Power,* 443.
66. Powell, with Persico, *My American Journey,* 438.
67. Murray, "Reform of the Joint Chiefs of Staff," 66.
68. Rearden, *Council of War,* 124.
69. Jablonsky, *War by Land, Sea, and Air.*
70. Rearden, *Council of War,* 124.
71. Weigley, *American Way of War,* 400–401.
72. Weigley, 201.
73. Endicott and Stafford, *American Defense Policy,* 65.
74. Eisenhower, *White House Years,* 543.
75. Eisenhower, 543–44.
76. Radford, *From Pearl Harbor to Vietnam,* 318–19.
77. Quoted in Jablonsky, *War by Land, Sea, and Air,* 234.
78. Rearden, *Council of War,* 135.
79. Barlow, *From Hot War to Cold,* 385.
80. Barlow, 20, 21.
81. Barlow, 20, 21.
82. Barlow, 22.
83. Ryan, *First Line of Defense,* 17.
84. Isenberg, *Shield of the Republic,* 290–91.
85. Isenberg, 295.
86. Ryan, *First Line of Defense,* 26.
87. Ryan, 26.
88. Isenberg, *Shield of the Republic,* 393.
89. Isenberg, 400.
90. Isenberg, 401.
91. Berman, *Zumwalt,* 119.
92. Allen and Polmar, *Rickover,* 81.
93. Lehman, *Command of the Seas,* 25–27.
94. Ryan, *First Line of Defense,* 28.
95. Metz, "Eisenhower as Strategist," 22.
96. Leighton, *History of the Office of the Secretary of Defense,* 29.
97. Stuart, *Organizing for National Security,* 41–44.
98. Millett, *Civilian Control of the Military,* 40.
99. Jablonsky, *War by Land, Sea, and Air,* 150.
100. Swartz, *Drawing Lines in the Sea,* 92.
101. Jablonsky, *War by Land, Sea, and Air,* 226.
102. Swartz, *Drawing Lines in the Sea,* 89.
103. Jablonsky, *War by Land, Sea, and Air,* 228.
104. Jablonsky, 229.
105. Jablonsky, 230.

106. Hone, *Power and Change,* 34.
107. Leighton, *History of the Office of the Secretary of Defense,* 373, 374.
108. Hone, *Power and Change,* 34.
109. Rosenberg, "Arleigh Burke."
110. Hone, *Power and Change,* 35.
111. Hone, 35.
112. Rosenberg, "Arleigh Burke."
113. Rosenberg.
114. Swartz, *Drawing Lines in the Sea,* 91.
115. Ryan, *First Line of Defense,* 23.
116. Hone, *Power and Change,* 36.
117. Swartz, *Drawing Lines in the Sea,* 90.
118. Jablonsky, *War by Land, Sea, and Air,* 296.
119. Bradford, *Quarterdeck and Bridge,* 379.
120. Hone, *Power and Change,* 43.
121. Hone, 43.
122. Hone, 41.
123. Rosenberg, "Origins of Overkill," 65.
124. Rosenberg, 5.
125. Rosenberg, 64.
126. Rosenberg, 58.
127. Millett, *Civilian Control of the Military,* 45.
128. Rearden, *Council of War,* 245.
129. Rearden, 246.
130. Enthoven and Smith, *How Much Is Enough,* 33.
131. Enthoven and Smith.
132. McMaster, *Dereliction of Duty,* 18–19.
133. McMaster, 18–19.
134. Endicott and Stafford, *American Defense Policy,* 71–72.
135. Endicott and Stafford, 71–72.
136. Bradford, *Quarterdeck and Bridge,* 376.
137. Bradford, 377.
138. Rosenberg, "Origins of Overkill," 53, 54.
139. Rearden, *Council of War,* 198.
140. Rearden, 215.
141. Ryan, *First Line of Defense,* 37, 38.
142. Rearden, *Council of War.*
143. McMaster, *Dereliction of Duty,* 333.
144. Polmar, *Aircraft Carriers,* 222–23.
145. Polmar, 223.
146. Polmar, 223, 224.
147. U.S. Congress, *Nuclear Propulsion for Surface Ships.*

148. Logevall, *Choosing War,* 401.
149. Ryan, *First Line of Defense,* 47.
150. Ryan, 49.
151. Cutler, *Brown Water, Black Berets,* xi.
152. Ryan, *First Line of Defense,* 56.
153. Clodfelter, *Limits of Air Power,* 82, 83, 106.
154. Ryan, *First Line of Defense,* 63.
155. Ryan, 51.
156. Millett, *Civilian Control of the Military,* 42–45.
157. Swartz, with Duggan, *U.S. Navy Capstone Strategies and Concepts: Introduction, Background and Analyses,* 74.
158. Swartz, with Duggan, 72–74.
159. Baer, *One Hundred Years of Sea Power,* 394–95.
160. Baer, 397.
161. Thaler, "Fifth Eskadra," 1, 2.
162. Hattendorf, *Evolution of the U.S. Navy's Maritime Strategy,* 25–26.
163. Hattendorf, 26.
164. Baer, *One Hundred Years of Sea Power,* 397.
165. Ryan, *First Line of Defense,* 73.
166. Ryan, 73.
167. Baer, *One Hundred Years of Sea Power,* 397.
168. Goldstein and Zhukov, "Tale of Two Fleets," 47.
169. Quoted in Hone, *Power and Change,* 80.
170. Hattendorf, *U.S. Naval Strategy in the 1970s,* xiii–xiv.
171. Hone, *Power and Change,* 87–88.
172. Hone, 87–88.
173. Sands, *On His Watch,* 58.
174. Sands, 18.
175. Hattendorf, *U.S. Naval Strategy in the 1970s,* 31.
176. Hattendorf, 4.
177. Hattendorf, 10.
178. Swartz, with Duggan, *U.S. Navy Capstone Strategies and Concepts, 1970–1980,* 18 (italics in the original).
179. Hattendorf, *Evolution of the U.S. Navy's Maritime Strategy,* 8.
180. Hattendorf, 5, 6; Prime, "Making of the Control School of Strategy," 24, 25.
181. Wylie, *Military Strategy,* xxxiv.
182. Turner, "Missions of the U.S. Navy," 2, 3.
183. Swartz, with Duggan, *U.S. Navy Capstone Strategies and Concepts, 1970–1980,* 25.
184. Swartz, with Duggan, 13.
185. Swartz, with Markowitz, *Organizing OPNAV,* 18.
186. Swartz, with Markowitz, 17.
187. Swartz, with Duggan, *U.S. Navy Capstone Strategies and Concepts, 1970–1980,* 15.

188. Swartz, with Duggan, 15.
189. Swartz, with Duggan, 15.
190. Hattendorf, *U.S. Naval Strategy in the 1970s*, 53.
191. Hattendorf, 54.
192. Swartz, with Duggan, *U.S. Navy Capstone Strategies and Concepts, 1970–1980*, 35.
193. Hattendorf, *U.S. Naval Strategy in the 1970s*, 105.
194. Kaufman, *Companion to Gerald R. Ford and Jimmy Carter*, 431, 435.
195. Swartz, with Duggan, *U.S. Navy Capstone Strategies and Concepts, 1970–1980*, 57.
196. Komer, "Maritime Strategy versus Coalition Defense," 1,132.
197. Swartz, email to author, 15 October 2015.
198. Hattendorf, *Evolution of the U.S. Navy's Maritime Strategy*, 10.
199. Hattendorf, 10.
200. Hattendorf, 12.
201. Swartz, with Markowitz, *Organizing OPNAV*, 28.
202. Hone, *Power and Change*, 104.
203. Swartz, with Duggan, *U.S. Navy Capstone Strategies and Concepts, 1970–1980*, 133.
204. Rearden, *Council of War*, 189.
205. Hattendorf, *Evolution of the U.S. Navy's Maritime Strategy*, 17; and Rearden, *Council of War*, 342.
206. Hone, *Power and Change*, 106.
207. Hattendorf, *Evolution of the U.S. Navy's Maritime Strategy*, 19.
208. Hattendorf, 37.
209. Swartz, with Duggan, *U.S. Navy Capstone Strategies and Concepts, 1970–1980*, 75–77.
210. Etzold, "The Navy and National Policy in the 1970s," 282.
211. Zackheim and Hamilton, *U.S. Naval Forces*, 39.
212. Polmar, *Aircraft Carriers*, 364.
213. Polmar, 364.
214. Boslaugh, *When Computers Went to Sea*, 385, 386.
215. Boslaugh, 386.
216. Boslaugh, 386.
217. Hattendorf, *U.S. Naval Strategy in the 1970s*, 110.
218. Polmar, *Aircraft Carriers*, 364.
219. Hughes, "Navy Operations Research," 108.
220. Hughes, 106.

CHAPTER 2. THE 1980s

1. Birkler et al., "Option for Funding Aircraft Carriers," 14.
2. C-SPAN, "Aircraft Carrier Replacement," 12 March 1987.
3. Healy, "Navy Secretary Resigns over Budget Cutbacks."
4. Yoshitani, *Reagan on War*, 17.
5. Bacevich, *New American Militarism*, 105.

6. Bacevich, 106.
7. Trauschweizer, "Adapt and Survive," 190.
8. Korb, "Where Did All the Money Go?," 7.
9. Ryan, *First Line of Defense*, 167.
10. Carter, "United States Defense Policy Remarks."
11. Korb, "Where Did All the Money Go?," 6.
12. Korb, 7.
13. Korb, 6–7.
14. Korb, 177.
15. Hattendorf, *U.S. Naval Strategy in the 1970s*, 113, 115–119.
16. Hattendorf, *Evolution of the U.S. Navy's Maritime Strategy*, 51.
17. Hattendorf, *U.S. Naval Strategy in the 1970s*, xiii.
18. Hattendorf, xiv, xv.
19. Republican Party, "Platform."
20. National Security Decision, Directive 32.
21. Hattendorf and Swartz, *U.S. Naval Strategy in the 1980s*, 25 (emphasis in the original).
22. Reagan, "Remarks at the Recommissioning Ceremony for the USS *New Jersey*."
23. Department of Defense, *Annual Report, Fiscal Year 1983*, I-30.
24. Department of Defense, *Annual Report, Fiscal Year 1988*, 165.
25. Wilson, "USS *Theodore Roosevelt* Joins Active Service as 15th Carrier," A21; Matthews, "Carrier *Theodore Roosevelt* 'Charges' to Life," 33, 37.
26. Grove, *Maritime Strategy and European Security*, 15.
27. Grove, 15, 16.
28. Till, *Seapower*, 45.
29. Till, 45.
30. Till, 45.
31. Sokolsky, *Seapower in the Nuclear Age*, 2.
32. Tarpgaard, *Building a 600-Ship Navy*, xxiii, xxiv.
33. Hone, *Power and Change*, 114.
34. Hunt, *Melvin Laird and the Foundation of the Post-Vietnam Military*, 17.
35. Hone, *Power and Change*, 51.
36. Hattendorf, *Evolution of the U.S. Navy's Maritime Strategy*, 4.
37. Hattendorf, 193.
38. Bush, "Remarks at the Aspen Institute Symposium."
39. Small, fax memorandum to Swartz, 2 October 1998.
40. Hattendorf, *Evolution of the U.S. Navy's Maritime Strategy*, 65.
41. Hattendorf, 67.
42. Hattendorf, 67.
43. Johnson, telephone interview, 1 July 2015.
44. Weeks, telephone interview, 16 February 2016.
45. Chipman and Lay, "Sea Power and the B-52 Stratofortress."

46. Hattendorf, *Evolution of the U.S. Navy's Maritime Strategy*, 70.
47. Weeks, telephone interview, 16 February 2016.
48. Hattendorf, *Evolution of the U.S. Navy's Maritime Strategy*, 57.
49. Hattendorf, 57.
50. Hattendorf, 57.
51. Hattendorf and Swartz, *U.S. Naval Strategy in the 1980s*, 20.
52. Williams, "The U.S. Navy under the Reagan Administration," 282.
53. Hattendorf and Swartz, *U.S. Naval Strategy in the 1980s*, 282.
54. Hattendorf and Swartz, 282.
55. Hattendorf and Swartz, 27.
56. Hattendorf and Swartz, 31–33.
57. Hattendorf and Swartz, 30.
58. Hattendorf and Swartz, 13.
59. Hattendorf and Swartz, 7.
60. Middleton, "U.S. and Allied Navies Starting Major Test Today."
61. Swartz, with Duggan, *U.S. Navy Capstone Strategies and Concepts, 1981–1990*, 12.
62. Swartz, with Duggan, 12.
63. Hone, *Power and Change*, 101.
64. Muir, *Black Shoes and Blue Water*, 211.
65. Boslaugh, *When Computers Went to Sea*, 386–87.
66. Baer, *One Hundred Years of Sea Power*, 428, 435.
67. Muir, *Black Shoes and Blue Water*, 232.
68. Thompson, *Brown Shoes, Black Shoes and Felt Slippers*, 45.
69. Muir, *Black Shoes and Blue Water*, 218.
70. Muir, 222.
71. Muir, 222.
72. Swartz, with Markowitz, *Organizing OPNAV*, 22.
73. "PPBE Process: Program Objective Memorandum."
74. Swartz, with Markowitz, *Organizing OPNAV, 1970–2009*, 39.
75. Hone, Smith, and Easton, "Aegis Evolutionary or Revolutionary Technology?," 50.
76. Swartz, with Markowitz, *Organizing OPNAV, 1970–2009*, 39.
77. Hone, Smith, and Easton, "Aegis Evolutionary or Revolutionary Technology?," 59.
78. Hone, Smith, and Easton, 50.
79. Hattendorf, *Evolution of the U.S. Navy's Maritime Strategy*, 45.
80. Hanley, "Creating the 1980s Maritime Strategy and Implications for Today," 14; Hattendorf, *Evolution of the U.S. Navy's Maritime Strategy*, 45.
81. Hattendorf, *Evolution of the U.S. Navy's Maritime Strategy*, 45.
82. Hattendorf, 46.
83. Hattendorf, 46.
84. Swartz, interview, 20 February 2015.
85. Swartz, 20 February 2015.
86. Swartz, 20 February 2015.

87. Swartz, 20 February 2015.
88. Swartz, 20 February 2015.
89. Armstrong, interview, 20 February 2015.
90. Armstrong, 20 February 2015.
91. Hattendorf, *Evolution of the U.S. Navy's Maritime Strategy*, 51.
92. Hay and Gile, *Global War Game*, 15, 16.
93. Neustadt and May, *Thinking in Time*, 132.
94. Ford and Rosenberg, *Admiral's Advantage*, 55.
95. Herrick, *Soviet Naval Strategy*, 143.
96. Herspring, *Soviet High Command*, 134, 135.
97. Ford and Rosenberg, *Admiral's Advantage*, 79; Hattendorf, *Evolution of the U.S. Navy's Maritime Strategy 1977–1986*, 13.
98. Sontag and Drew, with Drew, *Blind Man's Bluff*, 210.
99. Sontag and Drew, with Drew, 223.
100. Swartz, with Connell, *Understanding an Adversary's Strategic and Operational Calculus*, 19.
101. Ford and Rosenberg, *Admiral's Advantage*, 79.
102. Small, fax memorandum to Swartz, 2 October 1998.
103. Central Intelligence Agency, "Soviet Naval Strategy and Programs through the 1990s," 5.
104. Ford and Rosenberg, *Admiral's Advantage*, 83.
105. Ford and Rosenberg, 86.
106. Ford and Rosenberg, "Naval Intelligence Underpinnings of Reagan's Maritime Strategy," 401.
107. Rosenberg, "Realities of Formulating Modern Naval Strategy," 168.
108. Lehman, telephone interview, 2 December 2014.
109. Lehman, *Command of the Seas*, 56.
110. Naftali, interview of John Lehman, 4 October 2007, 7.
111. Lehman, *Command of the Seas*, 82.
112. Lehman, 61.
113. Lehman, 97, 98.
114. Lehman, email to author, 4 May 2020.
115. Lehman, *Command of the Seas*, 66.
116. Hone, *Power and Change*, 114.
117. Mearsheimer, "Review of John Lehman's *Command*," 14, 15.
118. Powell, with Persico, *My American Journey*, 298.
119. Barnett, *Navy Strategic Culture*, 91.
120. Hattendorf, *Evolution of the U.S. Navy's Maritime Strategy*, 73.
121. Hattendorf, 88.
122. Hattendorf, 88.
123. Lehman, *Command of the Seas*, 128.
124. Hattendorf, *Evolution of the U.S. Navy's Maritime Strategy*, 91.

125. Friedman, *Fifty-Year War,* 461.
126. Spector, *At War at Sea,* 377.
127. Howarth, *To Shining Sea,* 541.
128. Lehman, *Command of the Seas,* 128.
129. Lehman, 128.
130. Lehman, 43.
131. Lehman, 121, 122.
132. Enthoven and Smith, *How Much Is Enough?,* 13.
133. Enthoven and Smith, 74.
134. Lehman, *Command of the Seas,* 95.
135. Lehman, 95.
136. Swartz, with Markowitz, *Organizing OPNAV,* 36.
137. Ullman, email to author, 12 February 2016.
138. Zakheim et al., *Resources for Defense,* 40.
139. Congressional Budget Office, "Building a 600-Ship Navy," 1.
140. Woodall, "Analysis of the Future," 6.
141. Woodall, 6.
142. Swartz, with Markowitz, *Organizing OPNAV,* 35.
143. Brooks and Manthorpe, "Setting the Record Straight," 62.
144. Brooks and Manthorpe, 38.
145. Brooks and Manthorpe, 41.
146. Linn, *Echo of Battle,* 5.
147. Builder, *Army in the Strategic Planning Process,* 40 (emphasis in the original).
148. Builder, 69.
149. Wylie, *Military Strategy,* 125.
150. Jones, *Blowtorch,* 250.
151. Turner and Thibault, "Preparing for the Unexpected," 122–35.
152. Mearsheimer, "Strategic Misstep," 12.
153. Mearsheimer, 6.
154. Luttwak, *The Pentagon and the Art of War,* 264.
155. Posen, "Inadvertent Nuclear War and NATO's Northern Flank," 37.
156. Posen, 40, 41.
157. Swartz, telephone interview, 5 November 2015.
158. Hughes, "Navy Operations Research," 107.
159. Hughes, 108.
160. Swartz, telephone interview, 5 November 2015.
161. Barnett, email to author, 11 February 2016.
162. Hattendorf and Swartz, *U.S. Naval Strategy in the 1980s,* 49.
163. Swartz, telephone interview, 5 November 2015.
164. Hattendorf and Swartz, *U.S. Naval Strategy in the 1980s,* 51.
165. Brooks, "Naval Power and National Security," 79.
166. Falk, *Why Nations Put to Sea,* 30; Swartz, email to author, 10 January 2020.

167. Mustin, "Role of the Navy and the Marines in the Norwegian Sea," 2.
168. Hattendorf and Swartz, *U.S. Naval Strategy in the 1980s*, 43.
169. Swartz, email to author, 26 February 2015.
170. Swartz, 26 February 2015.
171. Hattendorf and Swartz, *U.S. Naval Strategy in the 1980s*, 2.
172. Hattendorf and Swartz, 2.
173. Swartz, with Markowitz, *Organizing OPNAV*, 37, 44.
174. Hattendorf and Swartz, *U.S. Naval Strategy in the 1980s*, 259, 260.
175. Trost, letter to Hattendorf, 2007.
176. Arkin, "Our Risky Naval Strategy Could Get Us All Killed."
177. Mohr, "Military Price on Coffee Cited as $7,622."
178. Tarpgaard and Mechanic, *Future Budget Requirements for the 600-Ship Navy*, 28.
179. Pierrot, *Naval Combat Aircraft*, 23.
180. Hartmann, *Naval Renaissance*, 270.
181. Mearsheimer, "Review of John Lehman's Command," 13–16.
182. Quoted in Hartmann, *Naval Renaissance*, 270.
183. Williams, "The U.S. Navy under the Reagan Administration," 279.
184. Swartz, with Markowitz, *Organizing OPNAV*, 43; Swartz, with Duggan, *U.S. Navy Capstone Strategies and Concepts, 1981–1990*, 91.
185. Hattendorf, *U.S. Naval Strategy in the 1990s*, 269.
186. Evans, "Navy Secretary Quits over $12 Billion Dollar Cut."
187. Hattendorf and Swartz, *U.S. Naval Strategy in the 1980s*, 309.
188. Swartz, with Duggan, *U.S. Navy Capstone Strategies and Concepts, 1981–1990*, 27.
189. Watkins and Kelley, *Amphibious Warfare Strategy*, 1.
190. Watkins and Kelley, 53.
191. Watkins and Kelley, 53.
192. Hattendorf and Swartz, *U.S. Naval Strategy in the 1980s*, 309.
193. Hattendorf, *U.S. Naval Strategy in the 1990s*, 1.
194. Hattendorf, 9.
195. Bush and Scowcroft, *A World Transformed*, 175, 318.
196. U.S. Congress, Senate, *Nomination of Admiral Frank B. Kelso*, 326, 327.

CHAPTER 3. THE GOLDWATER-NICHOLS ACT AND NAVY STRATEGY

1. Swartz, telephone interview, 5 November 2014; Sestak, email exchange, 9 February 2015.
2. Goldwater, with Casserly, *Goldwater*, 338.
3. Nemfakos et al., *Perfect Storm*, 15.
4. Haynes, *Toward a New Maritime Strategy*, 244.
5. Baer, *One Hundred Years of Sea Power*, 441, 442.
6. Wylie, *Military Strategy*, 42.
7. Wylie, 42.

8. Snider, "Strategy, Forces and Budgets," 15.
9. Snider, 15.
10. Sherry, *The Army Command Post and Defense Reshaping,* 27.
11. Snider, "Strategy, Forces and Budgets," 14.
12. Snider, 14.
13. Parcell, Cymrot, and Moore, *Officer Structure in the 21st Century,* 11.
14. McKee, with Winkler, Oral History of Admiral Kinnard McKee, 78.
15. Harrell et al., *Outside the Fleet,* 98.
16. Crowe, *In the Line of Fire,* 161.
17. DeYoung, *Soldier: The Life of Colin Powell,* 185.
18. Lovelace, "DoD Reorganization Act of 1986," 77.
19. Swartz, with Markowitz, *Reorganizing OPNAV,* 37.
20. Swartz, with Markowitz, 37.
21. U.S. Congress, Senate, *National Security Strategy: Hearings,* 453.
22. Brown, email to Swartz, 14 March 2008.
23. Swartz, with Markowitz, *Reorganizing OPNAV,* 54.
24. Rearden, *Council of War,* 450.
25. Jablonsky, *War By Land, Sea, and Air,* 319–21.
26. Lederman, *Reorganizing the Joint Chiefs of Staff,* 65; Lovelace, "DoD Reorganization Act of 1986," 71–73.
27. Korb, "Where Did All the Money Go?," 3.
28. Locher, *Victory on the Potomac,* 283–85.
29. "What Witnesses Had to Say," 18.
30. U.S. Congress, House, Committee on Armed Services, *Reorganization Proposals for the Joint Chiefs of Staff: Hearings,* 1.
31. Chiarelli, "Beyond Goldwater-Nichols," 71–72.
32. Roman and Tarr, "Joint Chiefs of Staff," 92.
33. "What Witnesses Had to Say," 20.
34. "What Witnesses Had to Say," 19.
35. Locher, *Victory on the Potomac,* 60, 61, and 88–90.
36. Moorer, memo to Lehman, 24 October 2012.
37. Worley, *Shaping U.S. Military Forces,* 39.
38. Weinberger, letter to Goldwater, 8 May 1986; Crowe, *In the Line of Fire,* 157.
39. Mustin, with Winkler, Oral History of Vice Admiral Henry C. Mustin, 185, 186.
40. Fedyszyn, "Maritime Perspective," 84.
41. Faller, *The Navy and Jointness,* 132.
42. Lehman, "Let's Stop Trying To Be Prussians," C7.
43. Ganley, "How's That Again, You're Opposed to What?," 18.
44. Goldwater, letter to Weinberger, 6 March 1986.
45. Locher, *Victory on the Potomac,* 71, 72; Train, Oral History of Admiral Harry DePue Train II.
46. Hughes, "Navy Operations Research," 107; Matloff, Oral History Interview with Dr. Alain Enthoven, 11.

47. Crowe, *In the Line of Fire*, 152.
48. Nemfakos et al., *Perfect Storm*, 14.
49. Goldwater, with Casserly, *Goldwater*, 357.
50. Cropsey, memorandum to Lehman, 23 December 1985.
51. Lehman, telephone interview, 2 December 2013.
52. U.S. Congress, Senate. *Defense Organization: Staff Report*, 10–12.
53. Locher, *Victory on the Potomac*, 329–31.
54. Punaro, with Poyer, *On War, On Politics*, 131.
55. Tower, *Consequences*, 247; Goldwater, with Casserly, *Goldwater*, 355–56.
56. Zegart, *Flawed by Design*, 138; Kaplan, Landa, and Drea, *History of the Office of the Secretary of Defense*, 18.
57. Faller, *The Navy and Jointness*, 61.
58. Faller, 61.
59. Faller, 57, 58.
60. Cropsey, memorandum to Lehman, April 1986.
61. Brooks, "Naval Power and National Security," 59.
62. Nemfakos et al., *Perfect Storm*, 48.
63. Cropsey, "Limits of Jointness," 29.
64. Mustin, with Winkler, Oral History of Vice Admiral Henry C. Mustin, 185.
65. Eilon and Lyon, "Evolution of Department of Defense Directive 5100.1," 22.
66. Harris, interview, 22 September 2014.
67. Ford and Rosenberg, "Naval Intelligence Underpinnings of Reagan's Maritime Strategy," 393.
68. Rubel, "What Critics of the Navy's Strategy Get Wrong."
69. Hattendorf, *Evolution of the U.S. Navy's Maritime Strategy*, 85.
70. U.S. Congress, Senate, *National Security Strategy: Hearings*, 452.
71. Swartz, with Duggan, *U.S. Navy Capstone Strategies and Concepts, 1970–1980*, 33.
72. Goldwater-Nichols Act, chap. 5, sec. 151.
73. Bolt, Colletta, and Shakleford, *American Defense Policy*, 152.
74. Goldwater-Nichols Act, chap. 5, sec. 151.
75. Goldwater-Nichols Act, sec. 153.
76. Hays, Vallance, and Van Tassel, *American Defense Policy*, 123.
77. Owens, "Hollow Promise of JCS Reform," 106, 107.
78. Jaffe, "Development of the Base Force," 2.
79. Jaffe, 2.
80. Jaffe, 7–9.
81. Hattendorf and Swartz, *U.S. Naval Strategy in the 1980s*, 259.
82. Hattendorf and Swartz, 309.
83. Hattendorf and Swartz, 271.
84. Jaffe, "Development of the Base Force," 9, 10.
85. Snider, "Strategy, Forces and Budgets," 10.
86. DeYoung, *Soldier: The Life of Colin Powell*, 188.
87. Snider, "Strategy, Forces and Budgets," 16.

88. Snider, 16.
89. Snider, 17.
90. Trost, "Maritime Strategy for the 1990s," 92.
91. Trost, 95.
92. Trost, 95.
93. Barlow, *From Hot War to Cold,* 83.
94. Jaffe, "Development of the Base Force," 45, 46.
95. Jaffe, 46.
96. Jaffe, 49.
97. Jaffe, 46.
98. Metz, *Iraq and the Evolution of American Strategy,* 5, 6.
99. Snider, "Strategy, Forces and Budgets," 12–17.
100. Snider, 28.
101. Kelso, with Stillwell, *Reminiscences,* 669.
102. Garrett, Kelso, and Gray, "The Way Ahead," 36.
103. Kelso, with Stillwell, *Reminiscences,* 669.
104. Kelso, 669.
105. Hattendorf, *U.S. Naval Strategy in the 1990s,* 6.
106. Goldwater-Nichols Act, chap. 6, sec. 161.
107. Johnson, telephone interview, 1 July 2015.
108. Drea et al., *History of the Unified Command Plan,* 70.
109. Snider, "Strategy, Forces and Budgets," 11.
110. Hattendorf, *U.S. Naval Strategy in the 1990s,* 6.
111. Drea et al., *History of the Unified Command Plan,* 70.
112. Drea et al., 62.
113. Drea et al., 63.
114. Drea et al., 63.
115. National Security Council, "Defense Planning Guidance," 4.
116. National Security Council, 4.
117. National Security Council, 8.
118. Miller, *War Plan Orange,* 368.
119. Hattendorf, *Evolution of the U.S. Navy's Maritime Strategy,* 76–79.
120. Sumida, *Inventing Grand Strategy and Teaching Command,* 21.
121. Hattendorf, *Evolution of the U.S. Navy's Maritime Strategy,* 8.
122. Hattendorf, 8.
123. Sands, *On His Watch,* 23, 59.
124. Johnson, telephone interview, 1 July 2015; Swartz, telephone interview, 28 August 2016.
125. Johnson, telephone interview, 1 July 2015.
126. Hattendorf, *Evolution of the U.S. Navy's Maritime Strategy,* 54.
127. Hattendorf, 45–46.
128. Swartz, telephone interview, 26 August 2016.

129. Harris, interview, 22 September 2014.
130. Mustin, with Winkler, Oral History of Vice Admiral Henry C. Mustin, 186.
131. Mustin, with Winkler, 188.
132. Fedyszyn, telephone interview, 5 May 2016.
133. Fedyszyn, 5 May 2016.
134. Swartz, with Markowitz, *Organizing OPNAV*, 49.
135. Swartz, with Markowitz, 42.
136. Hughes, "Navy Operations Research," 106.
137. Hughes, 106.
138. Hughes, email to Swartz, 29 October 2014.
139. Brown, email to author, 8 June 2016.
140. Swartz, with Markowitz, *Organizing OPNAV*, 54.
141. Meinhart, "Vice Chairman of the Joint Chiefs of Staff and the Leadership of the Joint Requirements Oversight Council," 145.
142. Owens, "JROC," 56.
143. Swartz, with Markowitz, *Organizing OPNAV*, 40.
144. Swartz, with Markowitz, 54.
145. Owens, *High Seas*, 126.
146. Owens, 127–28.
147. Owens, with Offley, *Lifting the Fog of War*, 166–67.
148. Powers, Sheldon, and Garrambone, "Oral History Interview of Mr. Bruce F. Powers," 119.
149. Powers, Sheldon, and Garrambone, 118.
150. Swartz, telephone interview, 26 August 2016.
151. Harris, interview, 22 September 2014.
152. Hattendorf and Swartz, *U.S. Naval Strategy in the 1980s*, 11.
153. "Budget of the United States Navy: 1794–2014."
154. U.S. Congress, Senate, *Nomination of Admiral Frank B. Kelso*, 344–45.
155. Garrett, Kelso, and Gray, "The Way Ahead," 3.
156. Kelso, with Stillwell, *Reminiscences*, 688–89.
157. Diamond, email to Hattendorf, 9 September 2006.
158. Giarra, email to author, 19 May 2015.
159. Hattendorf, *U.S. Naval Strategy in the 1990s*, 39.
160. Harris, interview, 22 September 2014.
161. Schirmer, *Challenging Time in DOPMA*, 14.
162. Parcell, Cymrot, and Moore, *Officer Structure in the 21st Century*, 16.
163. Parcell, Cymrot, and Moore, 11.
164. Diamond, email to Hattendorf, 9 September 2006.
165. Diamond, 9 September 2006.
166. Diamond, 9 September 2006.
167. Hattendorf, *U.S. Naval Strategy in the 1990s*, 8.
168. Harris, interview, 22 September 2014.

169. Johnson, telephone interview, 11 August 2014.
170. Lehman, telephone interview, 2 December 2013.

CHAPTER 4. THE GULF WAR, REVOLUTION IN MILITARY AFFAIRS, AND STRATEGIC CHANGE

1. Gordon and Trainor, *General's War*, 27.
2. Krepinevich, "Military Technical Revolution," i.
3. Summers, "Operations, Procurement, and Industrial Base," 76, 77.
4. Parker, *Military Revolution*, 1.
5. Parker, *Military Revolution*, 195–97.
6. Parker, *Military Revolution*, 1, 2.
7. Parker, 114.
8. Brodie, "War in the Atomic Age," 28, 29.
9. Gorshkov, *Seapower of the State*, 157.
10. FitzGerald, "Marshal Ogarkov," 8.
11. FitzGerald, 8.
12. FitzGerald, 8.
13. FitzGerald, 8.
14. FitzGerald, 8.
15. Gelb, "Who Won the Cold War."
16. Krepinevich, "Military Technical Revolution," i.
17. Department of Defense, *Annual Report, Fiscal Year 1982*, x.
18. "Harold Brown."
19. "Harold Brown."
20. Department of Defense, *Annual Report, Fiscal Year 1982*, 69.
21. Department of Defense, ix, 65–67, 115.
22. Tomes, *U.S. Defense Strategy*, 58.
23. Tomes, 58.
24. Tomes, 67.
25. Perry, "Technology and National Security," 4.
26. Tomes, *U.S. Defense Strategy*, 69.
27. Tomes, 69.
28. Coram, *Boyd*, 323–25.
29. Boyd, "Patterns of Conflict," 4, 5.
30. Boyd, 5.
31. Boyd, 5.
32. Coram, *Boyd*, 339, 340, 362.
33. Coram, 355.
34. Coram, 390, 391.
35. Coram, 391.
36. Hattendorf, *Evolution of the U.S. Navy's Maritime Strategy*, 232.
37. Winton, "Partnership and Tension," 101.

38. Swartz, *U.S. Navy–U.S. Air Force Relationships,* 59.
39. Swartz, 60.
40. Swartz, 70; O'Brasky, conversation with author, 2017–20.
41. Skinner, "Airland Battle Doctrine," 4.
42. Skinner, 3.
43. Trauschweizer, *Cold War U.S. Army,* 199.
44. Hattendorf and Swartz, *U.S. Naval Strategy in the 1980s,* 7.
45. Trauschweizer, *Cold War U.S. Army,* 235.
46. Romjue, *From Active Defense to AirLand Battle,* 7.
47. Trauschweizer, *Cold War U.S. Army,* 201.
48. Skinner, "Airland Battle Doctrine," 4.
49. Skinner, 4.
50. Trauschweizer, *Cold War U.S. Army,* 209.
51. Romjue, *From Active Defense to AirLand Battle,* 31, 32.
52. Linn, *Echo of Battle,* 207.
53. Linn, 214.
54. Linn, 50.
55. Starry, with Sorley, *Press On,* 1,264.
56. Starry, with Sorley, 1,264, 1,265.
57. Romjue, *From Active Defense to AirLand Battle,* 8.
58. Skinner, "Airland Battle Doctrine," 5.
59. Starry, with Sorley, *Press On,* 1,264.
60. Skinner, "AirLand Battle Doctrine," 6.
61. Starry with Sorley, *Press On,* 1,276.
62. Anderson, "ALSA Center Meets Immediate Needs of the Warfighter," 46.
63. Worden, *Rise of the Fighter Generals,* 224.
64. Worden, 224, 225.
65. Worden, 220.
66. Starry, with Sorley, *Press On,* 1,275.
67. Starry, with Sorley, 1,274.
68. Starry, with Sorley, 1,276.
69. Skinner, "Airland Battle Doctrine," 2.
70. Department of the Army, *FM 100-5,* 6.3.
71. Department of the Army, 7.1, 7.2.
72. Starry, with Sorley, *Press On,* 1,277.
73. Tomes, *U.S. Defense Strategy,* 113.
74. Tomes, 114.
75. Tomes, 114.
76. Tomes, 115, 116.
77. Tomes, "Cold War Offset Strategy."
78. Weeks, telephone interview, 6 February 2016.
79. Starry, with Sorley, *Press On,* 1,229, 1,238.

80. Huntington, *Soldier and the State*, 261.
81. Linn, *Echo of Battle*, 194, 195.
82. Summers, *On Strategy*, 21.
83. Huntington, *Soldier and the State*, 262.
84. Huntington, 263.
85. Wylie, *Military Strategy*, 41, 42.
86. Wylie, 48.
87. Builder, *Masks of War*, 138.
88. Romjue, *From Active Defense to AirLand Battle*, 58, 59.
89. Department of the Army, *FM 100-5*, 1–1.
90. Boyd, "Patterns of Conflict," 176.
91. Department of the Army, *FM 100-5*, 2–3.
92. Kelly and Brennan, *Alien*, 61.
93. Kelly and Brennan, 61, 62.
94. Romjue, *From Active Defense to AirLand Battle*, 109.
95. Skinner, "Airland Battle Doctrine," 23.
96. Friedman, *Seapower as Strategy*, 202.
97. Friedman, *Fifty-Year War*, 64.
98. Hattendorf, *U.S. Naval Strategy in the 1970s*, 31, 38.
99. Hattendorf and Swartz, *U.S. Naval Strategy in the 1980s*, 203.
100. Komer, with Farmer, Robert W. Komer Oral History, 6.
101. Komer, "Maritime Strategy versus Coalition Defense," 1,129–31.
102. Holloway, *Aircraft Carriers at War*, 383, 384.
103. Baer, *One Hundred Years of Sea Power*, 412, 413.
104. Werrell, *Evolution of the Cruise Missile*, 150, 154.
105. Department of Defense, *Annual Report, Fiscal Year 1979*, 173.
106. Friedman, *Fifty-Year War*, 463.
107. Hattendorf, *Evolution of the U.S. Navy's Maritime Strategy*, 79.
108. Boslaugh, *When Computers Went to Sea*, 53.
109. Boslaugh, 55.
110. Boslaugh, 56.
111. Boslaugh, 211, 212.
112. Isenberg, *Shield of the Republic*, 369.
113. Isenberg, 369.
114. Boslaugh, *When Computers Went to Sea*, 388.
115. Swartz, email to author, 16 September 2016.
116. Hughes, *Fleet Tactics and Coastal Combat*, 29.
117. Hughes, 29.
118. Hughes, 30.
119. Hughes, 33.
120. Romjue, *From Active Defense to AirLand Battle*, 58, 59.
121. Skinner, "Airland Battle Doctrine," 33.

122. Hattendorf, *U.S. Naval Strategy in the 1990s,* 101.
123. Builder, *Army in the Strategic Planning Process,* v.
124. Roberts, "Going in Harm's Way," 27.
125. Roberts, 27.
126. Pokrant, *Desert Storm at Sea,* x.
127. Pokrant, *Desert Shield at Sea,* 18.
128. Marolda and Schneller, *Shield and Sword,* 72.
129. Marolda and Schneller, 81.
130. Marolda and Schneller, 82.
131. Pokrant, *Desert Shield at Sea,* 18.
132. Marolda and Schneller, *Shield and Sword,* 186.
133. Marolda and Schneller, 186, 187.
134. Pokrant, *Desert Shield at Sea,* 169.
135. Pokrant, 169.
136. Pokrant, 19.
137. Pokrant, 169.
138. Pokrant, 169.
139. Pokrant, *Desert Storm at Sea,* 210.
140. Swartz, email to author, 16 September 2016.
141. Hallion, *Storm over Iraq,* 142, 143.
142. Hallion, 142, 143.
143. Swartz, email to author, 16 September 2016; Carter, Presidential Review Memorandum, 10.
144. Hallion, *Storm over Iraq,* 117.
145. Warden, *Air Campaign,* 6.
146. Warden, 151.
147. Warden, 116, 117, 151.
148. Gordon and Trainor, *General's War,* 99.
149. Marolda and Schneller, *Shield and Sword,* 112.
150. PBS, "Oral History: Charles Horner."
151. Gordon and Trainor, *General's War,* 95.
152. Metz, *Iraq and the Evolution of American Strategy,* 26, 27.
153. Pokrant, *Desert Shield at Sea,* 68.
154. Gordon and Trainor, *General's War,* 97.
155. Pokrant, *Desert Shield at Sea,* 64.
156. Marolda and Schneller, *Shield and Sword,* 114.
157. Pokrant, *Desert Shield at Sea,* 65.
158. Marolda and Schneller, *Shield and Sword,* 114.
159. Pokrant, *Desert Shield at Sea,* 68.
160. Pokrant, 68.
161. Boyne, "Route Pack 6."
162. Pokrant, *Desert Shield at Sea,* 68.

163. Cohen, *Gulf War Airpower Survey*, 52.
164. Pokrant, *Desert Shield at Sea*, 66.
165. Pokrant, 66.
166. Pokrant, 66.
167. "Joint Doctrine for Theater Counterair Operations," III-4.
168. Swartz, email to author, 16 September 2016.
169. Cohen, *Gulf War Airpower Survey*, 33–35.
170. Hallion, *Storm over Iraq*, 142.
171. "Joint Doctrine for Theater Counterair Operations," III-4, III-5.
172. Pokrant, *Desert Shield at Sea*, 71.
173. Pokrant, 66, 67.
174. Pokrant, 68.
175. Marolda and Schneller, *Shield and Sword*, 189.
176. Marolda and Schneller, 189.
177. Gordon and Trainor, *General's War*, 75.
178. Pokrant, *Desert Shield at Sea*, 73.
179. Gordon and Trainor, *General's War*, 115.
180. Gordon and Trainor, 115.
181. Gordon and Trainor, 115.
182. Gordon and Trainor, 115.
183. Pokrant, *Desert Shield at Sea*, 73.
184. Hallion, *Storm over Iraq*, 250, 251.
185. PBS, "Oral History: General Norman Schwarzkopf."
186. Bush and Scowcroft, *A World Transformed*, 316, 317.
187. Pokrant, *Desert Shield at Sea*, 79.
188. Pokrant, 79.
189. Pokrant, 83.
190. Marolda and Schneller, *Shield and Sword*, 118.
191. Marolda and Schneller, 254.
192. Marolda and Schneller, 254.
193. Scales, *Certain Victory*, 128.
194. Scales, 128.
195. Gordon and Trainor, *General's War*, 126.
196. Pokrant, *Desert Shield at Sea*, 84.
197. Marolda and Schneller, *Shield and Sword*, 117.
198. Gordon and Trainor, *General's War*, 159, 160.
199. Gordon and Trainor, 159–61.
200. Gordon and Trainor, 161, 162.
201. Scales, *Certain Victory*, 96.
202. Melson, Englander, and Dawson, *U.S. Marines in the Persian Gulf*, 16.
203. Quilter, *U.S. Marines in the Persian Gulf*, 20, 21.
204. Metz, *Iraq and the Evolution of American Strategy*, 34.

205. Winnefeld and Johnson, American "Unity of Control," 99.
206. Marolda and Schneller, *Shield and Sword,* 118.
207. Gordon and Trainor, *General's War,* 176.
208. Marolda and Schneller, *Shield and Sword,* 118.
209. Gordon and Trainor, *General's War,* 292, 294.
210. Marolda and Schneller, *Shield and Sword,* 150.
211. Scales, *Certain Victory,* 106.
212. Pokrant, *Desert Storm at Sea,* 209, 210.
213. Pokrant, 208, 209.
214. Owens, with Offley, *Lifting the Fog of War,* 90, 91.
215. Mustin, with Winkler, Oral History of Vice Admiral Henry C. Mustin, 191.
216. Mustin, with Winkler, 191.
217. Carlucci, with Kennedy, "Interview with Frank C. Carlucci III," 138, 139.
218. Carlucci, with Kennedy, 210.
219. Marolda and Schneller, *Shield and Sword,* 359.
220. Pokrant, *Desert Storm at Sea,* 215.
221. Marolda and Schneller, *Shield and Sword,* 359.
222. Gordon and Trainor, *General's War,* 471.
223. Pokrant, *Desert Storm at Sea,* 271.
224. Pokrant, 271.
225. Pokrant, 271, 272.
226. Marolda and Schneller, *Shield and Sword,* 231, 232.
227. Pokrant, *Desert Storm at Sea,* 273.
228. Pokrant, 272.
229. Pokrant, 177.
230. Pokrant, 177.
231. Marolda and Schneller, *Shield and Sword,* 117, 118.
232. Pokrant, *Desert Storm at Sea,* 225.
233. Pokrant, 228.
234. Pokrant, *Desert Shield at Sea,* 157.
235. Turley, *Journey of a Warrior,* 401, 402; Grady, "Book Review: *The Journey of a Warrior.*"
236. Pokrant, *Desert Storm at Sea,* 229.
237. Marolda and Schneller, *Shield and Sword,* 251.
238. Marolda and Schneller, 252, 253.
239. Gordon and Trainor, *General's War,* 173–75.
240. Gordon and Trainor, 174.
241. Pierce, *Warfighting and Disruptive Technologies,* 86.
242. Hattendorf and Swartz, *U.S. Naval Strategy in the 1980s,* 309.
243. Bouchard, email to Swartz, 28 June 2005.
244. Metz, *Iraq and the Evolution of American Strategy,* 29, 30.
245. Owens, *High Seas,* 4.

246. Owens, 4.
247. Owens, 4.
248. Owens, 125, 126.
249. O'Rourke, "Future of the U.S. Navy," 292, 293.
250. Hattendorf and Swartz, *U.S. Naval Strategy in the 1980s*, 309, 310.
251. Hattendorf and Swartz, 295.
252. Hattendorf and Swartz, 295, 296.
253. Hattendorf, *U.S. Naval Strategy in the 1970s*, 14–17.
254. Ryan, *First Line of Defense*, 17.

CHAPTER 5. MAKING THE CHANGE IN NAVY STRATEGY

1. Bush and Scowcroft, *A World Transformed*, 172, 173.
2. Jaffe, "Development of the Base Force," 2.
3. Vego, "On Littoral Warfare," 31.
4. Russell et al., "Navy Strategy Development in the 21st Century," 10.
5. Borrenson, "Alliance Naval Strategies in Norway," 99, 100.
6. Mustin, "Role of the Navy and the Marines in the Norwegian Sea," 4–6.
7. Hattendorf and Swartz, *U.S. Naval Strategy in the 1980s*, 127.
8. Michishita, Swartz, and Winkler, "Lessons of the Cold War in the Pacific," 14.
9. Hattendorf and Swartz, *U.S. Naval Strategy in the 1980s*, 4.
10. Coram, *Boyd*, 383.
11. Coram, 381.
12. Pierce, *Warfighting and Disruptive Technologies*, 96.
13. Pierce, 89.
14. Pierce, 90.
15. Department of the Navy, *FMFM 1: Warfighting*, 42.
16. Lee, Shiba, and Wood, *Integrated Management Systems*, 164.
17. Lee, Shiba, and Wood, 164.
18. Lee, Shiba, and Wood, 165.
19. Dunaway, email to Swartz, 2 May 2005.
20. DeYoung, *Soldier: The Life of Colin Powell*, 191.
21. Department of the Air Force, "Air Force and U.S. National Security," 4.
22. Department of the Air Force, 5.
23. Hallion, *Storm over Iraq*, 119, 120.
24. Swartz, with Duggan, *U.S. Navy Capstone Strategies and Concepts, 1991–2000*, 6.
25. Kelso, with Stillwell, *Reminiscences*, 668.
26. Jaffe, "Development of the Base Force," 2.
27. Jaffe, 61.
28. Garrett, Kelso, and Gray, "The Way Ahead," 36.
29. Joint OPNAV/SECNAV Memorandum: The Way Ahead.
30. Hattendorf, *U.S. Naval Strategy in the 1990s*, 9.
31. Diamond, email to Swartz, 7 July 2006.

32. Diamond, 7 July 2006.
33. Diamond, 7 July 2006.
34. Hattendorf, *U.S. Naval Strategy in the 1990s,* 9.
35. Hattendorf, 9.
36. Diamond, email to Hattendorf, 9 September 2006.
37. Jaffe, "Development of the Base Force," 12.
38. Jaffe, 40; Stark, email to Swartz, 3 September 2008.
39. Jaffe, "Development of the Base Force," 40.
40. Diamond, email to Hattendorf, 9 September 2006.
41. Diamond, 9 September 2006.
42. Dunaway, email to Swartz, 2 May 2005.
43. Diamond, email to Swartz, 7 July 2006.
44. Hattendorf, *U.S. Naval Strategy in the 1990s,* 11.
45. Hattendorf, 11.
46. Hattendorf, 11.
47. Diamond, email to Hattendorf, 9 September 2006.
48. Diamond, 9 September 2006.
49. Hattendorf, *U.S. Naval Strategy in the 1990s,* 11.
50. Diamond, email to Hattendorf, 9 September 2006.
51. Joint Memorandum from CNO Adm. Frank Kelso II and Secretary of the Navy H. Lawrence Garrett III.
52. Diamond, email to Hattendorf, 9 September 2006.
53. Diamond, 9 September 2006.
54. Diamond, 9 September 2006.
55. Diamond, email to Swartz, 7 July 2006.
56. Swartz and Byron, "Make the Word Become the Vision," 17; Hattendorf and Swartz, *U.S. Naval Strategy in the 1980s,* 1.
57. Swartz and Byron, "Make the Word Become the Vision," 72.
58. Garrett, Kelso, and Gray, "The Way Ahead," 38.
59. Garrett, Kelso, and Gray, 46.
60. Garrett, Kelso, and Gray, 45.
61. Dunaway, email to Swartz, 2 May 2005.
62. Dunaway, 2 May 2005.
63. Hattendorf, *U.S. Naval Strategy in the 1990s,* 12.
64. Haynes, *Toward a New Maritime Strategy,* 59.
65. Bouchard, email to Swartz, 28 June 2005.
66. Swartz, with Duggan, *U.S. Navy Capstone Strategies and Concepts, 1991–2000,* 19.
67. Durell-Young, "When Programming Trumps Policy and Plans," 2, 3.
68. Kelso, with Stillwell, *Reminiscences,* 669, 670.
69. Swartz, with Duggan, *U.S. Navy Capstone Strategies and Concepts, 1991–2000,* 20.
70. Truver, "Tomorrow's Fleet," 51.
71. Durell-Young, "When Programming Trumps Policy and Plans," 2, 3.

72. Swartz, with Duggan, *U.S. Navy Capstone Strategies and Concepts, 1991–2000,* 25.
73. "The Navy Policy Book," cover.
74. Diamond, email to Swartz, 7 July 2007.
75. Myers, email to Swartz, 6 June 2012.
76. Diamond, email to Swartz, 7 July 2006.
77. Holland, "Book Review: The Navy Policy Book," 113.
78. Hattendorf, *U.S. Naval Strategy in the 1990s,* 13.
79. Swartz, with Duggan, *U.S. Navy Capstone Strategies and Concepts, 1991–2000,* 23.
80. Cushman, "Admiral Frank B. Kelso Dies at 79."
81. Hattendorf, *U.S. Naval Strategy in the 1990s,* 14; Swartz, with Duggan, U.S. Navy Capstone Strategy and Concepts, 1991-2000, 35, 36.
82. O'Keefe, Kelso, and Mundy, ". . . From the Sea," 93–96.
83. O'Keefe, Kelso, and Mundy, 93–96.
84. O'Keefe, Kelso, and Mundy, 93–96.
85. Swartz, with Duggan, *U.S. Navy Capstone Strategies and Concepts, 1991–2000,* 36.
86. Pierce, *Warfighting and Disruptive Technologies,* 165.
87. Swartz, with Duggan, *U.S. Navy Capstone Strategies and Concepts, 1991–2000,* 52.
88. Hayes, "Keeping the Naval Service Relevant," 57.
89. Swartz, *U.S. Navy Capstone Strategy, Policy, Vision and Concept Documents: What to Consider before You Write One,* 46.
90. Swartz, with Duggan, *U.S. Navy Capstone Strategies and Concepts, 1991–2000,* 52.
91. Russell et al., "Navy Strategy Development," 4.
92. Diamond, email to Hattendorf, 9 September 2006.
93. Diamond, 9 September 2006.
94. Diamond, 9 September 2006.
95. Diamond, 9 September 2006.
96. Neider and Barnett, "Memorandum for the Record," 1.
97. Smith, "What '. . . From the Sea' Didn't Say," 11.
98. Swartz, with Duggan, *U.S. Navy Capstone Strategies and Concepts, 1991–2000,* 35.
99. O'Keefe, Kelso, and Mundy, ". . . From the Sea."
100. Swartz, with Duggan, *U.S. Navy Capstone Strategies and Concepts, 1991–2000,* 35, 36.
101. Smith, "What '. . . From the Sea' Didn't Say," 11.
102. Manthorpe, "Personal Reflections," 32.
103. Manthorpe, 32.
104. Barnett, *Pentagon's New Map,* 69, 70.
105. Manthorpe, "Personal Reflections," 32.
106. Smith, with Stillwell, *Reminiscences,* 641.
107. Smith, with Stillwell, 641.
108. Smith, with Stillwell, 642.
109. Kelso, with Stillwell, *Reminiscences,* 686.
110. Kelso, with Stillwell, 686, 687.

111. Swartz, with Duggan, *U.S. Navy Capstone Strategies and Concepts, 1991–2000,* 42.
112. Swartz, with Duggan, 42.
113. Smith, with Stillwell, *Reminiscences,* 642.
114. Smith, with Stillwell, 644.
115. Smith, with Stillwell, 644.
116. Swartz, with Duggan, *U.S. Navy Capstone Strategies and Concepts, 1991–2000,* 42.
117. Smith, with Stillwell, *Reminiscences,* 643.
118. Smith, with Stillwell, 643.
119. Smith, with Stillwell, 643.
120. Stavridis, email to Swartz, 28 June 2006.
121. O'Keefe, Kelso, and Mundy, ". . . From the Sea," 93.
122. O'Keefe, Kelso, and Mundy, 93.
123. Swartz, with Duggan, *U.S. Navy Capstone Strategies and Concepts, 1991–2000,* 44.
124. Hughes, "Naval Operations," 24.
125. Swartz, with Duggan, *U.S. Navy Capstone Strategies and Concepts, 1991–2000,* 57, 61.
126. O'Keefe, Kelso, and Mundy, ". . . From the Sea," 95.
127. O'Keefe, Kelso, and Mundy, 96.
128. Swartz, with Duggan, *U.S. Navy Capstone Strategies and Concepts, 1991–2000,* 46.
129. Smith, with Stillwell, *Reminiscences,* 645, 646.
130. Breemer, quoted in Thompson, *Brown Shoes, Black Shoes and Felt Slippers,* 57, 58.
131. Thompson, *Brown Shoes, Black Shoes and Felt Slippers,* 172, 173.
132. Engel, "Cruise Missiles and the Tomahawk"; Hayes and Smith, *The Politics of Naval Innovation,* 31; O'Keefe, Kelso, and Mundy, ". . . From the Sea," 95.
133. Kelso, with Stillwell, *Reminiscences,* 688.
134. Kelso, with Stillwell, 687.
135. Kelso, with Stillwell, 688.
136. Mundy, "Getting It Right," 70.
137. Mundy, 70.
138. Kelso, with Stillwell, *Reminiscences,* 687.
139. Kelso, with Stillwell, 687.
140. Kelso, with Stillwell, 687.
141. Smith, with Stillwell, *Reminiscences,* 647.
142. Hoffman, "Stepping Forward Smartly," 33.
143. Smith, "What '. . . From the Sea' Didn't Say," 24.
144. Smith, 24.
145. Smith, 24, 25.
146. Brooks, "Peacetime Influence," 1.
147. Dismukes, "National Security Strategy and Forward Presence," 65.
148. Rainbow and Miller, "Be Careful What You Ask For . . . ," 73.
149. Aspin, *Report on the Bottom-Up Review,* 7.
150. Dismukes, "National Security Strategy and Forward Presence," 70.

151. Kelso, with Stillwell, *Reminiscences,* 689, 690.
152. Hattendorf, *U.S. Naval Strategy in the 1990s,* 198.
153. Breemer, "The End of Naval Strategy," 49.
154. Breemer, 53.
155. Breemer, 44.
156. Till, *Seapower,* 67.
157. Till, 67, 68.
158. Preble, "Cold War Navy in the Post War World," 1.
159. Hattendorf, *U.S. Naval Strategy in the 1990s,* 14.
160. Dombrowski, *Naval Power in the 21st Century,* 154.
161. Kelso, with Stillwell, *Reminiscences,* 688.
162. " . . . From the Sea" Update.
163. Swartz, with Markowitz, *Organizing OPNAV,* 54.
164. Swartz, with Markowitz, 54.
165. Swartz, with Markowitz, 40, 57.
166. Swartz, with Markowitz, 57.
167. Swartz, with Markowitz, 40.
168. Kelso, with Stillwell, *Reminiscences,* 690.
169. Swartz, with Markowitz, *Organizing OPNAV,* 57.
170. Swartz, with Markowitz, 54.
171. Swartz, with Markowitz, 54.
172. Swartz, with Markowitz, 58.
173. Kelso, with Stillwell, *Reminiscences,* 686.
174. Kelso, with Stillwell, 686.
175. Kelso, with Stillwell, 686.
176. Hanley, "Creating the 1980s Maritime Strategy," 19.
177. Swartz, with Duggan, *U.S. Navy Capstone Strategies and Concepts, 1991–2000,* 37.
178. Owens, with Offley, *Lifting the Fog of War,* 167.
179. Owens, with Offley, 167.
180. Office of the Chief of Naval Operations, Follow-on Papers, 4, 5, 6.
181. Office of the Chief of Naval Operations, 6, 7.
182. Owens, "Quest for Consensus," 70.
183. Owens, 70.
184. Office of the Chief of Naval Operations, Follow-on Papers, 6.
185. Swartz, with Markowitz, *Organizing OPNAV 1970–2009,* 59.
186. Swartz, with Markowitz, 56.
187. Kelso, with Stillwell, *Reminiscences,* 688.
188. Swartz, with Markowitz, *Organizing OPNAV 1970–2009,* 54.
189. Kelso, with Stillwell, *Reminiscences,* 689.
190. Owens, "Quest for Consensus," 69.
191. Owens, *High Seas,* 4.
192. Summers, "Operations, Procurement, and Industrial Base," 76, 77.

193. Summers, 76.
194. Pokrant, *Desert Storm at Sea,* 302.
195. Owens, *High Seas,* 4.
196. Owens, 4.
197. Swartz, with Duggan, *U.S. Navy Capstone Strategies and Concepts, 1991–2000,* 78.
198. Swartz, with Duggan, 78.
199. White House, "National Security Strategy of Engagement and Enlargement," 8.
200. Department of Defense, "Report of the Bottom-Up Review," 28.
201. Diamond, email to Swartz, 2 December 2009.
202. Clemente, email to Swartz, 12 December 2009.
203. Swartz, with Duggan, *U.S. Navy Capstone Strategies and Concepts, 1991–2000,* 86.
204. "Forward . . . From the Sea," 1.
205. Aspin and Powell, "News Briefing on the Bottom-Up Review," 4.
206. Rhodes, "'. . . From the Sea' and Back Again," 32.
207. Swartz, with Duggan, *U.S. Navy Capstone Strategies and Concepts, 1991–2000,* 93.
208. Swartz, with Duggan, 93.
209. Powers, Sheldon, and Garrambone, "Oral History Interview of Mr. Bruce Powers," 118.
210. Hanley, "Creating the 1980s Maritime Strategy and Implications for Today," 15.
211. Swartz, with Duggan, *U.S. Navy Capstone Strategies and Concepts, 1991–2000,* 105.
212. Hattendorf, *U.S. Naval Strategy in the 1990s,* 17.
213. Hattendorf, 18.
214. Swartz, with Duggan, *U.S. Navy Capstone Strategies and Concepts, 1991–2000,* 109.
215. Hattendorf, *U.S. Naval Strategy in the 1990s,* 18; Haynes, *Toward a New Maritime Strategy,* 126.
216. Department of Defense, "Report of the Quadrennial Defense Review," 29.
217. Swartz, with Duggan, *U.S. Navy Capstone Strategies and Concepts, 1991–2000,* 105.
218. Swartz, with Duggan, 82.
219. Hughes, "Navy Operations Research," 107.
220. Ratcliff, "CNO and OPNAV Reorganization," 326–28.
221. Haynes, *Toward a New Maritime Strategy,* 153.
222. O'Rourke, "Navy Force Structure and Shipbuilding Plans," 8.
223. Swartz, with Duggan, *U.S. Navy Capstone Strategies and Concepts, 1991–2000,* 27.
224. Pandolfe, "Evolution of Modern U.S. Naval Strategy," 9.
225. Swartz, with Duggan, *U.S. Navy Capstone Strategies and Concepts, 1991–2000,* 101.
226. Swartz, with Duggan, 127.
227. Swartz, with Duggan, 136.
228. Swartz, with Duggan, 129.
229. Swartz, with Duggan, 138.

230. Swartz, with Duggan, 166.
231. Swartz, with Duggan, 189.
232. OPNAV Instruction 3050.27, Force Structure Assessments, 1.
233. "Report to Congress on the Annual Long-Range Plan for Construction of Naval Vessels for Fiscal Year 2016," 7.
234. Tangredi, "Running Silent and Algorithmic," 1.
235. Department of the Navy, Memorandum: POM Process Reorganization and OPNAV Staff Realignment.
236. McInnis, "Goldwater-Nichols at 30," 13.
237. McInnis, 15.
238. O'Rourke, "Navy Force Structure and Shipbuilding Plans," 12, 13.
239. Office of the Chief of Naval Operations, "Establishment of the Navy Strategy Subspecialty 230X."
240. Eckstein, "CNO Richardson Wants Aggressive Timelines."

CONCLUSION

1. Kelso, with Stillwell, *Reminiscences,* 688.
2. Hattendorf, *U.S. Naval Strategy in the 1990s,* 5.
3. Hattendorf, 5.
4. Hattendorf, 6.
5. Owens, "Quest for Consensus," 68.

BIBLIOGRAPHY

PRIMARY SOURCES

Government Documents and Publications

Aspin, Leslie. *Report on the Bottom-Up Review.* Washington D.C.: Office of the Secretary of Defense, October 1993.

Aspin, Leslie, and Colin L. Powell. "News Briefing on the Bottom-Up Review," official transcript, 1 September 1993. Office of the Assistant Secretary of Defense for Public Affairs, Washington, D.C.

Carlucci, Frank Charles, III. "Interview with Frank C. Carlucci III," by Charles Stuart Kennedy, 1 April 1997. Association of Diplomatic Studies and Training Foreign Affairs Oral History Project, Washington, D.C., 2000. https://cdn.loc.gov/service/mss/mfdip/2004/2004car04/2004car04.pdf.

Cohen, Eliot A., dir. *Gulf War Airpower Survey.* Vol. 1, *Planning and Command and Control.* Washington, D.C.: U.S. Government Printing Office, 1993.

Congressional Budget Office. "Building a 600-Ship Navy: Costs, Timing, and Alternative Approaches." Washington, D.C., March 1982.

Department of Defense. *Annual Report, Fiscal Year 1979.* Washington, D.C., 2 February 1978.

———. *Annual Report, Fiscal Year 1982.* Washington, D.C., 16 January 1981.

———. "Report on the Bottom-Up Review." Washington, D.C., October 1993.

———. "Report of the Quadrennial Defense Review." Office of the Secretary of Defense, Washington, D.C., May 1997.

Department of the Air Force. "The Air Force and U.S. National Security: Global Reach–Global Power. A White Paper." Washington, D.C., June 1990. https://secure.afa.org/EdOp/2012/GRGP_Rice_1990.pdf.

Department of the Army. *FM 100-5: Operations.* Field Manual. Washington, D.C., 20 August 1982.

Department of the Navy. *FMFM 1: Warfighting.* Washington, D.C., 6 March 1989.

———. Memorandum: POM Process Reorganization and OPNAV Staff Realignment, Washington D.C., 18 October 2016. https://www.public.navy.mil/bupers-npc/reference/messages/Documents/NAVADMINS/NAV2016/NAV16231.txt.

Elion, Lindsey, and Jack Lyon. "The Evolution of Department of Defense Directive 5100.1: Functions of the Department of Defense and Its Major Components." Office of the Secretary of Defense, Administration and Management, Organizational Management and Planning, Washington, D.C., April 2010.

"Forward . . . From the Sea." Department of the Navy, Washington, D.C., 9 November 1994.

". . . From the Sea: Preparing the Naval Service for the 21st Century." Washington, D.C.: Office of the Chief of Naval Operations, Chief of Naval Information, 30 September 1992.

" . . . From the Sea" Update: The OPNAV Assessment Process. Department of the Navy, Public Affairs Office, Washington, D.C., May 1993. From the personal and professional papers of Capt. Peter M. Swartz, USN (Ret.), "From the Sea" file, Washington, D.C.

Goldwater-Nichols Department of Defense Reorganization Act of 1986, Public Law 99–433.

"Joint Doctrine for Theater Counterair Operations." Joint Chiefs of Staff, Washington, D.C., 1 April 1986, III-4. http://www.davi.ws/doc/JointPub_3–01–2.pdf.

Joint Memorandum from CNO Adm. Frank Kelso II and Secretary of the Navy H. Lawrence Garrett III, SER 00/0U500222: The Way Ahead, 23 August 1990. Washington, D.C. From the personal and professional papers of Capt. Peter M. Swartz, USN (Ret.), The Way Ahead 1991 file, Washington, D.C.

Joint OPNAV/SECNAV Memorandum: The Way Ahead, 23 August 1990. Department of the Navy, Washington, D.C. From the personal and professional papers of Capt. Peter M. Swartz, USN (Ret.), Maritime Strategy Demise file, Washington, D.C.

Melson, Charles D., Evelyn A. Englander, and David A. Dawson. *U.S. Marines in the Persian Gulf, 1990–1991: Anthology and Annotated Bibliography.* Washington, D.C.: History and Museums Division, Headquarters, U.S. Marine Corps, 1992.

National Security Council. "Defense Planning Guidance: 1994–1999." Washington, D.C., 16 April 1992. http://www.archives.gov/declassification/iscap/pdf/2008-003-docs1–12.pdf.

"The Navy Policy Book." Alexandria, Va.: Office of the Chief of Naval Operations, OPNAV Executive Panel (00-K), May 1992.

Office of the Chief of Naval Operations. "Establishment of the Navy Strategy Subspecialty 230X." Washington, D.C., 14 January 2015. https://www.public.navy.mil/bupers-npc/reference/messages/Documents2/NAV2015/NAV15011.txt.

———. Follow-on Papers Expanding on " . . . From the Sea": Memorandum for the record, 22 February 1993. From the personal and professional papers of Capt. Peter M. Swartz, USN (Ret.), From the Sea file, Washington, D.C.

OPNAV Instruction 3050.27: Force Structure Assessments. Office of the Chief of Naval Operations, Washington, D.C., 12 February 2015. https://www.secnav.navy.mil/doni/Directives/03000%20Naval%20Operations%20and%20Readiness/03-00%20General%20Operations%20and%20Readiness%20Support/3050.27.pdf.

O'Rourke, Ronald. "Navy Force Structure and Shipbuilding Plans: Background and Issues for Congress." Congressional Research Service, 7–5700, Washington, D.C., 12 June 2015.

Quilter, Charles J., II. *U.S. Marines in the Persian Gulf, 1990–1991: With the I Marine Expeditionary Force in Desert Shield and Desert Storm*. Washington, D.C.: History and Museums Division, Headquarters, U.S. Marine Corps, 1993.

"Report to Congress on the Annual Long-Range Plan for Construction of Naval Vessels for Fiscal Year 2016." Office of the Chief of Naval Operations, Deputy Chief of Naval Operations, Integration of Capabilities and Resources, Washington, D.C., March 2015. https://news.usni.org/wp-content/uploads/2015/04/FY16–30-Year-Shipbuilding-Plan.pdf.

Scales, Robert H. *Certain Victory: The U.S. Army in the Gulf War*. Fort Leavenworth, Kans.: U.S. Army Command and General Staff College Press, 1994.

U.S. Congress. *Nuclear Propulsion for Surface Ships: Hearing before the Joint Committee on Atomic Energy*, 88th Cong., 1st sess., 13 November 1963.

U.S. Congress, House. Committee on Armed Services. *Reorganization Proposals for the Joint Chiefs of Staff: Hearings before the Investigative Subcommittee*, 98th Cong., 1st sess., 14 June 1983.

U.S. Congress, Senate. *National Security Strategy: Hearings before the Committee on the Armed Services*, 100th Cong., 1st sess., 21 January 1987.

———. *Nomination of Admiral Frank B. Kelso II for the Office of Chief of Naval Operations: Hearings before the Committee on Armed Services*, 101th Cong., 2nd sess., 14 and 21 June 1990.

Watkins, James D., and P. X. Kelley. *The Amphibious Warfare Strategy*. Department of the Navy, OPNAV 60 P-2–85/NAVMC-2790, Washington, D.C., 26 June 1985.

White House. "A National Security Strategy of Engagement and Enlargement." White House, Washington, D.C., July 1994. https://www.hsdl.org/?view&did=444939.

Additional Sources

Boyd, John R. "Patterns of Conflict." Presentation briefing to U.S. Army/U.S. Marine Corps, Washington, D.C., 1980. http://www.ausairpower.net/JRB/poc.pdf.

Bush, George H. W. "Remarks at the Aspen Institute Symposium in Aspen, Colorado," 2 August 1990. *The American Presidency Project*, edited by Gerhard Peters and John T. Woolley. https://www.presidency.ucsb.edu/documents/remarks-the-aspen-institute-symposium-aspen-colorado.

Carter, James Earl. Presidential Review Memorandum 10: Comprehensive Military Net Assessment and Posture Review, 18 February 1977. Jimmy Carter Presidential Library and Museum, Atlanta. https://www.jimmycarterlibrary.gov/assets/documents/memorandums/prm10.pdf.

———. "United States Defense Policy Remarks to the Members of the Business Council," 12 December 1979. *The American Presidency Project*, edited by Gerhard Peters and John T. Woolley. https://www.presidency.ucsb.edu/documents/united-states-defense-policy-remarks-members-the-business-council.

Central Intelligence Agency. "Soviet Naval Strategy and Programs through the 1990s: National Intelligence Estimate," NIE 11 15–82/D, March 1983. Central Intelligence Agency, Washington, D.C. http://www.foia.cia.gov/sites/default/files/document_conversions/89801/DOC_0000268225.pdf.

Cropsey, Seth. Memorandum from Deputy Under Secretary of the Navy Seth Cropsey to Navy Secretary John F. Lehman Jr.: DoD Organization, 23 December 1985. Papers of Navy Secretary John F. Lehman Jr., Defense Reorganization files, box 18. Navy History and Heritage Command, Washington, D.C.

———. Memorandum from Deputy Under Secretary of the Navy Seth Cropsey to Secretary of the Navy John Lehman Jr.: Defense Reorganization; Where Things Stand, April 1986. Papers of Navy Secretary John F. Lehman Jr., Defense Reorganization files, box 18. Naval History and Heritage Command, Washington, D.C.

Department of Defense. *Annual Report to the Congress, Fiscal Year 1983*. Washington, D.C.: Office of the Secretary of Defense, 8 February 1982.

———. *Annual Report to the Congress, Fiscal Year 1988*. Washington, D.C.: Office of the Secretary of Defense, 12 January 1987.

Forrestal, James. Memorandum from Secretary of Defense James Forrestal to the United States Joint Chiefs of Staff: Functions of the Armed Forces and the Joint Chiefs of Staff, 21 April 1948. Office of the Defense Secretariat, Washington, D.C.

Goldwater, Barry M. Letter to Caspar Weinberger, 6 March 1986. Papers of James Locher, Special Collections Series, box 14, folder 020, DoD (March), National Defense University, Washington, D.C.

Kelso, Frank B., II. *The Reminiscences of Admiral Frank B. Kelso II, U.S. Navy (Retired)*. In collaboration with Paul Stillwell. Annapolis, Md.: Naval Institute Press, 2009.

Komer, Robert W. Oral History Interview, with Elizabeth Farmer. JFK no. 4, 31 October 1964. John F. Kennedy Presidential Library, Boston. http://archive1.jfklibrary.org/JFKOH/Komer,%20Robert%20W/JFKOH-ROWK-04/JFKOH-ROWK-04-TR.pdf.

Matloff, Maurice. Oral History Interview with Dr. Alain Enthoven, 3 February 1986. U.S. Department of Defense, Historical Office, Stanford, Calif.

McKee, Kinnard R. Oral History: Admiral Kinnaird McKee, USN, pt. 2, 13 June 2000. In collaboration with David F. Winkler. Naval Historical Foundation, Washington, D.C. https://www.navyhistory.org/wp-content/uploads/2014/01/ADM-McKee-Oral-History-Part-2_June-2000.pdf.

Moorer, Thomas H. CSIS Military Reform Project Steering Group memo to Secretary of the Navy John Lehman, 28 February 1985. Papers of Secretary of the Navy John F. Lehman Jr., box 3, Defense Reorganization files, box 3. Naval History and Heritage Command, Washington, D.C.

Mustin, Henry C. Oral History of Vice Admiral Henry C. Mustin, USN (Ret.). In collaboration with David F. Winkler. Naval History and Heritage Command, Washington, D.C., July 2001.

National Security Decision, Directive 32: U.S. National Security Strategy, White House, 20 May 1982. Ronald Reagan Presidential Library Virtual Archive, Simi Valley, Calif. https://www.hsdl.org/?view&did=462986.

PBS. "Oral History: Charles Horner." Interview with Gen. Charles Horner, commander of the U.S. 9th Air Force, for *Frontline: The Gulf War,* aired 9 January 1996. https://www.pbs.org/wgbh/pages/frontline/gulf/oral/horner/1.html.

———. "Oral History: General Norman Schwarzkopf." Interview with Gen. Norman Schwarzkopf, commander in chief, Central Command, for *Frontline: The Gulf War,* aired 9 January 1996. https://www.pbs.org/wgbh/pages/frontline/gulf/oral/schwarzkopf/1.html.

Powers, Bruce, Bob Sheldon, and Mike Garrambone. "Military Operations Research Society (MORS) Oral History Project Interview of Mr. Bruce F. Powers." *Military Operations Research* 21, no. 2 (2016): 107–21.

Reagan, Ronald W. "Remarks at the Recommissioning Ceremony for the USS New Jersey in Long Beach, California," December 28, 1982. *The American Presidency Project,* edited by Gerhard Peters and John T. Woolley. https://www.presidency.ucsb.edu/documents/remarks-the-recommissioning-ceremony-for-the-uss-new-jersey-long-beach-california.

Republican Party. "Republican Party Platform of 1980," July 15, 1980. *The American Presidency Project,* edited by Gerhard Peters and John T. Woolley. https://www.presidency.ucsb.edu/documents/republican-party-platform-1980.

Smith, Leighton W., Jr. *The Reminiscences of Admiral Leighton W. Smith Jr., USN (Ret.).* In collaboration with Paul Stillwell. Annapolis, Md.: Naval Institute Press, 2010.

Tarpgaard, Peter T. *Building a 600-Ship Navy: Costs, Timing and Alternative Approaches.* Washington, D.C.: Congressional Budget Office, March 1982.

Train, Harry DePue. The Oral History of Admiral Harry DePue Train II, USN (Ret.). In collaboration with Paul Stillwell. U.S. Naval Institute, 1997. https://www.usni.org/press/oral-histories/train-harry.

U.S. Congress. *Defense Organization: The Need for Change: Staff Report to the Committee on Armed Services, United States Senate.* Washington, D.C.: U.S. Government Printing Office, 16 October 1985.

Warden, John A., III. *The Air Campaign: Planning for Combat.* Washington, D.C.: National Defense University Press, 1988.

Weinberger, Caspar W. Letter to Senator Barry M. Goldwater, 8 May 1986. Papers of James Locher, acc. no. 330–88–0038, box 14, folder 20, DoD, May 1986. National Defense University, Washington, D.C.

Woodall, Stephen R. "Analysis of the Future: Some Thoughts on the Utility of Resurrection of the Extended Planning Annex (EPA) in Support of Strategic Programming." Office of the Chief of Naval Operations, Strategic Programming Office (N816), Washington, D.C., 25 October 1997.

Interviews and Communications

Armstrong, Clarence "Skip," Rear Adm. USN. Interview, Arlington, Va., 20 February 2015.

Barnett, Roger W., Capt., USN (Ret.). Email to author, 11 February 2016.

Brown, Mitch, Prof., Naval Postgraduate School. Email to author, 8 June 2016.
Fedyszyn, Thomas, Capt., USN (Ret.). Telephone interview, 5 May 2016.
Giarra, Paul, Cdr., USN (Ret.). Email to author, 19 May 2015.
Harris, R. Robinson "Robby," Capt., USN (Ret.). Interview, Arlington, Va., 22 September 2014.
Johnson, William Spencer, Capt., USN (Ret.). Telephone interview, 11 August 2014.
———. Telephone interview, 1 July 2015.
Lehman, John F., Jr. Email to author, 4 May 2020.
———. Telephone interview, 2 December 2013.
O'Brasky, James, National War College. Occasional conversations, 2017–20.
Sestak, Joe, Rear Adm. USN (Ret.). Email to author, 9 February 2015.
Swartz, Peter M., Capt., USN (Ret.). Email to author, 16 September 2016.
———. Interview, Arlington, Va., 20 February 2015.
———. Interview, Arlington, Va., 15 November 2015.
———. Telephone interview, 5 November 2014.
———. Telephone interview, 26 August 2016.
Ullman, Harlan K. Cdr., USN (Ret.), and PhD. Email to author, 12 February 2016.
Weeks, Stanley B., Comm., USN (Ret.). Telephone interview, 16 February 2016.

Memoranda and Letters

Bouchard, Joseph, Capt., USN (Ret.), to Capt. Peter M. Swartz, USN (Ret.). Email: Capstone strategy concepts, 28 June 2005. Personal and professional papers of Swartz, The Way Ahead file, Washington, D.C.
Brown, Mitch, Prof., Naval Postgraduate School, to Capt. Peter Swartz, USN (Ret.). Email: Naval Postgraduate School curriculum, 14 March 2008. Personal and professional papers of Swartz, Maritime Strategy folder, Washington, D.C.
Clemente, Mark N., Capt., USN (Ret.), to Capt. Peter M. Swartz, USN (Ret.). Email: From the Sea, 12 December 2009. Personal and professional papers of Swartz, From the Sea file, Washington, D.C.
Diamond, Richard, Capt., USN (Ret.), to Capt. Peter M. Swartz, USN (Ret.). Email: Comments on Navy Policy Book, 7 July 2006. The personal and professional papers of Swartz, The Navy Policy Book file, Washington D.C.
Diamond, Richard, Capt., USN (Ret.), to Capt. Peter M. Swartz, USN (Ret.). Email: The Way Ahead and the Navy Policy Book, 7 July 2006. Personal and professional papers of Swartz, Demise of the Maritime Strategy file, Washington, D.C.
Diamond, Richard, Capt., USN (Ret.), to Capt. Peter M. Swartz, USN (Ret.). Email: First Sea Lord on UK defense, 2 December 2009. Personal and professional papers of Swartz, From the Sea file, Washington, D.C.
Diamond, Richard, Capt., USN (Ret.), to Prof. John B. Hattendorf, U.S. Naval War College. Email: Paper review status (unpublished narrative of the events leading up to the September 1992 publication of From the Sea), 9 September 2006. Copies

filed with the U.S. Naval War College and the Naval Historical Collection and among the papers of Prof. John B. Hattendorf, Newport, R.I., and the personal and professional papers of Capt. Peter M. Swartz, USN (Ret.), The Way Ahead 1991 file, Washington, D.C.

Dunaway, Michael, Capt., USN (Ret.), to Capt. Peter M. Swartz, USN (Ret.). Email: Drafting Adm. Frank Kelso's first Way Ahead document, 2 May 2005. Personal and professional papers of Swartz, The Way Ahead file, Washington, D.C.

Hughes, Wayne P., professor emeritus, Naval Postgraduate School, to Capt. Peter M. Swartz, USN (Ret.). Email: The lack of Navy strategy, 29 October 2014. Personal and professional papers of Swartz, N96 file, Washington, D.C.

Myers, Judith M., Capt., USN (Ret.), to Capt. Peter M. Swartz, USN (Ret.). Email: Remember the Navy Policy Book!, 6 June 2012. Personal and professional papers of Swartz, Policy Book file, Washington, D.C.

Small, William T., Adm. USN (Ret.), to Capt. Peter M. Swartz, USN (Ret.). Fax memorandum: Maritime Strategy development, 2 October 1998. Personal and professional papers of Swartz, Post-1991 Commentary on the Maritime Strategy file, Washington, D.C.

Stark, James R., Rear Adm., USN (Ret.), to Capt. Peter M. Swartz, USN (Ret.). Email: USN force goals, 1990s, 3 September 2008. Personal and professional papers of Swartz, The Way Ahead file, Washington, D.C.

Stavridis, James, Vice Adm., USN, to Capt. Peter M. Swartz, USN (Ret.). Email: Navy strategy, 28 June 2006. Personal and professional papers of Swartz, The Way Ahead file, Washington, D.C.

Trost, Carlisle A. H., Adm. USN (Ret.), to John B. Hattendorf. Letter: Maritime Strategy, 2007. Personal and professional papers of Swartz, Maritime Strategy post-1990 file, Washington, D.C.

SECONDARY SOURCES

Books and Reports

Allen, Thomas B., and Norman Polmar. *Rickover, Father of the Nuclear Navy.* Washington, D.C.: Potomac Books, 2007.

Bacevich, Andrew J. *The New American Militarism: How Americans Are Seduced by War.* New York: Oxford University Press, 2005.

Baer, George W. *One Hundred Years of Sea Power: The U.S. Navy, 1890–1990.* Stanford, Calif.: Stanford University Press, 1994.

Barlow, Jeffrey G. *From Hot War to Cold: The U.S. Navy and National Security Affairs, 1945–1955.* Stanford, Calif.: Stanford University Press, 2009.

Barnett, Rodger W. *Navy Strategic Culture: Why the Navy Thinks Differently.* Annapolis, Md.: Naval Institute Press, 2009.

Barnett, Thomas P. M. *The Pentagon's New Map: War and Peace in the 21st Century.* New York: Putnam, 2004.

Berman, Larry. *Zumwalt: The Life and Times of Admiral Elmo Russell "Bud" Zumwalt Jr.* New York: Harper Collins, 2012.

Birkler, John, John F. Schank, James Chiesa, Giles Smith, Irv Blickstein, Ronald D. Fricker Jr., and Denis Rushworth. "Option for Funding Aircraft Carriers." RAND Corporation, Santa Monica, Calif., 2002.

Bolt, Paul J., Damon Coletta, and Collins G. Shackelford Jr., eds. *American Defense Policy.* 8th ed. Baltimore. Md.: Johns Hopkins University Press, 2008.

Boslaugh, David L. *When Computers Went to Sea: The Digitalization of the United States Navy.* Los Alamitos, Calif.: IEEE Computer Society Press, 1999.

Bradford, James C. *America, Seapower and the World.* Oxford: John Wiley and Sons, 2016.

Bradford, James C., ed. *Quarterdeck and Bridge: Two Centuries of American Naval Leadership.* Annapolis, Md.: Naval Institute Press, 1997.

Brodie, Bernard. "War in the Atomic Age." In *The Absolute Weapon: Atomic Power and World Order,* edited by Bernard Brodie. New Haven: Yale Institute of International Studies, 15 February 1946. https://www.osti.gov/opennet/servlets/purl/16380564-wvLB09/16380564.pdf.

"The Budget of the US Navy: 1794–2014." Naval History and Heritage Command, 31 May 2016. https://www.history.navy.mil/research/library/online-reading-room/title-list-alphabetically/b/budget-of-the-us-navy-1794-to-2004.html.

Builder, Carl H. *The Army in the Strategic Planning Process: Who Shall Bell the Cat?* R-3515-A. Santa Monica, Calif.: RAND Corporation, April 1987.

———. *The Masks of War: American Military Styles in Strategy and Analysis.* Baltimore, Md.: Johns Hopkins University Press, 1989.

Bush, George H. W., and Brent Scowcroft. *A World Transformed: The Collapse of the Soviet Empire, the Unification of Germany, Tiananmen Square, and the Gulf War.* New York: Alfred Knopf, 1998.

Clodfelter, Mark. *The Limits of Air Power: The American Bombing of North Vietnam.* Lincoln: University of Nebraska Press, 2006.

Colomb, Philip H. *Naval Warfare: Its Ruling Principles and Practice Theoretically Treated.* 2nd ed. London: W. H. Allen and Company, 1895. https://archive.org/stream/navalwarfareoocologoog#page/n41/mode/2up.

Coram, Robert. *Boyd: The Fighter Pilot Who Changed the Art of War.* New York: Little Brown and Company, 2002.

Crowe, William J. *In the Line of Fire: From Washington to the Gulf, the Politics and Battles of the New Military.* New York: Simon and Schuster, 1993.

C-SPAN. "Aircraft Carrier Replacement," 12 March 1987. https://www.c-span.org/video/?56752–1/aircraft-carrier-replacement.

Cutler, Thomas J. *Brown Water, Black Berets: Coastal and Riverine Warfare in Vietnam.* Annapolis, Md.: Naval Institute Press, 2012.

DeYoung, Karen. *Soldier: The Life of Colin Powell.* New York: Alfred Knopf, 2006.

Dismukes, Bradford. "National Security Strategy and Forward Presence: Implications for Acquisition and Use of Forces." CRM 93–192. Center for Naval Analyses, Alexandria, Va., March 1994.

Dombrowski, Peter, ed. *Naval Power in the 21st Century: A Naval War College Review Reader.* Newport, R.I.: Naval War College Press, 2005.

Dorwart, Jeffrey M. *Eberstadt and Forrestal: A National Security Partnership, 1909–1949.* College Station: Texas A&M University Press, 1991.

Drea, Edward, et al. *History of the Unified Command Plan, 1946–2012.* Washington, D.C.: Office of the Chairman of the Joint Chiefs of Staff, Joint History Office, 2013.

Echevarria, Antulio. "American Operational Art, 1917–2008." In *The Evolution of Operational Art: From Napoleon to the Present,* edited by John Andreas Olsen and Martin Van Creveld. Oxford: Oxford University Press, 2011.

Eisenhower, Dwight D. *The White House Years: Mandate for Change, 1953–1956.* New York: Doubleday, 1963.

Endicott, John F., and Roy W. Stafford Jr., eds. *American Defense Policy.* 4th ed. Baltimore, Md.: Johns Hopkins University Press, 1980.

Engel, Gregory A. "Cruise Missiles and the Tomahawk." In *The Politics of Naval Innovation,* edited by Bradd C. Hayes, and Douglas V. Smith, 16–39. Strategic Research Department Research Report 4-94. Newport, R.I.: U.S. Naval War College, Center for Naval Warfare Studies, 1 August 1994.

Enthoven, Alain C., and K. Wayne Smith. *How Much Is Enough? Shaping the Defense Program, 1961–1969.* Santa Monica, Calif.: RAND Corporation, 1971.

Etzold, Thomas H. "The Navy and National Policy in the 1970s." In *Military Planning in the Twentieth Century: Proceedings of the Eleventh Military History Symposium, 10–12 October 1984,* edited by Harry R. Borowski. Washington, D.C. U.S. Air Force, Office of Air Force History, 1986.

Falk, Kevin. *Why Nations Put to Sea: Technology and the Changing Character of Seapower.* New York: Garland Publishing, 2000.

Faller, Craig S. *The Navy and Jointness: No Longer Reluctant Partners?* Monterey, Calif.: Naval Postgraduate School, 1991.

FitzGerald, Mary C. "Marshal Ogarkov and the New Soviet Revolution in Military Affairs." CRM-87-2. Center for Naval Analyses, Alexandria, Va., January 1987.

Ford, Christopher A., and David Alan Rosenberg. *The Admiral's Advantage: U.S. Navy Operational Intelligence in World War II and the Cold War.* Annapolis, Md.: Naval Institute Press, 2005.

Friedman, Norman. *The Fifty-Year War: Conflict and Strategy in the Cold War.* Annapolis, Md.: Naval Institute Press, 2000.

———. *Seapower as Strategy: Navies and National Interests.* Annapolis, Md.: Naval Institute Press, 2000.

Fulton, William B. *Vietnam Studies Series: Riverine Operations, 1966–1969.* Washington, D.C.: Department of the Army, 1973.

Gaddis, John Lewis. *Strategies of Containment: A Critical Appraisal of American Security Policy during the Cold War.* Rev. ed. Oxford: Oxford University Press, 2005.

Goldwater, Barry M. *Goldwater.* In collaboration with Jack Casserly. New York: Doubleday, 1988.

Gordon, Michael R., and Bernard E. Trainor. *The General's War: The Inside Story of the Conflict in the Gulf.* New York: Little Brown and Company, 1995.

Gorshkov, Sergey Georgiyevich. *The Seapower of the State*. Annapolis, Md.: Naval Institute Press, 1979.

Grove, Eric. *Maritime Strategy and European Security.* Common Security Studies 2. London: Brassey's, 1990.

Hallion, Richard P. *Storm over Iraq: Air Power and the Gulf War.* Washington, D.C.: Smithsonian Institution Press, 1992.

"Harold Brown." Historical Office, Office of the Secretary of Defense, Washington, D.C. http://history.defense.gov/Multimedia/Biographies/Article-View/Article/571287/harold-brown/.

Harrell, Margaret C., Harry J. Thie, Jefferson P. Marquis, Kevin Brancato, Ronald J. Yardley, Clifford M. Graf II, and Jerry Sollinger. *Outside the Fleet: External Requirements for Naval Officers.* Santa Monica, Calif., RAND Corporation, 2002.

Hartmann, Frederick H. *Naval Renaissance: The U.S. Navy in the 1980s.* Annapolis, Md.: Naval Institute Press, 1990.

Hattendorf, John B. *The Evolution of the U.S. Navy's Maritime Strategy, 1977–1986.* Newport, R.I.: Naval War College Press, 2004.

Hattendorf, John B., ed. *U.S. Naval Strategy in the 1970s: Selected Documents.* Newport, R.I.: Naval War College Press, September 2007.

———. ed. *U.S. Naval Strategy in the 1990s: Selected Documents.* Newport, R.I.: Naval War College Press, September 2006.

Hattendorf, John B., and Peter M. Swartz, eds. *U.S. Naval Strategy in the 1980s: Selected Documents.* Newport, R.I.: Naval War College Press, December 2008.

Hay, Bud, and Bob Gile. *Global War Game: The First Five Years.* Newport, R.I.: Naval War College Press, June 1993.

Hayes, Bradd C., and Douglas V. Smith, eds. *The Politics of Naval Innovation.* Strategic Research Department Research Report 4-94. Newport, R.I.: U.S. Naval War College, Center for Naval Warfare Studies, 1 August 1994.

Haynes, Peter D. *Toward a New Maritime Strategy: American Naval Thinking in the Post–Cold War Era.* Annapolis, Md.: Naval Institute Press, 2015.

Hays, Peter J., Brenda J. Vallance, and Alan R. Van Tassel, eds. *American Defense Policy.* 7th ed. Baltimore, Md.: Johns Hopkins University Press, 1997.

Herrick, Robert Waring. *Soviet Naval Strategy: Fifty Years of Theory and Practice.* Annapolis, Md.: Naval Institute Press, 1968.

Herspring, Dale Roy. *The Soviet High Command, 1967–1989: Personalities and Politics.* Princeton: Princeton University Press, 1990.

Hewes, James E., Jr. *From Root to McNamara: Army Organization and Administration, 1900–1963.* Special Studies Series. Washington, D.C.: U.S. Army Center of Military History, 1983.

Holloway, James L., III. *Aircraft Carriers at War: A Personal Retrospective of Korea, Vietnam, and the Soviet Confrontation.* Annapolis, Md.: Naval Institute Press, 2007.

Hone, Thomas C. *Power and Change: The Administrative History of the Office of the Chief of Naval Operations, 1946–1986.* Washington, D.C.: Naval Historical Center, 1989.

Hone, Thomas C., Douglas V. Smith, and Rodger C. Easton Jr. "Aegis Evolutionary or Revolutionary Technology?" In *The Politics of Naval Innovation,* edited by Brad C. Hayes and Douglas V. Smith. Strategic Research Department Report 4-94. Newport, RI: U.S. Naval War College, Center for Naval Warfare Studies, 1 August 1994, 59.

Howarth, Stephen. *To Shining Sea: A History of the United States Navy, 1775–1998.* Norman: University of Oklahoma Press, 1991.

Hughes, Wayne P. *Fleet Tactics and Coastal Combat,* 2nd ed. Annapolis, Md.: Naval Institute Press, 2000.

Hunt, Richard A. *Melvin Laird and the Foundation of the Post-Vietnam Military, 1969–1973.* Washington, D.C.: Office of the Secretary of Defense, Historical Office, 2015.

Huntington, Samuel P. *The Soldier and the State: The Theory and Politics of Military Relations.* Cambridge, Mass.: Harvard University Press, 1957.

Isenberg, Michael T. *Shield of the Republic: The United States Navy in an Era of Cold War and Violent Peace, 1945–1962.* New York: St. Martin's Press, 1993.

Jablonsky, David. *War by Land, Sea, and Air: Dwight Eisenhower and the Concept of Unified Command.* New Haven: Yale University Press, 2010.

Jaffe, Lorna S. "The Development of the Base Force, 1989–1993." Office of the Chairman of the Joint Chiefs of Staff, Joint History Office, Washington, D.C., 1993.

Jones, Frank Leith. *Blowtorch: Robert Komer, Vietnam, and American Cold War Strategy.* Annapolis, Md.: Naval Institute Press, 2013.

Kaplan, Lawrence S., Ronald D. Landa, and Edward J. Drea. *History of the Office of the Secretary of Defense.* Vol. 5, *The McNamara Ascendancy, 1961–65.* Washington, D.C.: Office of the Secretary of Defense, Joint History Office, 2006.

Kaufman, Scott, ed. *A Companion to Gerald R. Ford and Jimmy Carter.* Chichester, UK: John Wiley and Sons, 2016.

Kelly, Mike, and Justin Brennan. *Alien: How Operational Art Devoured Strategy.* Carlisle, Pa.: U.S. Army War College Strategic Studies Institute, 2009.

Korb, Lawrence J. "Where Did All the Money Go? The 1980s Defense Buildup and the End of the Cold War." In *Mysteries of the Cold War,* edited by Stephen J. Cimballa. Aldershot, UK: Ashgate Publishing Company, 1999.

Krepinevich, Andrew E., Jr. "The Military Technical Revolution: A Preliminary Assessment." Center for Strategic and Budgetary Assessments, Washington, D.C., 2002.

Lederman, Nathaniel Gordon. *Reorganizing the Joint Chiefs of Staff: The Goldwater Nichols Act of 1986.* Westport, Conn.: Greenwood Press, 1999.

Lee, Thomas H., Shoji Shiba, and Robert Chapman Wood. *Integrated Management Systems: A Practical Approach to Transforming Organizations.* New York: John Wiley and Sons, 1999.

Lehman, John F., Jr. *Command of the Seas.* Annapolis, Md.: Naval Institute Press, 2001.

Lehman, John F., and Harvey Sicherman, eds. *America the Vulnerable: Our Military Problems and How to Fix Them.* Philadelphia: Foreign Policy Research Institute, 2002.

Leighton, Richard M. *History of the Office of the Secretary of Defense.* Vol. 3, *Strategy, Money, and the New Look, 1953–1956.* Washington, D.C.: Office of the Secretary of Defense, Historical Office, 2001.

Linn, Brian McAllister. *The Echo of Battle: The Army's Way of War.* Cambridge, Mass.: Harvard University Press, 2007.

Locher, James R., III. *Victory on the Potomac: The Goldwater Nichols Act Unifies the Pentagon.* College Station: Texas A&M University Press, 2002.

Logevall, Fredirk. *Choosing War: The Lost Chance for Peace and the Escalation of the War in Vietnam.* Berkeley: University of California Press, 1999.

Lovelace, Douglas C. "The DoD Reorganization Act of 1986: Improving the Department through Centralization and Integration." In *Organizing for National Security,* edited by Douglas Stuart. Carlisle, Pa.: United States Army War College Strategic Studies Institute, November 2000.

Luttwak, Edward N. *The Pentagon and the Art of War: The Question of Military Reform.* New York: Simon and Schuster, 1984.

Mahan, Alfred Thayer. *The Problem of Asia and Its Effect upon International Policies.* Boston: Little Brown and Company, 1900.

Mansoor, Peter R., and Williamson Murray. *Grand Strategies and Military Alliances.* Cambridge: Cambridge University Press, 2016.

Marolda, Edward J. *The United States Navy and the Korean War.* Annapolis, Md.: Naval Institute Press, 2007.

Marolda, Edward J., and Robert J. Schneller, Jr. *Shield and Sword: The United States Navy and the Persian Gulf War.* Washington, D.C.: Naval Historical Center, 1998.

McInnis, Kathleen J. "Goldwater-Nichols at 30: Defense Reform and Issues for Congress." Congressional Research Service, Washington D.C., 2 June 2016.

McMaster, H. R. *Dereliction of Duty: Lyndon Johnson, Robert McNamara, the Joint Chiefs of Staff, and the Lies That Led to Vietnam.* New York: Harper Collins, 1997.

Metz, Steven K. *Eisenhower as Strategist: The Coherent Use of Military Power in War and Peace.* Carlisle, Pa.: U.S. Army War College, Strategic Studies Institute, 1992.

———. *Iraq and the Evolution of American Strategy.* Washington, D.C.: Potomac Books, 2008.

Michishita, Narushigue, Peter M. Swartz, and David F. Winkler. "Lessons of the Cold War in the Pacific: U.S. Maritime Strategy, Crisis, Prevention and Japan's Role." Wilson Center Asia Program, Washington, D.C., March 2016.

Miller, Edward S. *War Plan Orange: The U.S. Strategy to Defeat Japan, 1897–1945.* Annapolis, Md.: Naval Institute Press, 1991.

Millett, Allan R. *The American Political System and Civilian Control of the Military: A Historical Perspective.* Columbus: Mershon Center of the Ohio State University, 1979.

Muir, Malcolm, Jr. *Black Shoes and Blue Water: Surface Warfare in the United States Navy, 1945–1975.* Washington, D.C.: Naval Historical Center, 1996.

Murray, Robert J. "Reform of the Joint Chiefs of Staff." In *The Reorganization of the Joint Chiefs of Staff: A Critical Analysis.* Cambridge, Mass.: Institute for Foreign Policy Analysis, 1986.

Naftali, Timothy. Interview with John Lehman. Richard Nixon Presidential Library, 4 October 2007. https://www.nixonlibrary.gov/virtuallibrary/documents/histories/lehman-2007-10-04.pdf.

Neider, Ferd, and Thomas P. M. Barnett. "Memorandum for the Record: The Final Report of the Naval Force Capabilities Planning Effort, Phases I and II." CNA 92-0527. Alexandria, Va.: Center for Naval Analyses, 23 March 1992.

Nemfakos, Charles, Irv Blickstein, Aine Seitz McCarthy, and Jerry M. Sollinger. *The Perfect Storm: The Goldwater Nichols Act and Its Effects on Navy Acquisition.* Santa Monica, Calif.: RAND Corporation, 2010.

Neustadt, Richard E., and Ernest R. May. *Thinking in Time: The Uses of History for Decision Makers.* New York: Simon and Schuster, 1986.

O'Rourke, Ronald. "The Future of the U.S. Navy." In Fifty Years of Canada–United States Defense Cooperation: The Road from Ogdensburg, edited by Joel J. Sokolsky and Joseph Jockel. Lewiston, N.Y.: Edwin Mellen Press, 1992.

Owens, William A. *High Seas: The Naval Passage to an Uncharted World.* Annapolis, Md.: Naval Institute Press, 1995.

———. *Lifting the Fog of War.* In collaboration with Ed Offley. New York: Farrar, Strauss, and Giroux, 2000.

Palmer, Michael A. *The Origins of the Maritime Strategy.* Annapolis, Md.: Naval Institute Press, 1988.

Parcell, Anne D., Donald J. Cymrot, and Carol S. Moore. *The Officer Structure in the 21st Century.* CRM D0003570.A2. Alexandria, Va.: Center for Naval Analyses, May 2001.

Parker, Geoffrey. *The Military Revolution: Military Innovation and the Rise of the West, 1500–1800.* Cambridge: Cambridge University Press, 1996.

Perry, William J. "Technology and National Security: Risks and Responsibilities." Stanford, Calif.: Stanford University, France-Stanford Center for Interdisciplinary Studies, April 2003. http://stanford.edu/dept/france-stanford/Conferences/Risk/Perry.pdf.

Pierce, Terry C. *Warfighting and Disruptive Technologies: Disguising Innovation.* New York: Frank Cass Publishing, 2004.

Pierrot, Lane. *Naval Combat Aircraft: Issues and Options.* Washington, D.C.: Congressional Budget Office, November 1987.

Pokrant, Marvin. *Desert Shield at Sea: What the Navy Really Did.* Westport, Conn.: Greenwood Press, 1999.

———. *Desert Storm at Sea: What the Navy Really Did.* Westport, Conn.: Greenwood Press, 1999.

Polmar, Norman. *Aircraft Carriers: A History of Carrier Aviation.* Vol. 2, *1946–2005.* Washington, D.C.: Potomac Books, 2008.

Powell, Colin L. *My American Journey.* In collaboration with Joseph E. Persico. New York: Ballantine Books, 1995.

Preble, Christopher A. "The Cold War Navy in the Post War World." Policy Analysis 195. Cato Institute, Washington, D.C., 2 August 1993.

Prime, Nicholas. "The Making of the Control School of Strategy: Joseph C. Wylie, Henry Eccles and Herbert Rossinski at the Naval War College, 1950–1974." PhD diss., Kings College London, 2017.

Punaro, Arnold L. *On War, On Politics: The Battlefield inside Washington's Beltway.* In collaboration with David Poyer. Annapolis, Md.: Naval Institute Press, 2016.

Radford, Arthur W. *From Pearl Harbor to Vietnam: The Memoirs of Admiral Arthur W. Radford.* Stanford, Calif.: Hoover Institution Press, 1980.

Raines, Edward F., Jr., and David R. Campbell. *Evolution of Army Ideas on the Command, Control, and Coordination of the U.S. Armed Forces, 1942–1985.* Washington, D.C.: U.S. Army Center of Military History, 1986.

Ratcliff, Ronald. "CNO and OPNAV Reorganization." In *Case Studies in Policy Making and Implementation,* 6th ed., edited by David A. Williams. Newport, R.I.: Naval War College Press, 2002.

Rearden, Steven L. *Council of War: A History of the Joint Chiefs of Staff, 1942–1991.* Washington, D.C.: Joint Chiefs of Staff, Office of the Director of the Joint Staff, Joint History Office, 2012.

———. *History of the Office of the Secretary of Defense: The Formative Years.* Washington, D.C.: U.S. Government Printing Office, 1984.

Romjue, John L. *From Active Defense to AirLand Battle: The Development of Army Doctrine, 1973–1982.* Fort Monroe, Va.: U.S. Army Training and Doctrine Command Historical Office, 1984.

Rosenberg, David Alan. "Arleigh Burke: The Last CNO." Naval History and Heritage Command, Washington, D.C., 22 December 2015. https://www.history.navy.mil/research/library/online-reading-room/title-list-alphabetically/a/arleigh-burke-the-last-cno.html.

———. "The Realities of Formulating Modern Naval Strategy." In *Mahan Is Not Enough: The Proceedings of the Conference on the Writings of Sir Julian Corbett and Admiral Sir Herbert Richmond,* edited by James Goldrick, and John Hattendorf. Newport, R.I.: Naval War College Press, 1993.

Russell, James A., James Wirtz, Donald Abenheim, Thomas-Durrell Young, and Diana Wueger. "Navy Strategy Development: Strategy in the 21st Century." Naval Postgraduate School, Monterey, Calif., June 2015.

Ryan, Paul B. *First Line of Defense: The U.S. Navy since 1945.* Stanford, Calif. Hoover Institution Press, 1981.

Sands, Jeffrey I. *On His Watch: Admiral Zumwalt's Efforts to Institutionalize Strategic Change.* CRM 93-23. Alexandria, Va.: Center for Naval Analyses, July 1993.

Schirmer, Peter. *Challenging Time in DOPMA: Flexible and Contemporary Military Officer Management.* Santa Monica, Calif.: RAND Corporation, 2006.

Sherry, Mark D. *The Army Command Post and Defense Reshaping, 1987–1997.* Washington, D.C.: U.S. Army Center of Military History, 2008.

Skinner, Douglas W. "Airland Battle Doctrine." Professional Paper 463. Center for Naval Analyses, Alexandria, Va., September 1988.

Snider, Don M. "Strategy, Forces and Budgets: Dominant Influences in Executive Decision Making, Post–Cold War, 1989–1991." Carlilse, Pa.: U.S. Army War College Strategic Studies Institute, February 1993.

Snyder, William P., and James, Brown, eds. *Defense Policy in the Reagan Administration.* Washington, D.C.: National Defense University, 1988.

Sokolsky, Joel J. *Seapower in the Nuclear Age: The United States Navy and NATO, 1949–80.* Annapolis, Md.: Naval Institute Press, 1991.

Sontag, Sherry, and Christopher Drew. *Blind Man's Bluff: The Untold Story of American Submarine Espionage.* In collaboration with Lawrence Drew. New York: Public Affairs, 1998.

Spector, Ronald H. *At War at Sea: Sailors and Naval Warfare in the 20th Century.* New York: Viking Press, 2001.

Sprout, Harold H., and Margaret Sprout. *Toward a New Order of Seapower: American Naval Policy and the World Scene, 1918–1922.* New York: Greenwood Press, 1974.

Starry, Donn A., ed. *Press On: The Selected Works of General Donn A. Starry.* In collaboration with Lewis S. Sorley, Fort Leavenworth, Kans.: U.S. Army Combined Arms Center Combat Studies Institute Press, September 2009.

Stuart, Douglas T., ed. *Organizing for National Security.* Carlisle, Pa.: U.S. Army War College Strategic Studies Institute, November 2000.

Sumida, Jon T. *Inventing Grand Strategy and Teaching Command: The Classic Works of Alfred Thayer Mahan Reconsidered.* Baltimore, Md.: Johns Hopkins University Press, 1999.

Summers, Harry G., Jr. *On Strategy: The Vietnam War in Context.* Honolulu: University Press of the Pacific, 2002.

———."Operations, Procurement, and Industrial Base." In *America the Vulnerable: Our Military Problems and How to Fix Them,* edited by John F. Lehman and Harvey Sicherman. Philadelphia: Foreign Policy Research Institute, 2002.

Swartz, Peter M. *Drawing Lines in the Sea: The U.S. Navy Confronts the Unified Command Plan.* CRM 99-3.09. Alexandria, Va.: Center for Naval Analyses, January 1999.

———. *Organizing OPNAV, 1970–2009.* In collaboration with Michael Markowitz. CAB D0020997.A5/2Rev. Alexandria, Va.: Center for Naval Analyses, January 2010.

———. *Understanding an Adversary's Strategic and Operational Calculus: A Late Cold War Case Study with 21st Century Applicability.* In collaboration with Michael Connell. COP-2013-U-005622. Alexandria, Va.: Center for Naval Analyses, August 2013.

———. *U.S. Navy Capstone Strategies and Concepts: Introduction, Background and Analyses.* In collaboration with Karin Duggan. MISC D0026421.A1. Alexandria, Va.: Center for Naval Analyses, December 2011.

———. *U.S. Navy Capstone Strategies and Concepts, 1970–1980: Strategy, Policy, Concept and Vision Documents.* In collaboration with Karin Duggan. MISC D0026414.A1. Alexandria, Va.: Center for Naval Analyses, December 2011.

———. *U.S. Navy Capstone Strategies and Concepts, 1981–1990: Strategy, Policy, Concept and Vision Documents*. In collaboration with Karin Duggan. MISC D0026415.A1. Alexandria, Va.: Center for Naval Analyses, December 2011.

———. *U.S. Navy Capstone Strategies and Concepts, 1991–2000: Strategy, Policy, Concept and Vision Documents*. In collaboration with Karin Duggan. MISC D0026416.A2. Alexandria, Va.: Center for Naval Analyses, March 2012.

———. *U.S. Navy Capstone Strategy, Policy, Vision and Concept Documents: What to Consider before You Write One*. Alexandria, Va.: CNA, 2009.

———. *U.S. Navy–U.S. Air Force Relationships, 1970–2010*. In collaboration with Karin Duggan. MISC D0024022.A4/1Rev. Alexandria, Va.: Center for Naval Analyses, June 2011.

Tarpgaard, Peter T., and Robert E. Mechanic. *Future Budget Requirements for the 600-Ship Navy*. Washington D.C.: Congressional Budget Office, September 1985.

Thompson, Rodger. *Brown Shoes, Black Shoes and Felt Slippers: Parochialism and the Evolution of the Post-War U.S. Navy*. Strategic Research Department Report 5-95. Newport, R.I.: Naval War College Press, 1995.

Till, Geoffrey. *Seapower: A Guide for the 21st Century*. London: Frank Cass Books, 2009.

Tomes, Robert. *U.S. Defense Strategy from Vietnam to Operation Iraqi Freedom: Military Innovation and the New American Way of War, 1973–2003*. London: Routledge, 2007.

Tower, John G. *Consequences: A Personal and Political Memoir*. Boston: Little, Brown and Co., 1991.

Trauschweizer, Ingo. *The Cold War U.S. Army: Building Deterrence for Limited War*. Lawrence: University Press of Kansas, 2008.

Turley, Gerald H. *The Journey of a Warrior: The Twenty Ninth Commandant of the United States Marine Corps (1987–1991). General Alfred Mason Gray*. Arlington, Va.: Potomac Institute Press, 2010.

Weigley, Russell F. *The American Way of War: A History of United States Military Strategy and Policy*. Bloomington: Indiana University Press, 1973.

Werrell, Kenneth P. *The Evolution of the Cruise Missile*. Maxwell Air Force Base, Ala.: Air University Press, September 1985. https://www.airuniversity.af.edu/Portals/10/AUPress/Books/B_0006_WERRELL_EVOLUTION_CRUISE_MISSILE.pdf.

Williams, John Allen. "The U.S. Navy under the Reagan Administration." In *Defense Policy in the Reagan Administration*, edited by William P. Snyder and James Brown. Washington, D.C.: National Defense University Press, 1988.

Worden, R. Michael. *Rise of the Fighter Generals: The Problem of Air Force Leadership, 1945–1982*. Maxwell Air Force Base, Ala.: Air University Press, 1998.

Worley, Robert D. *Shaping U.S. Military Forces: Revolution or Relevance in a Post–Cold War World*. London: Praeger Security International, 2006.

Wylie, Joseph C. *Military Strategy: A General Theory of Power Control*. Annapolis, Md.: Naval Institute Press, 1989.

Yoshitani, Gail, E. S. *Reagan on War: A Reappraisal of the Weinberger Doctrine, 1980–1984*. College Station: Texas A&M University Press, 2012.

Zakheim, Dov S., and Andrew Hamilton. *U.S. Naval Forces: The Peacetime Presence Mission*. Washington, D.C.: Congressional Budget Office, December 1978.

Zakheim, Dov S., et al. *Resources for Defense: A Review of Key Issues for Fiscal Years 1982–1986*. Washington, D.C.: Congressional Budget Office, January 1981.

Zegart, Amy B. *Flawed by Design: The Evolution of the CIA, JCS, and NSC*. Stanford, Calif.: Stanford University Press, 1999.

Articles

Anderson, John R. "ALSA Center Meets Immediate Needs of the Warfighter." *Infantry Magazine*, May–June 2006.

Arkin, William. "Our Risky Naval Strategy Could Get Us All Killed." *Washington Post*, 3 July 1988.

Borrenson, Jacob. "Alliance Naval Strategies in Norway in the Final Years of the Cold War." *Naval War College Review* 64, no. 2 (Spring 2011).

Boyne, Walter J. "Route Pack 6." *Air Force Magazine*, 1 November 1999, http://www.airforcemag.com/MagazineArchive/Pages/1999/November%201999/1199pack.aspx.

Breemer, Jan S. "The End of Naval Strategy: Revolutionary Change and the Future of American Naval Power." *Strategic Review* 22, no. 2 (Spring 1994).

Brooks, Linton F. "Naval Power and National Security: The Case for the Maritime Strategy." *International Security* 11, no. 2 (Fall 1986).

Brooks, Thomas A., and William H. Manthorpe. "Setting the Record Straight: A Critical Review of *Fall from Glory* by Gregory I. Vistica." *Naval Intelligence Professional's Quarterly* (Spring 1996).

Chiarelli, Peter W. "Beyond Goldwater-Nichols." *Joint Forces Quarterly* (Autumn 1993).

Chipman, Donald D., and David Lay. "Sea Power and the B-52 Stratofortress." *Air University Review* (January/February 1986).

Cropsey, Seth. "The Limits of Jointness." *Joint Forces Quarterly* (Summer 1993).

Cushman, John H., Jr. "Admiral Frank B. Kelso Dies at 79, Tied to Tailhook Scandal." *New York Times*, 28 June 2013.

Davis Evans. "Navy Secretary Quits over $12 Billion Dollar Cut." *Chicago Tribune*, 23 February 1988.

Durell-Young, Thomas. "When Programming Trumps Policy and Plans: The Case of the U.S. Department of the Navy." *Journal of Strategic Studies* (10 May 2016).

Eckstein, Megan. "CNO Richardson Wants Aggressive Timelines for New Weapons, Operational Concepts in Updated Navy 'Design.'" *Naval Institute News*, 18 December 2018. https://news.usni.org/2018/12/17/cno-richardson-calls-aggressive-timelines-new-weapons-operational-concepts-updated-navy-design.

Fedyszyn, Thomas. "A Maritime Perspective." U.S. Naval Institute *Proceedings* (July 1985).

Ford, Christopher A., and David Alan Rosenberg. "The Naval Intelligence Underpinnings of Reagan's Maritime Strategy." *Journal of Strategic Studies* 28, no. 2 (April 2005).

Ganley, Michael. "How's That Again? You're Opposed to What?" *Armed Forces Journal* (March 1986).

Garrett, H. Lawrence, III, Frank B. Kelso II, and A. M. Gray. "The Way Ahead." U.S. Naval Institute *Proceedings* 117, no. 4 (April 1991).

Gelb, Leslie. "Foreign Affairs: Who Won the Cold War?" *New York Times*, 20 August 1992.

Goldstein, Lyle J., and Yuri M. Zhukov. "A Tale of Two Fleets: A Russian Perspective on the 1973 Naval Standoff in the Mediterranean." *Naval War College Review* (Spring 2004).

Grady, John. "Book Review: *The Journey of a Warrior: The Twenty Ninth Commandant of the United States Marine Corps (1987–1991),* Alfred Mason Gray." Naval Historical Foundation, 11 December 2012. http://www.navyhistory.org/2012/12/book-review-journey-of-a-warrior-29th-commandant-marine-corps-general-alfred-mason-gray/.

Hanley, John T. "Creating the 1980s Maritime Strategy and Implications for Today." *Naval War College Review* 67, no. 2 (Spring 2014).

Hayes, Bradd. "Keeping the Naval Service Relevant." U.S. Naval Institute *Proceedings* (October 1993).

Healy, Melissa. "Navy Secretary Resigns over Budget Cutbacks: Webb Says He Can't Back Carlucci, Plan to Mothball 16 Ships." *Los Angeles Times,* 23 February 1988.

Hoffman, Frank G. "Stepping Forward Smartly: 'Forward . . . From the Sea': The Emerging, Expanded Naval Strategy." *Marine Corps Gazette,* March 1995.

Holland, Jerry. "Book Review: The Navy Policy Book." U.S. Naval Institute *Proceedings* (October 1992).

Hughes, Wayne P. "Naval Operations: A Close Look at the Operational Level of War at Sea." *Naval War College Review* 65, no. 3 (Summer 2012).

———. "Navy Operations Research." *Operations Research* 50, no. 1 (2002). doi/pdf/10.1287/opre.50.1.103.17786.

Huntington, Samuel P. "National Policy and the Transoceanic Navy." U.S. Naval Institute *Proceedings* 80, no. 5 (May 1954).

Keller, Bill. "Last Soviet Soldiers Leave Afghanistan." *New York Times*, 16 February 1989. https://partners.nytimes.com/library/world/africa/021689afghan-laden.html.

Komer, Robert W. "Maritime Strategy versus Coalition Defense." *Foreign Affairs* 60, no. 5 (Summer 1982).

Lehman, John F., Jr. "Let's Stop Trying to Be Prussians." *Washington Post,* 10 June 1984.

Lind, William S., and Colin S. Gray. "The Maritime Strategy, 1988: Bad Strategy or Global Deterrent." U.S. Naval Institute *Proceedings* (February 1988).

Manthorpe, William H. J. "Personal Reflections on *The Pentagon's New Map: War and Peace in the 21st Century* by Thomas P. M. Barnett (New York: Putnam, 2004)." *Naval Intelligence Professionals Quarterly* 21, no. 3 (Fall 2005).

Matthews, William. "Carrier *Theodore Roosevelt* 'Charges' to Life." *Navy Times,* 10 November 1986.

McFarland, Keith D. "The 1949 Revolt of the Admirals." *US Army War College Quarterly: Parameters* 11, no. 2 (1981).

Mearsheimer, John J. "Review of John Lehman's *Command*." *US Army War College Quarterly: Parameters* (June 1990).

———. "A Strategic Misstep: The Maritime Strategy and Deterrence in Europe." *International Security* 11, no. 2 (Fall 1986).

Meinhart, Richard. "Vice Chairman of the Joint Chiefs of Staff and the Leadership of the Joint Requirements Oversight Council." *Joint Forces Quarterly*, no. 56 (2010).

Middleton, Drew. "U.S. and Allied Navies Starting Major Test Today." *New York Times*, 1 August 1981, http://www.nytimes.com/1981/08/01/world/us-and-allied-navies-starting-major-test-today-military-analysis.html.

Mohr, Charles. "Military Price on Coffee Cited as $7,622." *New York Times*, 20 September 1984.

Mundy, Carl E., Jr. "Getting It Right '. . . From the Sea.' " U.S. Naval Institute *Proceedings* (January 1994).

Mustin, Henry C. "The Role of the Navy and the Marines in the Norwegian Sea." *Naval War College Review* 39, no. 2 (March/April 1986).

O'Keefe, Sean, Frank B. Kelso II, and Carl E. Mundy. ". . . From the Sea: Preparing the Naval Service for the 21st Century." U.S. Naval Institute *Proceedings* 118, no. 11 (November 1992).

Owens, Mackubin Thomas. "The Hollow Promise of JCS Reform." *International Security* 10, no. 3 (Winter 1985/86).

Owens, William A. "JROC: Harnessing the Revolution in Military Affairs." *Joint Forces Quarterly* (Summer 1994).

———. "The Quest for Consensus." U.S. Naval Institute *Proceedings* 120, no. 5 (May 1994).

Pandolfe, Frank C. "The Evolution of Modern U.S. Naval Strategy." *Naval War College Review* 69, no. 4 (2016).

Parker, Geoffrey. "The Military Revolution, 1550–1650: A Myth?" *Journal of Modern History* 48, no. 2 (1976).

Pendley, William. "The New Maritime Strategy: A Lost Opportunity." *Naval War College Review* 61, no. 2 (2008).

Posen, Barry R. "Inadvertent Nuclear War and NATO's Northern Flank." *International Security* 7, no. 2 (Fall 1982).

"PPBE Process: Program Objective Memorandum." *AcqNotes*, 30 May 2018. http://acqnotes.com/acqnote/acquisitions/program-objective-memorandum-pom.

Rainbow, Fred, and John Miller. "Be Careful What You Ask For. . . ." U.S. Naval Institute *Proceedings* (January 1993).

Rhodes, Edward. "'. . . From the Sea' and Back Again: Naval Power in the Second American Century." *Naval War College Review* 70, no. 2 (Spring 1999).

Roberts, James. "Going in Harm's Way: The U.S. Navy in the Light of the Gulf Crisis." *Defense*, March 1991.

Roman, Peter J., and David W. Tarr. "The Joint Chiefs of Staff: From Parochialism to Jointness." *Political Science Quarterly* 113, no. 1 (Spring 1998).

Rosenberg, David Alan. "The Origins of Overkill: Nuclear Weapons and American Strategy, 1945–1960." *International Security* 7, no. 4 (Spring 1983).

Rubel, Robert C. "What Critics of the Navy's Strategy Get Wrong." *War on the Rocks,* 6 January 2015. http://warontherocks.com/2015/01/what-critics-of-the-navys-strategy-get-wrong/.

Smith, Edward A., Jr. "What '. . . From the Sea' Didn't Say." *Naval War College Review* 48, no. 1 (Winter 1995).

Swartz, Peter M., and John L. Byron. "Make the Word Become the Vision." U.S. Naval Institute *Proceedings,* 118, no. 11 (November 1992).

Tangredi, Sam J. "Running Silent and Algorithmic: The U.S. Navy Strategic Vision in 2019." *Naval War College Review* 72, no. 2 (2020).

Thaler, David E. "The Fifth Eskadra: Soviet Maritime Power in the Mediterranean." *Jewish Institute of National Security Affairs* 5, no. 3 (March 1987).

Tomes, Robert. "The Cold War Offset Strategy: Assault Breaker and the Beginning of the RSTA Revolution." *War on the Rocks,* 20 November 2014. http://warontherocks.com/2014/11/the-cold-war-offset-strategy-assault-breaker-and-the-beginning-of-the-rsta-revolution/.

Trost, Carlisle A. H. "Maritime Strategy for the 1990s." U.S. Naval Institute *Proceedings* 116, no. 5 (May 1990).

Truver, Scott C. "Tomorrow's Fleet." U.S. Naval Institute *Proceedings* (June 1992).

———. "Why America Needs Aircraft Carriers." *BreakingDefense.com,* 2 October 2015.

Turner, Stansfield. "Missions of the U.S. Navy." *Naval War College Review* 26, no. 5 (March/April 1974).

Turner, Stansfield, and George E. Thibault. "Preparing for the Unexpected: The Need for a New Military Strategy." *Foreign Affairs* (Fall 1982).

Vego, Milan. "On Littoral Warfare." *Naval War College Review* 68, no. 2 (Spring 2015).

"What Witnesses Had to Say." *Armed Forces Journal International* (February 1984). Congress/Administration section.

Wheeler, Gerald E. "Naval Aviation in the Korean War." U.S. Naval Institute *Proceedings* 83, no. 7 (July 1957).

Wilson, George. "USS *Theodore Roosevelt* Joins Active Service as 15th Carrier." *Washington Post,* 26 October 1986.

Winnefeld, James A., and Dana J. Johnson. "Unity of Control: Joint Air Operations in the Gulf." *Joint Forces Quarterly* (Summer 1993).

Winton, Harold R. "Partnership and Tension: The Army and the Air Force between Vietnam and Desert Shield." *US Army War College Quarterly: Parameters* (Spring 1996).

INDEX

ABOUT THE AUTHOR

Steven T. Wills is an expert in U.S. Navy strategy and policy at the Center for Naval Analyses (CNA) in Arlington, Virginia. He served for twenty years as a U.S. Navy surface warfare officer. He also holds a PhD and MA in history from Ohio University, an MA from the U.S. Naval War College, and a BA in history from Miami University, Oxford, Ohio.